First World War
and Army of Occupation
War Diary
France, Belgium and Germany

Rhine Cavalry Brigades
Dragoon Brigade: Headquarters,
1st Dragoons (Royals),
6th Dragoon Guards (Carabineers),
6th Dragoons (Inniskilling),
Dragoon Brigade Machine Gun Squadron,
Hussar Brigade Headquarters,
3rd (King's Own) Hussars,
10th (Prince of Wales' Own Royal) Hussars,
15th (The King's) Hussars,
Hussar Brigade 9 Machine Gun Squadron,
Lancer Brigade Headquarters,
Lancer Brigade 9 (Queen's Royal) Lancers,
Lancer Brigade 12 (Prince of Wales's) Lancers,
17th Lancers (Duke of Cambridge's Own)
and Lancer Brigade 2 Machine Gun Squadron
1 April 1919 - 31 August 1919

WO95/1166

The Naval & Military Press Ltd
www.nmarchive.com
Published in association with The National Archives

Published by

The Naval & Military Press Ltd

Unit 10 Ridgewood Industrial Park,

Uckfield, East Sussex,

TN22 5QE England

Tel: +44 (0) 1825 749494

www.naval-military-press.com

www.nmarchive.com

This diary has been reprinted in facsimile from the original. Any imperfections are inevitably reproduced and the quality may fall short of modern type and cartographic standards.

© Crown Copyright
Images reproduced by permission of The National Archives, London, England, 2015.

Contents

Document type	Place/Title	Date From	Date To
Heading	B.E.F. Cav Div Dragoon Bde H.Q. Formerly I Cav Bde 1919 Apr To 1919 Aug		
Heading	War Diary Of Headquarters Dragoon Brigade From 1st To 30th April 1919 Volume No LVII		
War Diary	Zieverich (Germany)	01/04/1919	30/04/1919
Heading	War Diary Of Headquarters Dragoon Brigade From 1st To 31st May 1919		
War Diary	Zieverich (Germany)	01/05/1919	31/05/1919
Miscellaneous	Dragoon Brigade Order No. 1 Appendix 1	23/05/1919	23/05/1919
Miscellaneous	Instructions For The Advance.	22/05/1919	22/05/1919
Heading	War Diary Of Headquarters Dragoon Brigade Period 1st To 30th June 1919 Volume LIX		
War Diary	Zieverich (Germany)	01/06/1919	30/06/1919
Heading	War Diary Of Headquarters Dragoon Brigade From 1st To 31st July 1919		
War Diary	Zieverich (Germany)	01/07/1919	31/07/1919
Heading	War Diary Of Headquarters Dragoon Brigade From 1st To 31st August 1919		
War Diary	Zieverich (Germany)	01/08/1919	31/08/1919
Heading	B E F Cav. Div. Dragoon Bde. Royal 1 Dragoon S 1919 Apr To 1919 Aug From 3 Cav Div 6 Cav Bde Box 1153		
Heading	War Diary Of The 1st (Royal) Dragoons From 1st To 30th April 1919 Volume No LVII		
War Diary	Paffendorf. (Germany)	01/04/1919	30/04/1919
Heading	War Diary Of The 1st (Royal) Dragoons From 1st To 31st May 1919		
War Diary	Germany.	01/05/1919	31/05/1919
Heading	War Diary Of The 1st (Royal) Dragoons Period 1st To 30th June 1919 Volume No LIX		
War Diary	Germany	01/06/1919	30/06/1919
Heading	War Diary Of 1st (Royal) Dragoons. From 1st To 31st July 1919		
War Diary	Paffendorf Germany	01/07/1919	31/07/1919
Heading	War Diary Of 1st (Royal) Dragoons. From 1st To 31st August 1919		
War Diary	Germany	01/08/1919	31/08/1919
War Diary			
Heading	BEF Cav. Div. Dragoon Bde. 6 Dragoon Gds. 1919 Apr To 1919 Aug From 2 Cav Div 4 Cav Bde Box 1137		
Heading	War Diary Of 6th Dragoon Guards (The Carabiniers) From 1st To 30th April 1919 Volume No LVII		
War Diary	Elsdorf Germany	01/04/1919	30/04/1919
Heading	War Diary Of 6th Dragoon Guards (The Carabiniers) From 1st To 31st May 1919		
War Diary	Elsdorf	01/05/1919	31/05/1919
Heading	War Diary Of 6th Dragoon Guards (Carabiniers) Period 1st To 30th June 1919 Volume No LIX		
War Diary	Elsdorf	01/06/1919	02/06/1919

War Diary	Germany	03/06/1919	30/06/1919
Heading	War Diary Of 6th Dragoon Guards (The Carabiniers) From 1st To 31st July 1919		
War Diary	Elsdorf	01/07/1919	31/07/1919
Heading	War Diary Of 6th Dragoon Guards (The Carabiniers) From 1st To 31st August 1919		
War Diary	Elsdorf Germany	01/08/1919	31/08/1919
Heading	B E F Cav Div. Dragoon Bde. 6 Innisk Dragoons 1919 Apr To 1920 Feb From 3 Cav Div 7 Cav Bde Box 1155		
War Diary	Niederembt	01/04/1919	17/04/1919
War Diary	Sindorf	18/04/1919	30/04/1919
Heading	War Diary Of 6th (Inniskilling) Dragoons From 1st To 31st May 1919		
War Diary	Sindorf	01/05/1919	31/05/1919
Heading	War Diary Of The 6th (Inniskilling) Dragoons Period 1st To 30th June 1919 Volume No LIX		
War Diary	Sindorf Germany	01/06/1919	30/06/1919
Heading	War Diary Of 6th (Inniskilling) Dragoons From 1st To 31st July 1919		
War Diary	Sindorf	01/07/1919	31/07/1919
Heading	War Diary Of 6th (Inniskilling) Dragoons From 1st To 31st August 1919		
War Diary	Sindorf	01/08/1919	31/08/1919
Heading	War Diary Of The Innis Killing Dragoons Sept 1st 1919 To Sept 30th 1919		
War Diary	Sindorf	01/09/1919	27/09/1919
War Diary	Cologne	28/09/1919	05/10/1919
Heading	War Diary Of Inniskilling Dragoons From Nov 1st 1919 To Nov 30th 1919		
War Diary	Cologne	01/11/1919	30/11/1919
Heading	War Diary Of The Inniskilling Dragoons. From 1/12/19 To 31/12/19		
War Diary	Cologne	01/12/1919	31/12/1919
Heading	War Diary Of The Inniskilling Dragoons From Feb 1st 1920 To Feb 29th 1920		
War Diary	Deutz Bk Cologne	02/02/1920	27/02/1920
Heading	BEF Cav. Div. Dragoon Bde. Machine Gun Sdn 1919 Apr To 1919 Aug From 1 Cav Div 1 Bde Box 1108		
War Diary	Berrendorf	01/04/1919	30/04/1919
Heading	War Diary Of 1st Machine Gun Squadron From 1st To 31st May 1919		
War Diary	Berrendorf	02/05/1919	31/05/1919
Heading	War Diary Of Dragoon Machine Gun Squadron Period 1st To 30th June 1919 Volume LIX		
War Diary	Berrendorf	05/06/1919	30/06/1919
Heading	War Diary Of Dragoon Machine Gun Squadron From 1st To 31st July 1919		
War Diary	Berrendorf	01/07/1919	30/07/1919
Heading	War Diary Of The Dragoon Machine Gun Squadron From 1st To 31st August 1919		
War Diary	Berrendorf Germany	01/08/1919	31/08/1919
Heading	BEF Cav. Div Hussar Bde H.Q. 1919 Apr To 1919 July		
Heading	War Diary Of Headquarters Hussar Brigade April 1919 Volume No. 1		

War Diary	Harff.	01/04/1919	07/04/1919
War Diary	Bergerhausen	07/04/1919	30/04/1919
Miscellaneous	Hussar Brigade Order No. 1 Appendix 1	05/04/1919	05/04/1919
Miscellaneous	March Table (Issued With Hussar Brigade Order No. 1)		
Miscellaneous	Hussar Brigade Order No. 2 Appendix 2	23/04/1919	23/04/1919
Miscellaneous	Hussar Brigade. Effective Strength in Hussar Brigade for week ending 26/4/19	26/04/1919	26/04/1919
Miscellaneous	Hussar Brigade. Effective Strength in Hussar Brigade for week ending 19/4/19	19/04/1919	19/04/1919
Miscellaneous	Hussar Brigade. Effective Strength in Hussar Brigade for week ending 12/4/19	12/04/1919	12/04/1919
Miscellaneous	Hussar Brigade. Effective Strength in Hussar Brigade for week ending 5/4/19	05/04/1919	05/04/1919
Heading	War Diary Of Hussar Brigade Headquarters. May 1919 Volume No. 2		
War Diary	Bergerhausen	01/05/1919	31/05/1919
Miscellaneous	Hussar Brigade. Effective Strength in Hussar Brigade for week ending 3/5/19	03/05/1919	03/05/1919
Miscellaneous	Hussar Brigade. Effective Strength in Hussar Brigade for week ending 10/5/19	10/05/1919	10/05/1919
Miscellaneous	Hussar Brigade Effective Strength in Hussar Brigade for week ending 17/5/19	17/05/1919	17/05/1919
Miscellaneous	Hussar Brigade Effective Strength in Hussar Brigade for week ending 24th May 1919	24/05/1919	24/05/1919
Miscellaneous	Hussar Brigade Effective Strength in Hussar Brigade for week ending 31st May 1919	31/05/1919	31/05/1919
Miscellaneous	Mobile Striking Force. Appendix III	30/05/1919	30/05/1919
Miscellaneous	Mobile Striking Force. Appendix III	24/05/1919	24/05/1919
Miscellaneous	Mobile Striking Force. Appendix I	23/05/1919	23/05/1919
Miscellaneous	Mobile Striking Force.	23/05/1919	23/05/1919
Heading	War Diary Of Hussar Brigade Headquarters. June 1919 Volume No. 3		
War Diary	Bergerhausen	01/06/1919	28/06/1919
Miscellaneous	Hussar Brigade Effective Strength in Hussar Brigade for week ending 24th May 1919	24/05/1919	24/05/1919
Miscellaneous	9th M.G. Squadron	17/06/1919	17/06/1919
Miscellaneous	Hussar Brigade. Effective Strength in Hussar Brigade for week ending 8th June 1919	08/06/1919	08/06/1919
Miscellaneous	Hussar Brigade Effective Strength in Hussar Brigade for week ending 14th June 1919	14/06/1919	14/06/1919
Miscellaneous	Hussar Brigade Effective Strength in Hussar Brigade for week ending 21st June 1919	21/06/1919	21/06/1919
Miscellaneous	Hussar Brigade Effective Strength in Hussar Brigade for week ending 28st June 1919	28/06/1919	28/06/1919
Heading	War Diary Of Hussar Brigade Headquarters. July 1919 Volume No. 4		
War Diary	Bergerhausen	01/07/1919	28/07/1919
Miscellaneous	Hussar Brigade Effective Strength in Hussar Brigade for week ending 5th July 1919	25/07/1919	25/07/1919
Miscellaneous	Hussar Brigade Effective Strength in Hussar Brigade for week ending 12th July 1919	12/07/1919	12/07/1919
Miscellaneous	Hussar Brigade Effective Strength in Hussar Brigade for week ending 19th July 1919	19/07/1919	19/07/1919
Miscellaneous	Hussar Brigade Effective Strength in Hussar Brigade for week ending 26th July 1919	26/07/1919	26/07/1919

Heading	War Diary Of Headquarters Hussar Brigade August 1919 Volume No. 5		
War Diary	Bergerhausen	06/08/1919	30/08/1919
Miscellaneous	Detail Of Personnel Horse And Equipment Trains. Appendix 1		
Miscellaneous	Hussar Brigade Effective Strength in Hussar Brigade for week ending 2nd August 1919	02/08/1919	02/08/1919
Miscellaneous	Hussar Brigade Effective Strength in Hussar Brigade for week ending 9th August 1919	09/08/1919	09/08/1919
Miscellaneous	Hussar Brigade Effective Strength in Hussar Brigade for week ending 16th August 1919	16/08/1919	16/08/1919
Miscellaneous	Hussar Brigade Effective Strength in Hussar Brigade for week ending August 23rd 1919	23/08/1919	23/08/1919
Miscellaneous	Hussar Brigade Effective Strength in Hussar Brigade for week ending 30th August 1919	30/08/1919	30/08/1919
Heading	BEF Cav Div Hussar Bde 3 K. O. Hussars 1919 Apr 1919 Aug		
Heading	War Diary Of 3rd King's Own Hussars From 1st April 1919 To 30th April 1919 Volume LVI		
War Diary	Grotten Hirten	01/04/1919	25/04/1919
War Diary	Duren	26/04/1919	31/04/1919
Miscellaneous	To All Ranks Of The Second Cavalry Division.	11/03/1919	11/03/1919
Miscellaneous	3rd (K.O.) Hussars. App C.		
Miscellaneous	3rd (K.O.) Hussars. App D		
Miscellaneous	Army Of The Rhine G. I. 43/14 IV Corps No. 16/26 (G) App E		
Miscellaneous	Mobile Striking Force. Appendix "B"		
Heading	War Diary of 3rd (Kings Own) Hussars. From 1st May 1919 To 31st May 1919 Volume LVII		
War Diary	Duren	01/05/1919	31/05/1919
Miscellaneous	Mobile Striking Force App A		
Miscellaneous	3rd (K.O.) Hussars. App B		
Miscellaneous	3rd (K.O.) Hussars. App C		
Heading	War Diary Of 3rd King's Own Hussars. 1st June 1919 To 31st June 1919 Volume LVIII		
War Diary	Duren	01/06/1919	30/06/1919
Miscellaneous	Duren	30/06/1919	30/06/1919
Miscellaneous	Details Of Attached App A		
Miscellaneous	Roll Of Officers By Squadrons App B		
Heading	War Diary 3rd King's Own Hussars. From 1st July 1919 To 31st July 1919 Volume LIX		
War Diary	Duren	01/07/1919	28/07/1919
Miscellaneous	3rd (K.O.) Hussars. App A		
Miscellaneous	Strength And Distribution Of Regiment On 31st July 1919 App B		
Heading	War Diary Of 3rd (K.O.) Hussars. From 1st August 1919 To 31st August 1919 Volume LX.		
War Diary	Nideggen	17/08/1919	17/08/1919
War Diary	Duren	20/08/1919	30/08/1919
War Diary	Duren	01/08/1919	15/08/1919
Miscellaneous	3rd (K.O) Hussars.		
Miscellaneous	3rd (K.O) Hussars. App B		
Miscellaneous	3rd (K.O) Hussars.		
Miscellaneous	3rd (K.O) Hussars. App D.		
Heading	BEF Cav Div Hussar Bde 10 Hussars 1919 Apr To 1919 Aug From 3 Cav Div 6 Bde Box 1153		

Heading	War Diary Of 10th (P.W.O.) Royal Hussars. For April 1919 Volume No. 41		
War Diary	Konigshoven	01/04/1919	07/04/1919
War Diary	Turnich	08/04/1919	30/04/1919
War Diary	Turnich	01/05/1919	31/05/1919
Heading	War Diary Of 10th (P.W.O.) Royal Hussars. June 1919 Volume No. 43		
War Diary	Turnich	01/06/1919	30/06/1919
Heading	War Diary Of 10th (P.W.O.) Royal Hussars. July 1919 Volume. No. 44		
War Diary	Turnich	01/07/1919	31/08/1919
Heading	BEF Cav Div Hussar Bde 15 Hussars 1919 Apr To 1919 Aug From 1 Cav Div 9 Bde Box 1114		
Heading	War Diary Of 15th "The King's" Hussars. For April 1919 Volume XLIX.		
War Diary	Bedburg	01/04/1919	07/04/1919
War Diary	Kerpen	08/04/1919	30/04/1919
War Diary			
Heading	War Diary Of 15th "The King's" Hussars May 1919 Volume No. XIX.		
War Diary	Kerpen	01/05/1919	31/05/1919
War Diary			
War Diary	Summary Of Casualties During May 1919		
Heading	15th "The King's" Hussars. War Diary For June, 1919 Volume L.		
War Diary	Kerpen	01/06/1919	30/06/1919
War Diary	Summary Of Training For Month Of June 1919		
Miscellaneous	Summary Of Training For Month Of June 1919		
Heading	War Diary Of 15th "The King's" Hussars. For July 1919 Volume LI.		
War Diary	Kerpen	01/07/1919	31/07/1919
War Diary	Summary Of Training For Month Of July 1919		
Miscellaneous	Summary Of Casualties During July 1919		
Heading	War Diary Of XVth (The King's) Hussars. For August 1919 Volume LII.		
War Diary	Kerpen	01/08/1919	31/08/1919
Miscellaneous	Summary Of Training For Month Of August 1919		
War Diary	Summary Of Casualties During August 1919		
Heading	BEF Cav Div Hussar Bde 9 M.G. Sdn 1919 Apr To 1919 Aug From 1 Cav Div 9 Bde Box 1116		
Heading	War Diary Of 9th Machine Gun Squadron For April 1919 Volume XXXIX.		
War Diary	Kaster	01/04/1919	07/04/1919
War Diary	Blatzheim	08/04/1919	30/04/1919
War Diary	9th Machine Gun Squadron May 1919 Volume 40		
War Diary	Blatzheim	01/05/1919	31/05/1919
War Diary	June 1919 Volume Number 41		
War Diary	Blatzheim	01/06/1919	30/06/1919
War Diary	Hussar M.G. Squadron July 1919 Volume No 42		
War Diary	Blatzheim	01/07/1919	31/07/1919
Heading	August 1919 Volume No. 43		
War Diary	Blatzheim	01/08/1919	31/08/1919
Heading	BEF Cav. Div Lancer Bde H.Q. 1919 Apr To 1919 Sept		
Heading	War Diary "Lancer" Brigade Headquarters. For The Month Of April 1919		

War Diary	Cologne.	01/04/1919	30/04/1919
Miscellaneous	Grooming State 2nd Cavalry Brigade-April 1st. 1919 Appendix I		
Miscellaneous	Appendix "A" Attached To Lancer Brigade War Diary For The Month Of April 1919		
Heading	War Diary "Lancer" Brigade Headquarters. For The Month Of May 1919 Volume LVIII		
War Diary	Cologne.	01/05/1919	31/05/1919
Miscellaneous	Appendix "A" Attached To Lancer Brigade War Diary For The Month Of May. 1919		
Miscellaneous	Appendix I 9th Lancers.	08/05/1919	08/05/1919
Heading	War Diary Of Lancer Brigade Headquarters. For The Month Of June 1919		
War Diary	Cologne.	01/06/1919	30/06/1919
Operation(al) Order(s)	Lancer Brigade Order No. 3	28/06/1919	28/06/1919
Miscellaneous			
Miscellaneous	Appendix "A" Attached to Lancer Brigade War Diary For the Month of June 1919		
Miscellaneous	Appendix "B" The following are the numbers of reinforcements recieved by this Brigade for the month of June 1919		
Heading	War Diary. For The Month Of July 1919 Lancer Brigade Headquarters Volume LX		
War Diary		01/07/1919	30/07/1919
War Diary	War Diary Of Lancer Brigade Headquarters. For The Month Of August 1919 Volume IX		
War Diary	Cologne	01/08/1919	13/08/1919
Heading	BEF Cav. Div. Lancer Bde. 9 Lancers 1919 Apr To 1919 Aug From 1 Cav Div 2 Bde Box 1113		
War Diary	Daren	01/04/1919	30/04/1919
War Diary	Cologne	01/05/1919	31/05/1919
Heading	War Diary Of 9th (Q R) Lancers. From 1st June 1919 To 30th June 1919		
War Diary	Cologne	01/06/1919	30/06/1919
Heading	War Diary Of The 9th (QR) Lancers. From 1-7-19 To 31-7-19 Volume 19		
War Diary	Cologne	01/07/1919	31/07/1919
Heading	War Diary Of The 9th (QR) Lancers From 1-8-19 To 31-8-19		
War Diary	Cologne	01/08/1919	31/08/1919
Heading	Bef Cav. Div. Lancer Bde 12 Lancers 1919 Apr To 1919 Aug From 2 Cav Div 5 Bde Box 1140		
War Diary		01/04/1919	31/05/1919
Heading	War Diary 12th (Prince Of Wales's Royal) Lancers. June 1919		
War Diary	Cologne	01/06/1919	30/06/1919
War Diary		01/07/1919	31/07/1919
War Diary	Cologne	01/08/1919	31/08/1919
Heading	Bef Cav Div Lancer Bde 17 Lancers 1919 Apr To 1919 Aug From 3 Cav Div 7 Bde Box 1155		
War Diary	Cologne	02/04/1919	28/04/1919
Miscellaneous	War Diary Of The 17th Lancers Cavalry Division Army Of The Rhine		
War Diary	Cologne	04/05/1919	30/05/1919
Miscellaneous	War Diary Of The 17th Lancers Cavalry Division Army Of The Rhine		

War Diary		Cologne	01/06/1919	28/06/1919
Heading		War Diary Of The 17th Lancers. Cavalry Division. British Army Of The Rhine. Vol VI Page For Period 1st To 31st July 1919		
War Diary		Cologne	01/07/1919	31/07/1919
Heading		War Diary Of The 17th Lancers. Cavalry Division British Army Of The Rhine. Vol. VI. Pages. For The Period 1st To 31st August 1919		
War Diary		Cologne	12/08/1919	31/08/1919
Heading		BEF Cav. Div. Lancer Bde. 2 Machine Gun Sdn 1919 Apr to 1919 Aug. From 1 Cav Div 2 Bde Box 1111		
War Diary		Deutz	01/04/1919	30/04/1919
War Diary		Cologne	01/05/1919	31/05/1919
War Diary		Deutz.	01/06/1919	01/06/1919
War Diary		Cologne	02/06/1919	30/06/1919
War Diary		Deutz Cologne	01/07/1919	31/07/1919
War Diary			01/08/1919	31/08/1919

BEF
CAV. DIV

DRAGOON Bde H.Q
formerly 1 Cav Bde

1919 APR to 1919 AUG

Confidential

War Diary

Headquarters 7 Dragoon Brigade

From 1st to 30th April 1919

Volume No LVII

Army Form C. 2118.

WAR DIARY
or
INTELLIGENCE SUMMARY of HEADQUARTERS, DRAGOON BRIGADE.

(Erase heading not required.)

Instructions regarding War Diaries and Intelligence Summaries are contained in F. S. Regs., Part II. and the Staff Manual respectively. Title pages will be prepared in manuscript.

Place	Date	Hour	Summary of Events and Information	Remarks and references to Appendices
ZIEVERICH. (Germany)	April 1st to 7th		Nothing to report.	
"	8th		Brigdr: General A.E.W. Harman, D.S.O. assumed command of Dragoon Brigade.	
"	9th to 19th		Nothing to report.	
"	20th		Captain G. Babington, M.C., North Som: Yeomy: assumed duties of Staff Captain, Dragoon Brigade vice Captain J. J. Kingstone, M.C., Queen's Bays, to England.	
"	21st to 23rd		Nothing to report.	
"	24th		Captain C. A. Heydeman, M.C., Queen's Bays, assumed duties of Brigade Major, Dragoon Brigade.	
"	25th		G. O. C. inspected composite Regiment of the Mobile Force.	
"	26th		Commander-in-Chief visited the Brigade and inspected The Carabiniers and Royals. "E" Batty: R. H. A. moved from ESCH to ICHENDORF.	
"	27th to 30th		Nothing to report.	

P.A. Heydeman Captain.
for G. O. C., Dragoon Brigade.

Confidential

War Diary

of

Headquarters, Dragoon Brigade.

from 1st to 31st May 1919

Army Form C. 2118.

WAR DIARY
or
INTELLIGENCE SUMMARY.
(Erase heading not required.)

of HEADQUARTERS, DRAGOON BRIGADE.

May, 1919.

Instructions regarding War Diaries and Intelligence Summaries are contained in F. S. Regs., Part II. and the Staff Manual respectively. Title pages will be prepared in manuscript.

Place	Date	Hour	Summary of Events and Information	Remarks and references to Appendices
ZIEVERICH (Germany)	1st		Nothing to report.	
	2nd		Cavalry Memorial Service, 10.30 hrs in Y.M.C.A. building, BERGHEIM.	
	3rd) 4th) 5th)		Nothing to report.	
	6th.		The Duke of Connaught passed through ELSDORF, ZIEVERICH and PAFFENDORF. A small detachment of the Inniskillings was inspected by the Duke at ZIEVERICH.	
	7th.		Nothing to report.	
	8th.		G. O. C. inspected all horses of the Carabiniers at ELSDORF.	
	9th.		G. O. C. inspected the composite Squadron of the Carabiniers.	
	10th to 14th		Nothing to report.	
	15th		G. O. C. inspected all horses of the Royals.	
	16th		G. O. C. inspected all horses of the Inniskillings.	
	17th to 19th		Nothing to report.	
	20th to 22nd		Nothing to report.	

Army Form C. 2118.

WAR DIARY
INTELLIGENCE SUMMARY of HEADQUARTERS, DRAGOON BRIGADE.

(Erase heading not required.)

Instructions regarding War Diaries and Intelligence Summaries are contained in F. S. Regs., Part II. and the Staff Manual respectively. Title pages will be prepared in manuscript.

Place	Date	Hour	Summary of Events and Information	Remarks and references to Appendices
ZIEVERICH. (Germany)	23rd		Divisional Commander's Conference at Brigade Headquarters, attended by the Brigadier, Commanding Officers and Squadron Leaders. Lecture at HORREM by Lieut: Colonel Tysham on BOLSHEVISM. Dragoon Brigade Order No, 1 and "Instructions for the Advance" issued.	I.
	24th 25th 26th		Nothing to Report.	
	27th.		Dragoon Brigade will not now find the Headquarters of the Composite Regiment; Headquarters to be found by the Lancer-Brigade. The G. O. C. inspected the composite Dragoon Squadron at THORR, and was highly pleased with the turn-out.	
	28th to 31st		Nothing to report.	

C.A. Heyderman Major.

for G. O. C., Dragoon Brigade.

APPENDIX. I.

SECRET. Copy No. 11.

DRAGOON BRIGADE ORDER No. 1.

Ref: 1/200,000 Map. 23rd May, 1919.

1. If an advance is ordered, the X, VI and II Corps will advance with Advanced Guards in lorries, in accordance with instructions for their advance attached.
   The Mobile Cavalry Force, constituted as under, will be attached to VI Corps and would be concentrated in COLOGNe in accordance with para: 3 below.
   "J" day being the day on which the advance commences.

Under the command of Lt. Col: H. Sadler, and Regtl: Staff found by 6th Dgn: Gds:	)))))))	A Composite Regiment - formed from 1 Sqdn: per Cav: Bde: each Regt: finding a strong troop. "G" Battery, R.H.A. 1 Composite M.G. Sqdn: - Formed of 1 Section of each M.G. Sqdn:

2. The mission of the Cavalry would probably be to keep in touch between the Advanced Guards in lorries (which would advance about 30 miles a day), and the main body.

3. In consequence, the Mobile Force would concentrate in the Lancer Brigade Area in COLOGNE on J - 3 days, as under :-

   Lancer Brigade   ) as billeted at present.
   "G" Batt: R.H.A.   )

   Dragoon Brigade   accommodation from 9th Lancers,
   (less 1 Sectn: White City.
   M. G. Sqdn:)

   Hussars Brigade   accommodation from 12th Lancers,
   (less 1 Sectn: Artillery Barracks.
   M. G. Sqdn:)

   1 Sectn: M.G. Sqdn: accommodation from 2nd M. G. Sqdn:
   from Dgn: and Hussars   Cavalry Barracks, COLOGNE.
   Bde:

4. Troops would come under orders of the G. Os. C. Divisions at dawn J - 2 days, as follows :-

   Lancer Squadron.   under G. O. C. London Division.

   Regtl: H.Q.   )
   Dragoon Sqdn:)
   Hussar Sqdn:) Under G. O. C. Northern Division.
   "G" Batt: R.H.A.   )
   1 Sqdn: M. Gs.   )

5. A. D. M. S. and A. D. V. S. are getting into touch with A.D.M.S. and A.D.V.S. London and Northern Divisions, as regards Med Medical and Veterinary arrangements.

6. A.A. & Q.M.G. is arranging to issue one iron ration forthwith. These will not be issued to the troops until as move is ordered.

7. On receipt of the code message "Perhaps" the above orders will come into force. Date of "J" day would be sent out as soon as received.

8. "B" Echelon will be taken up to the Concentration Area COLOGNE, and left there to be sent up if required.

9. ACKNOWLEDGE.

(Signed) C. A. Heydeman.   Captain.
Brigade Major, Dragoon Brigade.

Issued at 17.00 hours.

Distribution normal.

SECRET.   Cav: Div: No. S.G. 91/1.

INSTRUCTIONS FOR THE ADVANCE.

Ref: 1/200,000 Map.
Sheets HANNOVER.
        MUNSTER.
        COLN.   May 22nd, 1919.
        CASSELL.

1. Under certain eventualities, it may be necessary for the Allied Armies to seize as rapidly as possible the RUHR Basin, and to secure the railway communications, which are essential for a further advance North-eastwards.

The essential points to be reached with all speed are :-

    for the Americans - FRANKENBERG.
    for the British   - SOEST.
    for the Belgians - HAMM

In seizing the railways our object is to ensure that the German rolling stock on the lines is not evacuated in front of us and that the German personnel complete remain at their posts and work the railway for us. The main railway communication runs COLOGNE - CALIGS - ELBERFELD - HAGEN - UNNA. Important subsidiary lines are ALTENA - PLETTENBERG - KIRCHHUNDEM - KROMBACH - SIEGEN and SCHWERTE - ARNSBERG - MESCHEDE.

2. The intention is for the British Army to advance on a three Corps front, with the Xth Corps on the right, the VIIth Corps in the Centre and the IInd Corps on the left.

3. The VIth Corps will advance on a two Division front, with the London Division on the right and the Northern Division on the left. The London Division will advance on a one Brigade front, and the Northern Division on a two Brigade front on the first day and on a one Brigade front on the second day.

4. The earliest day on which the advance will be ordered (called "J" day hereafter) will be the 26th May.

5. The Eastern Division of the Xth Corps will advance on the Right of the VIth Corps, and the Southern Division of the IInd Corps on the left.

6. The objectives for the march are as follows :-

	"J" Day.	Distance Miles.	"J" + 1 day.	Distance Miles.
London Div. 'A' Bde.Group.	ATTENDORF via OLPE with detachment at NEUBRUCKE 6 miles further on.	33.	ARNSBERG.	29
Northern Div. 'A' Bde.Group.	SCHWERTE - HAGEN via LENNEP and SCHWELM.	32.	SOESTWERL.	30.
'B' Bde.Group.	ALTENA - LUDENSCHIED.via WIPPERFURTH.	30.	UNNA - SCHWERTE - MENDEN.	15 - 20.

Contd.....

	"J" day.	Distance Miles.	"J" + 1 Day.	Distance Miles.
Eastern Div. (Xth Corps).	WISSEN with detachment at KIRCHEN.	—	KIRCHMUNDEN – KROMBACH.	—

The Southern Division (IInd Corps) seize ELBERFELD and 291 on "J" day, HAGEN on "J" day – 2 day, SCHWERTE on "J" – 3 day, and UNNA on "J" – 4 day.

The following Division will leave troops in HAGEN, SCHWERTE and UNNA until relieved by the Southern Division, when they will rejoin their formations under Northern Division arrangements.

7. The rapid advance of the above Brigade Groups of the VIth Corps will be carried out in Motor busses. Each Brigade Group will be organized to contain in addition to the Brigade :–

> One Machine Gun Company.
> One Squadron Cavalry.
> A proportion of R.E. and R.A.M.C.
> A detachment of VIth Corps Cyclists.

8. It is proposed to convey the Cyclists in motor vehicles across the Neutral zone, and to debus them this side of, and well clear of, the German Neutral Zone Posts. The position of these posts (in so far as they are known will be notified later. The Cyclists would be used to cover the advance of the troops and will be supported by lorries with Machine Guns mounted in them, the bulk of the troops following in busses in rear.

9. Instructions will be issued later as to the attitude to be adopted in regard to the German Civil Population.

10. On no account will the present frontier be crossed by British Troops before "J" day.

11. The 12th Squadron R.A.F. will provide aeroplanes to reconnoitre the country immediately on our front, and to bring back information of the progress of the advance. Their machines are provided with W/T to communicate with H.Qrs. of each of the leading Brigades.

12. All Map references will be made to the 1/200,000 copies of which will be issued direct by G.H.Q. to Divisions. A limited number of 1/100,000 (German) Maps will also be issued to Divisions for local use.

13. Care must be taken to see that the line is disconnected in front of the most advanced telegraph office in use, to prevent messages being read by the enemy.

14. Information regarding the German Administrative Centres and Boundaries in the new area will be issued shortly.

German operatives working on this line will be instructed to remain at their posts, and proclamations to be distributed to them are being prepared, and will be issued to all concerned.

15. Advanced VIth Corps Headquarters will be established by 18.00 hours on "J" – 1 Day at LUDENSCHEID.

Distribution :–

(sd) G. REYNOLDS, Major.
G.S. Cavalry Division.

As for Divisional Order.
No. 1.

Confidential

"War Diary"

of

Headquarters, Dragoon Brigade

Period 1st to 30th June, 1919

Volume LIX.

Army Form C. 2118.

WAR DIARY of HEADQUARTERS, DRAGOON BRIGADE.

~~INTELLIGENCE SUMMARY~~   JUNE 1919.

(Erase heading not required.)

Instructions regarding War Diaries and Intelligence Summaries are contained in F. S. Regs., Part II. and the Staff Manual respectively. Title pages will be prepared in manuscript.

Place	Date	Hour	Summary of Events and Information	Remarks and references to Appendices
ZIEVERICH. (Germany)	1st to 12th		Nothing to report.	
	13th.		General HARMAN proceeded on leave to United Kingdom. Lieut: Colonel SADLER, The Carabiniers, assumed Temporary Command of the Brigade.	
	14th to 16th		Nothing to report.	
	17th.		Orders received that "J" day with be "A", i.e., 20th July; Composite Dragoon Squadron to march to COLOGNE forthwith.	
	18th to 27th		Nothing to report.	
	28th.		Peace signed. General HARMAN returned from leave.	
	29th.		Nothing to report.	
	30th.		Composite Squadron returns from forward area.	

C.A. Heyman
Major.
for G. O. C., Dragoon Brigade.

Confidential

War Diary

of 1 Dragoon Brigade.

Headquarters, 1 Dragoon Brigade
from 1st to 31st July 1919.

Army Form C. 2118.

WAR DIARY

HEADQUARTERS, DRAGOON BRIGADE.

INTELLIGENCE SUMMARY.

JULY, 1919.

(Erase heading not required.)

Instructions regarding War Diaries and Intelligence Summaries are contained in F. S. Regs., Part II. and the Staff Manual respectively. Title pages will be prepared in manuscript.

Place	Date	Hour	Summary of Events and Information	Remarks and references to Appendices
ZIEVERICH (Germany)	1st.		Brigadier General A.E.W. HARMAN, C.B., D.S.O., proceeded to United Kingdom to take over command of the Cavalry School, NETHERAVON. Brigadier General D'A. LEGARD, C.M.G., D.S.O., took over command of DRAGOON BRIGADE vice General HARMAN.	
	2nd.		Nothing to report.	
	3rd.		G. O. C. inspected billets and stables of Brigade Headquarters.	
	4th.		G. O. C. inspected billeting area of The Royal Dragoons.	
	5th.) 6th.)		Nothing to report.	
	7th.		G. O. C. inspected billeting area of Dragoon Machine Gun Squadron.	
	8th.		IV Corps Peace Celebration Holiday.	
	9th.		Divisional Commander inspected the Royal Dragoons at THORR 09.30 hours - Training of N. C. Os as Instructors. The Corps Commander visited each Regiment, Battery and Machine Gun Sqdn: in the morning.	
	10th.		Divisional Commander inspected The Inniskilling Dragoons at SINDORF 09.30 hours, and the Dragoon Machine Gun Squadron at SITTARDORF 11.00 hours - Training of N.C.O. Instructors. Rained heavily all day.	
	11th.		Divisional Commander inspected The Carabiniers at ELSDORF 10.00 hours. A special "ride" which it is proposed to insert in the Cavalry Training Manual, was carried out by The Carabiniers. Instructors Classes were also inspected.	
	12th.		Nothing to report. Rained heavily all day.	

Army Form C. 2118.

WAR DIARY

of HEAD QUARTERS, DRAGOON BRIGADE.

~~INTELLIGENCE SUMMARY~~ Sheet 2.

(Erase heading not required.)

Instructions regarding War Diaries and Intelligence Summaries are contained in F. S. Regs., Part II. and the Staff Manual respectively. Title pages will be prepared in manuscript.

Place	Date	Hour	Summary of Events and Information	Remarks and references to Appendices
ZIEVERICH (Germany)	13th		Nothing to Report.	
	14th.		Victory March of Allied Troops in PARIS. Two officers and 36 selected N. C. Os and men taken from the Carabiniers, Royals and Inniskillings represented the Dragoon Brigade. The guidons of the three Regiments also took part in the procession. G. O. C. inspected billeting area of The Inniskillings.	
	15th.		G. O. C. inspected billeting area of Dragoon Field Amce: at HEPPENDORF.	
	16th.		Nothing to report.	
	17th.		G. O. C. inspected billeting area of The Carabiniers, ELSDORF. Examination of candidates for 3rd Class Army School Certificate of Education held at QUADRATH.	
	18th) 19th) 20th) 21st)		Nothing to report.	
	22nd.		Examination of candidates for/1st Class Army School Certificate of Education held at QUADRATH. Group I of	
	23rd.		" " " for Group II of 1st Cl. ditto. ditto.	
	24th.		" " " for 1st Class (Bookkeeping, Languages etc) ditto.	
	25th.		G. O. C. inspected horses of The Carabiniers at ELSDORF. The Commander-in-Chief visited Brigade and lunched at B. H. Q.	
	26th.) 27th.)		Nothing to report.	

Army Form C. 2118.

WAR DIARY
of HEADQUARTERS, DRAGOON BRIGADE.
INTELLIGENCE SUMMARY. Sheet 3.

(Erase heading not required.)

Instructions regarding War Diaries and Intelligence Summaries are contained in F. S. Regs., Part II. and the Staff Manual respectively. Title pages will be prepared in manuscript.

Place	Date	Hour	Summary of Events and Information	Remarks and references to Appendices
ZIEVERICH (Germany)	28th.		The Commander-in-Chief again visited the Brigade and inspected the Carabiniers at ELSDORF, The Royal Dragoons at PAFFENDORF and The Inniskillings at SINDORF.	
	29th.		Classification of horses of The Royal Dragoons by the Brigade Board completed.	
	30th.		Classification of horses of The Carabiniers by the Brigade Board completed.	
	31st.		Nothing to report.	
			Weather was wet and cold throughout the month.	
			Regimental Classes in Equitation, Footdrill and Musketry were continued.	
			Educational training progressing satisfactorily in the Brigade. A large number of candidates attended the examinations for the 2nd and 3rd Class Certificates held at QUADRATH during the month.	

C.A. Heydeman Major.
for G. O. C., DRAGOON BRIGADE.

"War Diary"

of

Headquarters Dragoon Brigade

from

1st to 31st August, 1919.

Army Form C. 2118.

WAR DIARY
of HEADQUARTERS, DRAGOON BRIGADE.
INTELLIGENCE SUMMARY.
AUGUST, 1919.

(Erase heading not required.)

Instructions regarding War Diaries and Intelligence Summaries are contained in F. S. Regs., Part II. and the Staff Manual respectively. Title pages will be prepared in manuscript.

Place	Date	Hour	Summary of Events and Information	Remarks and references to Appendices
ZIEVERICH (Germany)	1st) 2nd)		Cavalry Division Sports.	
	3rd		Nothing to report.	
	4th) 5th)		Cavalry Division Meeting.	
	6th) to) 10th)		Nothing to report.	
	11th		G. O. C. inspected Royals recruits at Equitation, and attended Ceremonial Parade of "Y" Battery, R. H. A.	
	12th		G. O. C. /ceremonial drill of Royal Dragoons. inspected	
	13th		G. O. C. ceremonial drill of The Carabiniers.	
	14th		G. O. C. attended a tactical exercise, without troops, for all Officers of Inn-iskilling Dragoons.	
	15th		The Composite Dragoon Regiment marched to COLOGNE to take part in a Review for the Army Council. The Regiment was commanded by Lieut: Colonel G. R. Terrot, D.S.O., Inniskilling Dragoons. G. O. C. inspected the column en route at ICHENDORF.	
	16th) 17th)		Nothing to report.	
	18th) 19th)		Army Horse Show.	

Army Form C. 2118.

WAR DIARY

HEADQUARTERS, DRAGOON BRIGADE.
INTELLIGENCE SUMMARY.

(Erase heading not required.)

Instructions regarding War Diaries and Intelligence Summaries are contained in F. S. Regs., Part II. and the Staff Manual respectively. Title pages will be prepared in manuscript.

Place	Date	Hour	Summary of Events and Information	Remarks and references to Appendices
ZIEVERICH Germany.	20th to 26th		Nothing to report.	
	27th		Dragoon Brigade Entraining Order No. 1. issued (re transfer of the Brigade to the United Kingdom), copy attached.	APP: I
	28th to 31st		Nothing to report.	
			The weather was fine throughout the month. Training of recruits in Equitation, Musketry and physical drill etc., was carried out by all units.	

[signature]
Captain.
for G. O. C., DRAGOON BRIGADE.

BEF
CAV. DIV.
DRAGOON Bde
1st Royal DRAGOONS

1919 APR to 1919 AUG

FROM 3 CAV DIV 6 CAV BDE
Box 1153

Confidential

War Diary

of

The 1st K.(Royal) Dragoons.

from 1st to 30th April 1919

Volume No. LVII

DUPLICATE

Army Form C. 2118.

WAR DIARY
or
INTELLIGENCE—SUMMARY.

(Erase heading not required.)

Instructions regarding War Diaries and Intelligence Summaries are contained in F. S. Regs., Part II. and the Staff Manual respectively. Title pages will be prepared in manuscript.

Place	Date	Hour	Summary of Events and Information	Remarks and references to Appendices
PAFFENDORF. (Germany.)	April 1919.			
	1st.		The Regiment is now administered by 1st Cavalry Brigade to be known as "The Dragoon Brigade".	
	3rd.		3 Officers and 104 other ranks of the London Regiment lent to the Regiment to help in work. Lieut. R.W. Heyworth-Savage rejoined from Paris leave and Lieut.D.P.Lithgow rejoined from leave in the U.K.	
	4th.		70 riders transferred to the Carabiniers.	
	6th.		Lieut. S. Jackson and 2 other ranks proceeded to the U.K. for Dispersal.	
	7th.		The Divisional Commander (Major General Sir W.E.PEYTON, K.C.B.,K.C.V.O., D.S.O.) visited the Regiment. Lieut. A.S. Casey proceeded on leave to the U.K. 70 other ranks lent to the 10th Hussars to assist in move. 2/Lieut.R.Allan in charge of this party.	
	8th.		Lieut. F.W. Rhodes proceeded to the U.K. on leave.	
	9th.		Information received that Lieut. R.B. Bowesmen and 7 other ranks proceeded to the U.K. for Dispersal 26/3/19.	
	10th.		Lieut.R.C.G.Joy proceeded to the U.K. on leave.	
	12th.		Lieut.Hon.G.R.D. Browne proceeded on leave to the U.K.	
	13th.		Corps Commander (Lieut.General Sir A.J.Godley, K.C.B., K.C.M.G.,) visited the Regiment. Lieut.S.C.Dumbreck rejoined from sick leave.	

DUPLICATE

Army Form C. 2118.

Instructions regarding War Diaries and Intelligence
Summaries are contained in F. S. Regs., Part II.
and the Staff Manual respectively. Title pages
will be prepared in manuscript.

WAR DIARY
or
INTELLIGENCE-SUMMARY.

(Erase heading not required.)

Sheet II.

Place	Date	Hour	Summary of Events and Information	Remarks and references to Appendices
	April 1919.			
	15th.		Lieut. J.R.Wingfield-Digby detained in the U.K. and struck off the strength.	
	16th.		Received information that Lieut. J.F.Houstoun-Boswall and 84 other ranks, left at JEHAY-BODEGNEE, had proceeded home for Dispersal.	
			Lieut.P.L.Wilson rejoined from leave in the U.K.	
	18th.		Capt.C.W.Turner and Lieut.P.R.Davies-Cooke rejoined from leave in the U.K.	
	19th.		Lieut.W.H.W.Gossage and 40 other ranks lent to the Inniskillings to assist in move to SINDORF area.	
			Lieut.D'A.F.H.Harris M.C. proceeded on leave to U.K.	
	22nd.		No.1 Cinema showed to the Regiment at GLESCH.	
			Lecture at THORR by the Veterinary Officer.	
			Lieut.Col.F.W.Wormald D.S.O. proceeded to the U.K. on leave.	
			Major T.S.Irwin assumed command of the Regiment.	
			41 other ranks (band) joined the Regiment from England.	
	23rd.		Greys detachment at GROUVEN posted to Squadrons.	
	26th.		Capt.C.T.O'Callaghan M.C. to leave in U.K.	
			Lieut.P.R.Davies-Cooke performed duties of a/Adjutant.	
	28th. to 30th.		Nothing to report.	

DUPLICATE

Army Form C. 2118.

WAR DIARY
or
INTELLIGENCE-SUMMARY.

(Erase heading not required.)

Instructions regarding War Diaries and Intelligence Summaries are contained in F. S. Regs., Part II. and the Staff Manual respectively. Title Pages will be prepared in manuscript.

Place	Date	Hour	Summary of Events and Information	Remarks and references to Appendices
	April 1919.		Sheet III.	
			APPENDIX I.	
			NIL.	
			APPENDIX. II.	
			NIL.	
			APPENDIX. III.	
			NIL.	
			STRENGTH on 1st. April. 34 Offrs. 226 other ranks.	
			STRENGTH on 30th. April. 28 Offrs. 275 other ranks.	
			[signature] Lieut.& a/Adjt.	
			1/5/19. The Royal Dragoons.	

Confidential

War Diary

of

The 1st (Royal) Dragoons

from 1st to 31st May, 1919.

ORIGINAL

Army Form C. 2118.

WAR DIARY
or
INTELLIGENCE SUMMARY

(Erase heading not required.)

Sheet I.

Instructions regarding War Diaries and Intelligence Summaries are contained in F.S. Regs., Part II. and the Staff Manual respectively. Title pages will be prepared in manuscript.

Place	Date	Hour	Summary of Events and Information	Remarks and references to Appendices
Germany.	May 1919.			
	1st.		Lieuts. WYNN and DUMBRECK proceeded to ST.VITH Area for topographical reconnaissance Duty.	
	2nd.		Major R.Houstoun and Lieut.G.R.D.Browne returned from leave in U.K.	
	3rd.		Sergt.R.Mynard proceeded to ALDERSHOT to attend a Course at the Physical Training School. No.1 Army Cinema performed at PAFFENDORF.	
	4th.		Lieut.D.P.Lithgow proceeded to COLOGNE to take over duties of A.D.C. to Commander-in-Chief.	
	5th.		"B" Squadron Sports at GLESCH. The Band played during the afternoon.	
	6th.		H.R.H.Field Marshall The Duke of Connaught passed through the Regimental Area today and stopped to watch the football match between "B" & "C" Squadrons on the ground at GLESCH.	
	8th.		14 Riding horses to IVth Corps Animal Collecting Camp DUREN, prior to going to ROUEN.	
	9th.		The Band and Regimental Football team went over to WERMELISCHEN (H.Qrs.51st Hants.Regt.) and stayed the night.	
	10th.		Regimental Football team played the Hampshire Regiment which resulted in a draw = 2 goals all.	
	11th.		Regimental Team and Band returned to the Regiment. Lieut.S.L.Jeffrey proceeded to the U.K. on Leave. Lieut.R.H.W.Henderson proceeded to Paris on Leave.	
	12th.		Major T.S.Irwin proceeded to the U.K. on leave. Major R.Houstoun assumed command of the Regiment. Sergt.Bowles proceeded to NETHERAVON to attend a course at the Cavalry School. Pte.Gallagher proceeded to NETHERAVON as servant to Lieut.Jeffrey.	
	13th.		Lieut.R.F.Heyworth-Savage and Lieut.F.W.Rhodes returned from Leave in the U.K.	
	14th.		Regimental Football team played 9th London Regiment and won - 1goal to 0.	

Continued.

ORIGINAL

Army Form C. 2118.

WAR DIARY
or
INTELLIGENCE SUMMARY.

(Erase heading not required.)

Sheet II.

Place	Date	Hour	Summary of Events and Information	Remarks and references to Appendices
Germany.	May 1919.			
	15th.		G.O.C. The Dragoon Brigade inspected the horses of the Regiment. 2/Lieut.D.A.Longbotton proceed to the U.K. on leave, 2 other ranks proceeded to Concentration Camp for Dispersal. 8 Riders proceeded to IVth Corps Animal Collecting Camp.	
	16th.		Lieut.D'A.F.H.Harris M.C. rejoined from leave. 4 other ranks proceeded to Concentration Camp for re-enlistment furlough. Lieut.E.St.G.Stedall M.C. re-joined from leave in U.K.	
	17th.		Lieut.C.G.H.Hilton-Green rejoined from Reserve Regiment.	
	18th.		Capt.C.T.O'Callaghan M.C. rejoined from leave in U.K.	
	19th.		Lieut.S.H.Bromley struck off the Strength on demobilization. Lieut.S.L.Jeffrey to Cavalry School, NETHERAVON.	
	20th.		10 other ranks joined from Northants Yeomanry.	
	21st.		"C" Squadron played Field Squadron at Cricket at QUADRATH.	
	23rd.		Lieut.E.St.G Stedall M.C. proceeded to the U.K. to report to the W.O. in writing.	
	24th.		Regiment played the Carabiniers at Football. Won 2-1.	
	27th.		G.O.C. inspected the Composite Squadron at THORR. Lieut.R.H.W.Henderson rejoined from leave at PARIS.	
	28th.		Brigade Polo commenced at ICHENDORF.	
	29th.		Major T.S.Twin rejoined from leave in the U.K. and assumed command of the Regiment Regimental Football played the 63rd Rifle Brigade. result Royals 4 R.B. 0.	

Continued.

ORIGINAL

Sheet III. Army Form C. 2118.

WAR DIARY
or
INTELLIGENCE SUMMARY.
(Erase heading not required.)

Instructions regarding War Diaries and Intelligence Summaries are contained in F.S. Regs., Part II. and the Staff Manual respectively. Title pages will be prepared in manuscript.

Place	Date	Hour	Summary of Events and Information	Remarks and references to Appendices
Germany.	May 1919.			
	30th.		Lieuts. W. Williams Wynn and S.C. Dumbreck rejoined from reconnaissance Duty.	
	31st.		"C" Squadron held Sports at THORR.	
			Weather was consistently fine throughout the month. Each Squadron turned out 30 or 40 horses to graze. Polo started at ICHENDORF - all officers playing.	
			APPENDIX I. NIL.	
			APPENDIX II. NIL.	
			APPENDIX III. 10 other ranks from Northants Yeomanry.	
			STRENGTH ON 1st May. 35 Officers. 202 other ranks.	
			STRENGTH ON 31st May. 33 Officers. 253 other ranks.	
Germany. 1st June 1919.				

C.G. Callahan
Captain and Adjutant.
The Royal Dragoons.

Dragoon Guards

Confidential.

√ F

War Diary

of

The 1st (Royal) Dragoons

period 1st to 30th June, 1919.

Volume No. LLX

ORIGINAL.

Instructions regarding War Diaries and Intelligence Summaries are contained in F. S. Regs., Part II. and the Staff Manual respectively. Title pages will be prepared in manuscript.

THE ROYAL DRAGOONS.

WAR DIARY
or
INTELLIGENCE SUMMARY.

(Erase heading not required.)

Army Form C. 2118.

Sheet N°..

Place	Date	Hour	Summary of Events and Information	Remarks and references to Appendices
Germany.	June 1.		2/Lieut.D.A.Longbottom from leave. Colonel (Hon.Major General) J.F.Burn Murdoch, C.B.,C.M.G., to be Colonel, 1st.Royal Dragoons, in succession to Major General J.E.Lindley, who has resigned the appointment, with effect from 16th.April 1919.	
	3.		Cinematograph at Paffendorf. Lieut.W.R.Birch awarded Military Cross and S.S.M.B.Wischhusen and Sergt.W.J.Seaton awarded D.C.M., London Gazette dated 3rd. June 1919.	
	5.		Royals versus Inniskillings - Won 5 goals to one. Lieut.R.F.Heyworth Savage to leave.	
	6.		Miss Lena Ashwell's concert Party at Bergheim.	
	7.		Capt.C.W.Turner and Lieuts.R.H.W.Henderson and P.R.Davies Cooke to U.K. for Regimental Dinner.	
	10.		39 O.R. Labour Corps attached to Regiment for grooming. Major R.Houstoun, Capt.G.T.O'Callaghan, and Lieuts.W.Williams Wynn and S.C.Dumbreck to U.K. for Regimental Dinner.	
	11.		Regimental Dinner at Cafe Royal, Major General J.F.BurnMurdoch in the Chair.	
	13.		Memorial Service at Turnich (Hqrs.X.R.Hussars) for the late Lieut-Col.P.E.Hardwick, D.S.O., Cinema at Paffendorf. (Lieut-Col.Hardwick, wounded at Arras, 1917, died in London after a (long illness.	
	14.		Royals versus 51st.Hampshire Regt. - Won 3 goals to nil.	
	15.		Major H.A.Tomkinson, D.S.O., rejoined from U.K. and assumed Command of the Regiment.	
	16.		Lieut.D.P.Lithgow struck off strength on being seconded as A.D.C., to C-in-C.,Army of the Rhine. Draft of 32 O.R. joined from England.	
	17.		Composite Squadron moved up to White City, Cologne, under Command of Capt.W.P.Browne, M.C.	
	18.		Composite Squadron moved to Born.	
	19.		70 O.R. Labour Corps attached for grooming. Capt.F.W.Wilson Fitzgerald, D.S.O.,M.C., rejoined Regiment from leave.	
			(Continued)	CD Callaghan Capt. and Adjt., The Royal Dragoons.

ORIGINAL.

THE ROYAL DRAGOONS.

WAR DIARY

or

INTELLIGENCE SUMMARY

SHEET II.

Army Form C. 2118.

(Erase heading not required.)

Instructions regarding War Diaries and Intelligence Summaries are contained in F. S. Regs., Part II. and the Staff Manual respectively. Title pages will be prepared in manuscript.

Place	Date	Hour	Summary of Events and Information	Remarks and references to Appendices
Germany.	June 20.		Lieut.W.H.W.Gossage to leave in U.K.	
	21.		Lieut.R.F.Heyworth Savage from leave and Capt.J.Lyons, R.A.M.C., to leave.	
	24.		Draft of 12 O.R., from 6th.Reserve Regiment joined Regiment and taken on strength. Capt. C.G.W.Swire from leave to U.K. Capt.T.H.Hannan, attached IV Corps, struck off strength on proceeding for demobilisation.	
	26.		2/Lieut.C.W.Fox struck off strength whilst attached to No.4 area as P.R.O.,	
	27.		Draft of 15 O.R. from 6th.Reserve Regiment taken on strength.	
	28.		Peace was signed at Versailles.	
	29.		String Band played at British Empire Leave Club.	
	30.		General Harman relinquished Command of Brigade on proceeding to Command of the Cavalry School, Netheravon. General D'Arcy Legard assumed Command of the Brigade.	
			-:-;-:-;-:-;-:-;-:-;-:-;-:-;-:-;-:-;-:-	
			SUMMARY.	
			Weather broke on June 22nd. and remained stormy for remainder of the month. Training was suspended owing to the move of the Composite Squadron to a point of concentration. Precautionary Orders were issued as regards the Regimental area in the event of civil disturbances.	
			-:-;-:-;-:-;-:-;-:-;-:-;-:-;-:-;-:-;-:-	

C. Callaghan
Capt. and Adjt.,
The Royal Dragoons.

ORIGINAL.

THE ROYAL DRAGOONS.   SHEET III.

WAR DIARY
or
INTELLIGENCE SUMMARY.

(Erase heading not required.)

Army Form C. 2118.

Instructions regarding War Diaries and Intelligence Summaries are contained in F. S. Regs., Part II. and the Staff Manual respectively. Title pages will be prepared in manuscript.

Place	Date	Hour	Summary of Events and Information	Remarks and references to Appendices
GERMANY	June.			

Strength of 1st. June 1919   Offrs.   O.R.
Strength on 30th. June 1919.   33   250
                                                            29   309

APPENDIX I.

REINFORCEMENTS WHO HAVE JOINED DURING JUNE 1919.

Major H.A.Tomlinson, D.S.O., joined 15-6-19.
32 O.R. from England, joined 16-6-19.
12 O.R. from England, joined 24-6-19.
15 O.R. from England, joined 27-6-19.

APPENDIX II.

HONOURS AND AWARDS.

Lieut.W.R.Birch. awarded Military Cross,   ) London Gazette
S.S.M.B.Wischhusen awarded Distinguished Conduct Medal.) Supplement, dated
Sergt.W.J.Seaton, awarded Distinguished Conduct Medal,) 3-6-19.

APPENDIX III.

CASUALTIES.

Nil.

C.B.Callaghan
Capt. and Adjt.,
The Royal Dragoons.

Confidential

War Diary

of

1st (Royal) Dragoons.

From 1st to 31st July, 1919.

"ORIGINAL."

Army Form C. 2118.

WAR DIARY
or
INTELLIGENCE SUMMARY.

Sheet. I.

(Erase heading not required.)

Instructions regarding War Diaries and Intelligence Summaries are contained in F. S. Regs. Part II. and the Staff Manual respectively. Title pages will be prepared in manuscript.

Place	Date	Hour	Summary of Events and Information	Remarks and references to Appendices
PAFFENDORF, Germany. July, 1919.	1st.		Mobile Squadron rejoined Regiment.	
	2nd.		Lieut.E.St.G.STEDALL M.C. resigned Commission. (Lon.Gaz.Supp.dated 22-6-19.)	
	4th.		G.O.C., Dragoon Brigade, inspected Regimental Area.	
	5th.		31 other ranks London Regiment, returned to their Unit. No.1 Army Cinema at PAFFENDORF. Extract from London Gazette Supplement dated 5th July,1919.:- "Lieut.A.S.Casey,) "Lieut.J.F.Houstoun-Boswall,) "S.S.M.Angus G,) Mentioned in Despatches. "Sadd.S.Sergt.Dorling R,) "Sergt.Sampson J.)	
	7th.		Capt.F.W.Wilson-Fitzgerald D.S.O.,M.C.) Sergts.Allsebrooke, Boag, Buckham, and Dickenson, proceeded to PARIS to take part in the Victory March to be held on 14th.	
	8th.		67 other ranks London Regiment, transferred to the Regiment. Lieut.R.F.Heyworth-Savage proceeded to PARIS with the Regimental Guidon to take part in the Victory March. Peace Day celebrated in IVth Corps. Regiment held an inter-Squadron Football Tournament which was won by "A" Squadron, followed by a high tea and impromptu concert. Lieut.H.Harrison resigns his Commission.	
	11th.		Cinema performance at PAFFENDORF.	
	13th.		Lieut.S.C.Dunbreck proceeded to the U.K. on leave.	

Army Form C. 2118.

WAR DIARY
or
INTELLIGENCE SUMMARY.
(Erase heading not required.)

Sheet II.

"ORIGINAL".

Instructions regarding War Diaries and Intelligence Summaries are contained in F. S. Regs., Part II. and the Staff Manual respectively. Title pages will be prepared in manuscript.

Place	Date	Hour	Summary of Events and Information	Remarks and references to Appendices
July, 1919.	14th.		Victory March took place in PARIS.	
	17th.		Classification of horses carried out by the Commanding Officer. Paris party rejoined.	
	18th.		Eliminating heats for the Cavalry Divisional Sports held at GLESCH. 33 other ranks Labour Corps attached to the Regiment.	
	20th.		Major H.A.Tomkinson D.S.O. won the "Prix de JOORIS" at CREFELD in a meeting held by 1st Belgian Guides. Major T.S.Irwin granted one months leave to the U.K.	
	21st.		Maj-General J.F.Burn-Murdoch C.M.G.,D.S.O.,Colonel of 1st Royal Dragoons, visited PAFFENDORF and remained until 26th.	
	23rd.		Lieut.W.S.Phillips granted one months leave to the U.K. 33 other ranks Labour Corps attached to the Regiment.	
	24th.		Polo on Hussar Brigade ground. Gallimaxy for Handicap Tournament, Royals beat Div.H.Qrs. Preliminary/	
	25th.		Polo on Husser Brigade ground. Preliminary for Subalterns Tournament, Royal beat 10th Hussars. Capt.C.W.Turner M.C. proceeded to the U.K. for duty at the Royal Military College, SANDHURST.	
	26th.		9 Officers and 192 other ranks proceeded on a Rhine trip. 10 other ranks Labour Corps attached to the Regiment.	
	27th.		Cinema performance at PAFFENDORF.	
	28th.		Polo on Hussar Brigade ground. 2nd Round Handicap Tournament Hussar Brigade H.Qrs.,beat Regiment. Commander-in-Chief inspected the Regimental Foot-drill and Musketry Classes.	
	29th.		Horse classification carried out by the Brigade Board.	

"ORIGINAL".

Army Form C. 2118.

WAR DIARY
or
INTELLIGENCE SUMMARY.

Sheet III.

(Erase heading not required.)

Instructions regarding War Diaries and Intelligence Summaries are contained in F.S. Regs., Part II. and the Staff Manual respectively. Title pages will be prepared in manuscript.

Place	Date	Hour	Summary of Events and Information	Remarks and references to Appendices
July,1919.	30th.		Polo on Hussar Brigade ground. 2nd round Subalterns Tournament, Inniskillings beat Royals.	
	31st.		Lieut.P.R.Davies-Cooke and Lieut.Hon.GR.D.Browne proceeded to the U.K. on leave.	
			Weather was wet and cold throughout the month. Regimental Classes in Equitation. Footdrill and Musketry were continues and Recruit training was carried out under Squadron arrangements.	
			Strength on 1st of month. 29 Officers. 209 other ranks.	
			Strength on 31st of month. 28 Officers. 371 other ranks.	
Germany. 1st August, 1919.			C O'Callahan
Captain and Adjutant.
The Royal Dragoons.	

Dragoons
√F

Confidential

"War Diary"

of

1st (Royal) Dragoons.

from 1st to 31st August 1919.

ORIGINAL.

THE ROYAL DRAGOONS.

WAR DIARY

or

~~INTELLIGENCE SUMMARY~~

(Erase heading not required.)

SHEET 1.

Army Form C. 2118.

Instructions regarding War Diaries and Intelligence Summaries are contained in F. S. Regs., Part II. and the Staff Manual respectively. Title pages will be prepared in manuscript.

Place	Date August.	Hour	Summary of Events and Information	Remarks and references to Appendices
Germany.	1.		Divisional Horse Show. - Sergt.Mynard won N.C.Os. jumping. Pte.Allen was 6th.	
	2.		Divisional Races. Major Tomkinson 1st. on Madeleine, 3rd. on Torpedo, Lieut.W.W.Wynn 3rd. on Norah.	
	3.		Band at British Empire Leave Club for concert. Capt.C.A.Gordon struck off on being seconded as A.D.C., to C-in-C. Lieut.P.R.D.Cooke proceeded to Cav.School, Netheravon. to replace Lieut.S.L.Jeffrey.	
	4.		Band played at Divisional Horse Show. Sergt.Mynard and Pte.Allen in Open Jumping.	
	5.		Lieut.R.H.W.Henderson to leave in U.K. for one month. Divisional concert at Horrem.	
	9.		Lieut.R.C.G.Joy to leave in U.K.	
	11.		Lieut.A.S.Casey to leave in U.K.	
	15.		Cinema at Paffendorf. Composite Squadron under Capt.F.W.Wilson Fitzgerald, D.S.O.,M.C., to Cologne for Army Council's review. IV Corps Tattoo at Niedeggen.	
	16.		"Fancies" concert at Paffendorf. Lieut.G.R.D.Browne from leave.	
	18.		Army Horse Show. "B" Sqdn.limber 4th. Army Council review held at Cologne.	
	19.		Composite Squadron rejoined Regiment.	
	20.		Lieut.S.C.Dumbreck struck off strength on proceeding to U.K. for demobilisation.	
	21.		Major R.Houstoun to U.K. on leave.	
	23.		Races at Cologne. Major Tomkinson 3rd. on Madeleine, 2/Lieut.Longbottom 3rd. on Torpedo. Lieut.W.S.Phillips from leave.	

ACullffe
Capt. and Adjt.,
The Royal Dragoons.

Army Form C. 2118.

THE ROYAL DRAGOONS. SHEET II.

WAR DIARY
or
~~INTELLIGENCE SUMMARY.~~

(Erase heading not required.)

Instructions regarding War Diaries and Intelligence
Summaries are contained in F. S. Regs., Part II.
and the Staff Manual respectively. Title pages
will be prepared in manuscript.

Place	Date August	Hour	Summary of Events and Information	Remarks and references to Appendices
Germany.	24.		Lieut.R.C.G.Joy from leave.	
	25.		Royals versus 15th.Hussars at polo. Royals won.	
	27.		Lieut.C.C.H.Hilton Green to leave. 2/Lieut.J.W.Walker resigns his commission and receives a gratuity. (London Gazette dated 26/8/19.)	
	28.		Lieut.D.A.F.H.Harris, M.C., from leave. Royals versus 10th.Hussars at polo and won - 3 to 2. Band to British Empire Leave Club for Officers' dance.	
	30.		Royals versus 17th.Lancers at Polo and lost - 7 to 2. Cologne Races. Major Tomkinson 1st.in Rhine St.Leger Stakes on Madeleine. Lieut.Phillips and 7 O.Rs. to Antwerp with Equipment train.	
	31.		Racing at Crefeld under auspices of 1st.Belgian Guides.	

****

The weather has been fair during the month.   Definite orders were received that
the Regiment would move to England but destination has not definitely been given.

****
-%-

Capt.and Adjt.,
The Royal Dragoons.

ORIGINAL.

Instructions regarding War Diaries and Intelligence Summaries are contained in F. S. Regs., Part II. and the Staff Manual respectively. Title pages will be prepared in manuscript.

THE ROYAL DRAGOONS

WAR DIARY

or

INTELLIGENCE SUMMARY

(Erase heading not required.)

Army Form C. 2118.

SHEET III.

Place	Date	Hour	Summary of Events and Information	Remarks and references to Appendices
	AUGUST 1919. **********			
			Reinforcements received during the month:—	
			NIL.	
			Casualties sustained during the month:—	
			NIL.	
			Honours and rewards:—	
			NIL.	
			**************************	

C V Callaghan
Capt. and Adjt.,
The Royal Dragoons.

ORIGINAL.

THE ROYAL DRAGOONS. SHEET IV.
WAR DIARY

or

INTELLIGENCE SUMMARY.

Army Form C. 2118.

(Erase heading not required.)

Instructions regarding War Diaries and Intelligence Summaries are contained in F. S. Regs., Part II. and the Staff Manual respectively. Title pages will be prepared in manuscript.

Place	Date	Hour	Summary of Events and Information	Remarks and references to Appendices
			Strength of Regiment on 1st August 1919 .... Officers. 29 O.R. 375	
			Strength of Regiment on 31st August 1919 .... 26 372	
			********************************	
			en Callaghan Capt. and Adjt., The Royal Dragoons.	

BEF
CAV. DIV.
DRAGOON Bde
6 DRAGOON GDS
1919 APR to 1919 AUG

FROM 2 CAV DN 4 CAV Bde
Box 1137

Joins Dragoon Bde
18-3-19

Box 825

Confidential

War Diary

6th Dragoon Guards (the Carabiniers)
From 1st to 30th April 1919.

Volume No. XIII

Army Form C. 2118.

WAR DIARY
or
INTELLIGENCE SUMMARY
(Erase heading not required.)

Instructions regarding War Diaries and Intelligence Summaries are contained in F. S. Regs., Part II. and the Staff Manual respectively. Title pages will be prepared in manuscript.

Place	Date	Hour	Summary of Events and Information	Remarks and references to Appendices
ELSDORF Germany	APRIL 1st		Exercise & stables under squadron arrangements. WB	
"	2nd		Exercise under squadron. Stables 11.00hrs & 17.00hrs. S.O.E. Dragoon Bde inspected the horses at stables. 3 ors B.U.K. on leave. WB	
"	3rd		Exercise & stables under squadron. 2 ors to U.K. on leave. 7 officers & O.R.s of 1st Seaforths arrived to help with the horses. Lt. A. E. C. & C.O. proceeded to join Armistice Commission at SPA. Lt. H. Price rejoined from Base Remount Depot. Lt. A. E. Phillips to U.K. for army golf championship. Horses inspected by the M.O. WB	
"	4th		Exercise under squadron. Stables 11.00hrs & 17.00hrs. 70 horses from Rupals. Horse accounts inspected by Maj Carliss D.S.O. 1st Battn R.A. WB	
"	5th		Exercise with squadrons. Stables 11.00hrs & 17.00hrs. 1 or. to U.K. on leave. Lt A.M. Taylor to U.K. for demob. WB	
"	6th		Stables under squadrons. 1 or. to U.K. on leave. 60 cavalrymen sent at 16.00hrs to help move the 16th Hussars. WB	
"	7th		Exercise under squadrons. Stables as usual. 1 or. to U.K. on leave. 1/A 9.25 ors. 1st Seaforths to M.S. squadron at BERRENDORFF. G.O.C. Cav. Div: & Dragoon Bde inspected the horses at stables. WB	
"	8th		Exercise under squadrons. Stables as usual. 1 or. to U.K. on leave. Gen. A.W. Hanman D.S.O. took over command Dragoon Bde WB	
"	9th		Exercise under squadron. Stables as usual. 1 or. & Maj P.N. Smith M.C. to U.K. on leave. A.D.V.S. saw 2 horses for casting ob 17 bchns. Horse accounts inspected by Maj C. Munroriff 6th Dragoons. WB	
"	10th		Exercise with squadron. Stables as usual. 1 or. to U.K. on leave. Health inspection by M.O. WB	
"	11th		Exercise under sqdns. Stables as usual. 1 or. to U.K. on leave. Capt. S.P.C. Kinsey rejoined from leave. WB	
"	12th		Exercise under sqdns. Stables as usual. 1 or. to U.K. on leave. WB	
"	13th		Stables under sqdn. 1 or. to U.K. on leave. All R.C.s to church under P.R. Regrave. S.O.E. Cav Div to enquiry & divine WBs.	
"	14th		Exercise & stables as usual. 1 or. to U.K. on leave. S.O.E. IV Corps inspected horses Gills & also A.D.M.S. Cav Div. Baths allotted to the regiment. WB	
"	15th		Exercise & stables as usual. 1 or. to U.K. on leave. Summary of evidence taken re case of 5819 Pte A.E. Tilden. WB	
"	16th		Exercise & stables as usual. 1 or. to U.K. on leave. Conference & C.O. at Bde H.Q. 1 horse destroyed. Lt. M. J. Anderson to U.K. on Court. WB	

Army Form C. 2118.

WAR DIARY
or
INTELLIGENCE SUMMARY.
(Erase heading not required.)

Instructions regarding War Diaries and Intelligence Summaries are contained in F. S. Regs., Part II. and the Staff Manual respectively. Title pages will be prepared in manuscript.

Place	Date	Hour	Summary of Events and Information	Remarks and references to Appendices
ILSDORF Germany	APRIL 17th		Exercise & stables as usual. 1 or to U.K. on leave. S.O.C. Dragoon Bdr inspected lines & stables. D.C.O. inspected S.B.R's Health inspection by M.O. A draft of 1 Off & 18 O.R. from Graffrath. Capt J. N. Partinwlyk rejoined from leave. LtB.	
	18th		Stables under arrangements. 1 or to U.K. on leave. 1 saddler & Pte J.S.S. to U.K. on démob. Conference of officers are 30 hrs. LtB.	
	19th		Exercise & stables as usual. 1 or to U.K. on leave. 45 Recruits retained by 5.3rd Gardens at noon. 40 or to Galop 6th Dragoon same. LtB	
	20th		Stables under arrangements. 1 or to U.K. on leave. Also Pte P.S. Hammond. Church Parade at 10 onbu. LtB	
	21st		Exercise & stables as usual. 1 or to U.K. on leave LtB.	
	22nd		Exercise & stables as usual. 1 or to U.K. on leave. Cpe Allen rejoined from M.G. Cojt. Baths allotted the regiment. LtB.	
	23rd		Exercise & stables as usual. 1 or to U.K. on leave also 2/Lt A. F. Holland. Conference of C.O.'s at Bdr N.Q.H 10 o'clock. LtB.	
	24th		Exercise & stables as usual. 1 or to U.K. on leave. 1 S.C.M. & Pte Triber. Health inspection by M.O. LtB	
	25th		Exercise & stables as usual. 1 or to U.K. on leave. S.O.C. Dragoon Bdr inspected comforts &c at THOOR. LtB	
	26th		Exercise & stables as usual. 1 or to U.K. on leave. Gen. C. visited the regiment. LtB.	
	27th		Stables under arrangements. 1 or to U.K. on leave. Nine formists Church parade at 10 o'clock. LtB.	
	28th		Exercise & stables as usual. 1 or & Capt R.H. Barnsley to U.K. on leave. Lieut Cotton & D.O. & O.R.S. Edwards rejoined. LtB.	
	29th		Exercise & stables as usual. 1 or to U.K. on leave. LtB	
	30th		Exercise & stables as usual. 1 or to U.K. on leave. 2 rejoined from U.K. LtB	

Hammond Captain
for O.C. Carabiniers.

Confidential 1/t

War Diary

6th Dragoon Guards (The Carabiniers)

From 1st to 31st May, 1919.

Army Form C. 2118.

WAR DIARY
~~INTELLIGENCE SUMMARY.~~
(Erase heading not required.)

Instructions regarding War Diaries and Intelligence Summaries are contained in F. S. Regs., Part II. and the Staff Manual respectively. Title pages will be prepared in manuscript.

Place	Date MAY	Hour	Summary of Events and Information	Remarks and references to Appendices
ELSDORF	1st to 5th		Routine as usual &c.	
	6th		H.R.H. The Duke of Connaught inspected the regiment at 15.30 hrs. expressed himself as highly pleased with the parade. &c.	
	7 & 8th		Routine as usual &c.	
	9th		G.O.C. Dragoon Bde inspected the Composite Squadron at 16.45 hrs. C.O. went to BERLIN as courier. &c.	
	10–23rd		Routine as usual &c.	
	24th		C.O. inspected Composite Squadron at 10.30 hrs. &c.	
	25 & 26		Routine as usual &c.	
	27th		G.O.C. Dragoon Bde inspected composite regiment at THORR &c.	
	28,29,30,31		Routine as usual &c.	

W. Sarsaparel Capt
for O.C. Carabiniers.

Confidential ✓

War Diary

6th Dragoon Guards (Carabiniers)

Period 1st to 30th June 1919.

Volume No LIX

Army Form C. 2118.

WAR DIARY
or
INTELLIGENCE SUMMARY.
(Erase heading not required.)

Instructions regarding War Diaries and Intelligence Summaries are contained in F. S. Regs., Part II. and the Staff Manual respectively. Title pages will be prepared in manuscript.

Place	Date	Hour	Summary of Events and Information	Remarks and references to Appendices
ELSDORF Germany	JUNE 1st 2nd		Routine as usual. WES.	
	3rd		King's Birthday parade. WES.	
	4th to 9th		Routine as usual. WES.	
	10th		Routine as usual. 33 O.Rs from Labour Corps joined WES.	
	11th to 15th		Routine as usual. WES.	
	16th		Routine as usual. 35 O.Rs from 4.R.R.E. & 40 O.Rs from Labour Corps joined WES.	
	17th		Mobile force of 2 off. & 75 O.Rs left at 10.30 hrs for Cologne. 50 O.Rs Labour Corps joined. WES.	
	18th		Exercises, paying attacks. Draft of 23 O.Rs arrived from 6 R.R. Caw.	
	19th to 30th		Routine as usual. WES.	

Wayward Capt & ADW
for O.C. Cn & Paratroopers.

Dragoons &c

Confidential.

War Diary
of
6th Dragoon Guards (The Carabiniers)
From 1st to 31st July, 1919

Army Form C. 2118.

WAR DIARY
or
INTELLIGENCE SUMMARY.
(Erase heading not required.)

Instructions regarding War Diaries and Intelligence Summaries are contained in F.S. Regs., Part II. and the Staff Manual respectively. Title pages will be prepared in manuscript.

Place	Date July	Hour	Summary of Events and Information	Remarks and references to Appendices
ELSDORF	1		Routine as usual. Staff Capt returned from out post line. wd.	
"	2			
"	3		Routine & training as usual. wd.	
"	4			
"	5			
"	6			
"	7		Routine training as usual. Capt fild left 4 peace party to Paris. Country hopping in Rhineland declared. wd.	
"	8		Routine training as usual. wd.	
"	9		Peace Celebrations. G.O.C. IV Corps Major Genl visited rept at 11.15 & lunch. 33rd gordon reformed Highland Div. wd.	
"	10		Routine training as usual. wd.	
"	11		Routine training as usual & G.O.C. Cow: Div: inspected all claims at winter. wd.	
"	12		Routine as usual. wd.	
"	13			
"	14		Half the regiment to OPLADEN etc under Capt R.M. Bamsley. wd.	
"	15		Routine as usual. wd.	
"	16		Routine as usual. 1st OPLADEN party returned. wd.	
"	17		Routine as usual. 2nd half regiment to OPLADEN etc. wd.	
"	18		Routine as usual. Paris Peace party returned. wd.	
"	19			
"	20		Routine as usual. wd.	
"	21			
"	22			

Army Form C. 2118.

WAR DIARY
or
INTELLIGENCE SUMMARY.
(Erase heading not required.)

Instructions regarding War Diaries and Intelligence Summaries are contained in F. S. Regs., Part II. and the Staff Manual respectively. Title pages will be prepared in manuscript.

Place	Date JULY	Hour	Summary of Events and Information	Remarks and references to Appendices
ELSDORF	23rd		Routine as usual. 2nd OPLADEN party returned. HJS	
"	24th 25th		} Routine of training as usual. HJS	
"	26th		Routine & training as usual. O.C. Dragoon B.de inspected billets etc. HJS	
"	27th		Routine as usual. HJS	
"	28th		Two squadrons classified by V/O. C-in-C. visited divisional HJS	
"	29th		Remainder of regt classified by V/O. HJS	
"	30th		Two squadrons classified by B.de Bd. Left 09.00 hrs, remainder at 12.00 hrs. HJS	
"	31st		Routine under squadrons. First day Car. Bn. west HJS.	

H Garrard Capt
a/N Carabiniers
for O. C. Carabiniers.

Dragoon Gds
√ (F)

Confidential

War Diary

of

6th Dragoon Guards (The Carabiniers)

from

1st to 31st August, 1919.

Army Form C. 2118.

WAR DIARY
or
INTELLIGENCE SUMMARY
(Erase heading not required.)

ORDERLY ROOM
No...........
1 - SEP 1919
THE CARABINIERS.
6TH DRAGOON GUARDS

Instructions regarding War Diaries and Intelligence Summaries are contained in F. S. Regs., Part II. and the Staff Manual respectively. Title pages will be prepared in manuscript.

Place	Date	Hour	Summary of Events and Information	Remarks and references to Appendices
ELSDORF Germany	Aug 1st		Routine as usual. Cav Divl. Week. Itd.	
	2nd			
	3rd			
	4th			
	5th			
	6th			
	7th			
	8th		Training as usual. Draft sent to U.K. for 3rd D.G. Itd	
	9th			
	10th			
	11th			
	12th		Training as usual. Itd.	
	13th		Training as usual. S.O.C. Dragoon Bde attended. D.R's visited refresher stand "A" etc" Itd.	
	14th		Training as usual. B's V.S sports 18.00hrs. Itd.	
	15th		Combined Squadron under Capt R.N. Bamsley left for Cologne Water Park in review for Army Council Itd	
	16th		Routine as usual. Itd.	
	17th			
	18th			
	19th		Cologne Review party returned Itd.	
	20-27		Routine under Squadrons. Packing prior to leaving Army of Rhine Itd.	
	28th		Routine under Squadrons. Taking over party left for Ireland. Itd.	
	29th		Routine under Squadrons. Equipment left for ANTWERP. Itd	
	30th		Routine under Squadrons. Itd	
	31st		Routine under Squadrons Itd	

Harvard Captain(?)
for O.C. Carabiniers.

BEF
CAV. DIV.
DRAGOON Bde

6 INNISK DRAGOONS

1919 APR ~~MAY~~ 1920 FEB

From 3 Cav Div. > Cav Bde

Box 1155

WAR DIARY or INTELLIGENCE SUMMARY

Army Form C. 2118.

Place	Date	Hour	Summary of Events and Information	Remarks and references to Appendices
NIEDEREMBT	APRIL 1–17		The Commanding Officer inspected the Regiment by Troops during this period. Riding School for Young Officers & the Band.	
	18–23		The Regiment moved from NIEDEREMBT to SINDORF. Riding School for Band.	
SINDORF	24		The Regiment paraded as a mobile squadron at 10am & was inspected by the G.O.C. Dragoon Bde. Lt. Colonel C.R. Tenet D.S.O. in command of the Hybrid Regt. composed of a Sqdn. Carbiniers, Royals & Innis Killings. Riding School for Young Officers & the Band.	
	25–30		Training of Recruits was carried out by all officers of the Regiment throughout this month.	

Ian Maindrie Capt & Adjutant
Innis Killing Dragoons

Dragoon Bar

Confidential

"War Diary

of

6th (Inniskilling) Dragoons.

From 1st to 31st May, 1919.

Army Form C. 2118.

WAR DIARY
or
INTELLIGENCE SUMMARY.
(Erase heading not required.)

Instructions regarding War Diaries and Intelligence Summaries are contained in F. S. Regs., Part II. and the Staff Manual respectively. Title pages will be prepared in manuscript.

Place	Date	Hour	Summary of Events and Information	Remarks and references to Appendices
SINDORF	June 1st	1914	Riding School for Young Officers & for the Band. Elementary Training in Tactics for above Officers.	DM
	14			DM
	15		The G.O.C. Dragoon Brigade inspected the horses of the Regiment	DM
	16		As for 1st – 14th June.	DM
	23		Empire Day. "C" Squadron held a Gymkhana.	DM
	24		Riding School etc. as above.	DM
	25/26		The "Mobile Troop" paraded for inspection by the C.O.C. Dragoon Brigade	DM
	29		Riding School for Young Officers for the Band	DM
	30 31		Elementary Training in Tactics for Young Officers	DM

Lt-Monetype Captain Adjutant
The Senior Hilbrick Dragoons

Confidential

"War Diary"
of
The 6th (Inniskilling) Dragoons
Period 1st to 30th June, 1919.
Volume No LIX

Army Form C. 2118.

CONFIDENTIAL

WAR DIARY
or
INTELLIGENCE SUMMARY.
(Erase heading not required.)

Instructions regarding War Diaries and Intelligence Summaries are contained in F. S. Regs., Part II. and the Staff Manual respectively. Title pages will be prepared in manuscript.

Place	Date	Hour	Summary of Events and Information	Remarks and references to Appendices
SINDORF GERMANY.	1st	—	Riding School for Young Officers and Band boys. King's Birthday Holiday.	
	2nd	—	King's Birthday. Regimental parade at 0945 hrs. with Band, in honour of King's Birthday.	
	3rd to 13th	—	Riding School for last joined Subaltern Officers and Band boys. Elementary training in tactics for last joined subalterns under the Adjutant.	
	14th to 16th	—	Training of recruits, transfers & Band boys daily in Riding School, Musketry, Football and Physical training.	
	17th	"	A mobile force, consisting of 4 Officers, 86 O.R. (left SINDORF and proceeded to BOGNE (under Capt BROWNE, ROYAL DRAGOONS, Commanding Dragoon Composite Squadron) in readiness for resumption of hostilities.	
	18th	30d	Training of recruits and transfers in Riding also and foot drill continued. Recruits Educational School for recruits and transfers for 2nd & 3rd Class Certificate.	
			102 Recruits joined from Home Stations during month. Following awards appears in London Gazette dated 3rd June and 7th June: Birthday List : Lt. Col. (T. Brig. Gen.) B. VINCENT, CMG to be Commander of the Bar for valuable services rendered in connection with military operations in France as Reserve Major (Actg. Lt Col) C.P. Verot, DSO, to be Bt. Lt. Col. for distinguished service in connection with Military Operations in France & Flanders.	

Commanding The Inniskilling Dragoons

WAR DIARY
INTELLIGENCE SUMMARY

(Page 2)

Birthday List (continued).

Captains + Quartermasters W. Macpherson to be Major on the provisions of Art. 33(a) and 331 of R. Warrant.

5/21094. Farr. Qr. Sergt. C. LANDGRAF, awarded the Distinguished Conduct Medal for distinguished service in connection with military operations in France and Flanders.

Lt. (Actg Captain) H. TOTTENHAM, awarded the Military Cross for valuable services rendered in connection with military operations in France and Flanders.

Lt. Colonel (T/Brig. Gen.) E. Makinson D.S.O. to be Brevet Colonel for distinguished service in connection with military operations in France & Flanders.

2/Lt. M.B Christie to be Lieutenant, 8th May 1919.

E.B. [signature]

Commanding the Inniskilling Dragoons.

Confidential

War Diary

of

5th (Inniskilling) Dragoons

From 1st to 31st July, 1919.

Army Form C. 2118.

WAR DIARY
or
INTELLIGENCE SUMMARY.
(Erase heading not required.)

Instructions regarding War Diaries and Intelligence Summaries are contained in F.S. Regs., Part II. and the Staff Manual respectively. Title pages will be prepared in manuscript.

Place	Date	Hour	Summary of Events and Information	Remarks and references to Appendices
SINDORF	July 1919			
	1		Riding School for Recruits & Transfers from Infantry + to Band.	SM
	2		" " " " " "	SM
	3		" " " " " "	SM
	4		Foot Drill " " " " " "	SM
	5		Squadrons practised for Regimental Gymkhana	SM
	6/7		As for July 1st (above). Divine Service, Peace Day.	SM
	8		As for July 1st. Musketry Instruction (afternoon).	SM
	9		Major General Sir W.E. Peyton K.C.B. K.C.V.O. D.S.O. Commanding Cavalry Division of the Rhine inspected Recruits etc at Riding School.	SM
	10		As for July 4th. S.M.R.D.V.S. inspected the horses of the Regiment. Eliminating Trials for entries to Div Div Horse Show.	SM SM
	11		As for July 1st. The following extract from the London Gazette dated July 5th 1919, containing Sir Douglas Haig's Despatch of 9 March 1919 authorising names dressing of special	
	12		mention for gallant service in France, ~~published~~ distribution	
	13			SM

Lieut. Colonel C.R. Turnor DSO   Captain G.D. Lupton   D/20991 S.Q.M.S. B. Toombs
Capt/Adjt D.L. Macintyre   Capt D.F. Escier-Smith   B/21033 Pte J. Voisin

2353 Wt W2544/1454 700,000 5/15 L.D.&L.   A:D.S.S./Forms/C. 2118.

Army Form C. 2118.

WAR DIARY
or
INTELLIGENCE SUMMARY.
(Erase heading not required.)

Instructions regarding War Diaries and Intelligence Summaries are contained in F.S. Regs., Part II. and the Staff Manual respectively. Title pages will be prepared in manuscript.

Place	Date	Hour	Summary of Events and Information	Remarks and references to Appendices
SINDORF	July 1919			
	14		Riding School for Recruits. Transfers from Infantry &c. for the Band.	DMcK
	15		"	DMcK
	16		Foot Drill	DMcK
	17		As for July 14th (above). Examinations for Third Class Certificates.	DMcK
	18		"	DMcK
	19		Peace Day observed as a holiday.	DMcK
	20		As for July 14th (above). Classification of all horses by a Divisional Committee.	DMcK
	21		"	DMcK
	22		"	DMcK
	23		Foot drill as for July 16th.	DMcK
	24		As for July 14th (above). Musketry Instruction.	DMcK
	25		"	DMcK
	28		The Commander in Chief General Sir William Robertson GCB, GCMG, KCVO DSO, ADC inspected the Recruits & Band at Riding School. Also the Billets, Cookhouses, & Recreational Room, Canteen. The GOC Dragoon Gds inspected the horses in training order.	DMcK
	29		As for July 14th (above).	

Army Form C. 2118.

WAR DIARY
or
INTELLIGENCE SUMMARY.
(Erase heading not required.)

Place	Date	Hour	Summary of Events and Information	Remarks and references to Appendices
SINDORF	Jan 29/1919			
	30.		Riding School for Recruits, Infantry Transfers & the Band.	DMcM DMcM
	31.		" " Foot Drill " " " "	
			Instructional Training was also carried out regularly under the following subjects: Musketry for young Officers & NCO Instructors. Instruction in the Lewis Gun for the Recruits who had not passed 1st, 2nd or 3rd Class. Squadron Trumpet Practice for all Trumpeters. School under an Educational Officer for all Recruits who had not passed 1st, 2nd or 3rd Class Examination. Instruction of two Recruits per Squadron in the Saddlers & Tailor's shop.	DMcM

W. Mannly Capt & Adjutant
Lewis Wilkins Dragoons

Confidential

War Diary

of

6th (Inniskilling) Dragoons

from

1st to 31st August, 1919.

Army Form C. 2118.

WAR DIARY
or
INTELLIGENCE SUMMARY.
(Erase heading not required)

Place	Date	Hour	Summary of Events and Information	Remarks and references to Appendices
SINDORF	1-8-19	—	First day of Cavalry divisional week. Horse show. The training was suspended. About seventy men from the Regiment went to the show.	JRO. Lt
"	2-8-19	—	2nd Day of the week. Racing about the same number of men attended.	JRO. Lt
"	3-8-19	—	Sunday	JRO. Lt
"	4-8-19	—	August Bank Holiday and was observed as such. Horse show. The regt. was 3rd with the pack horses.	JRO. Lt
"	5-8-19	—	2nd Day's racing. Lt R.S. Orton "Golden Sunset" was second in a stifleshase final of the Subalterns polo (Tournament). The Regt beat the 17th Lancers	JRO. Lt
"	6-8-19	—	by 2 goals to 1. Classification of horses by a board. They were classified as T.T.-T.S.E.	JRO. Lt
"	7-8-19	—	Riding School etc as usual.	JRO. Lt
"	8-8-19	—	as usual.	JRO. Lt
"	9-8-19	—	Sunday	JRO. Lt
"	10-8-19	—	Regimental parade all I miss holidays attended.	JRO. Lt
"	11-8-19	—	Riding School etc as usual.	RAHK Lt
"	12-8-19	—	Major & Brevet Colonel B. Vincent C.B. C.M.G. to be Lieut. Colonel vice Lt Col. E. Paterson D.S.o who is removed from the Regimental List July 2nd 1919." Extract London Gazette.	RAHK Lt
"	13-8-19	—	" Lieut B.L. Lewis retires on retired pay on account of ill health contracted on active service. (August 3rd 1919) London Gazette.	RAHK Lt

Army Form C. 2118.

WAR DIARY
or
INTELLIGENCE SUMMARY.
(Erase heading not required.)

Instructions regarding War Diaries and Intelligence Summaries are contained in F. S. Regs., Part II. and the Staff Manual respectively. Title pages will be prepared in manuscript.

Place	Date	Hour	Summary of Events and Information	Remarks and references to Appendices
Sindorf	14.8.19		Staff ride for all Officers	
"	15.8.19		Composite Squadron for Review in Cologne marched to Cologne today.	
"	16.8.19		Riding School etc.	
"	17.8.19		" "	
"	18.8.19		Review of horse show in Cologne	
"	19.8.19		Composite Squadron returns from Cologne	
"	20.8.19		Riding School etc.	
"	21.8.19		" "	
"	22.8.19		" "	
"	23.8.19		Races in Cologne	
"	24.8.19		London Gazette "2nd Lieut W. R. Simeons resigns his commission 12/8/19." Sunday.	
"	25.8.19		Riding School etc.	
"	26.8.19		Lecture by Major Spencer Johnson on "Her Savings" Complimentary	

Army Form C. 2118.

WAR DIARY
or
INTELLIGENCE SUMMARY
(Erase heading not required.)

Place	Date	Hour	Summary of Events and Information	Remarks and references to Appendices
Sindluf	26.8.19		Menage received from Commander-in-Chief & Corps Commander re turn out of several squadrons of Troops at the review on the 18th.8.19 at Cologne	AAH5th
"	27.8.19		Foot drill & classes of instruction as usual	AAH5th
"	28.8.19		Riding etc as usual	AAH5th
"	29.8.19		" " "	AAH5th
"	30.8.19		Band practice mounted. Races at Cologne.	AAH5th
"	31.8.19		Sunday.	AAH5th

W.H. Elliot Lieut. for Acting Adjt.

Dragoon Bk

CONFIDENTIAL

War Diary
of
The Inniskilling Dragoons

From Sept 1st 1914 to Sept. 30th 1914.

Army Form C. 2118.

WAR DIARY
or
INTELLIGENCE SUMMARY
(Erase heading not required.)

Instructions regarding War Diaries and Intelligence Summaries are contained in F. S. Regs., Part II. and the Staff Manual respectively. Title pages will be prepared in manuscript.

Place	Date	Hour	Summary of Events and Information	Remarks and references to Appendices
SINDORF	1/9/19		Regt. Parade.	RSOF RSLT RSSLT
"	2/9/19		Regt Parade with Standard & mounted Band.	
"	3/9/19		Foot drill & classes of instruction.	
"	4/9/19		The Regt. was inspected by Brig. General N.W. Haig C.B. CMG. as a farewell visit on his returning to England. Polo in the afternoon. The afternoon was observed as a holiday.	RSOF RSLT RSSLT
"	5/9/19		Band practice mounted & Riding School in the morning. School & classes of Instruction as usual in the morning	RSSL RSLT
"	6/9/19		No riding school or classes. "A" Sqn held a gymkhana at AHE in the morning	RSSL RSLT
"	7/9/19		Sunday. Football v R.A.S.C. HORREM.	RSSL

Army Form C. 2118.

WAR DIARY
or
INTELLIGENCE SUMMARY
(Erase heading not required.)

Instructions regarding War Diaries and Intelligence Summaries are contained in F. S. Regs., Part II. and the Staff Manual respectively. Title pages will be prepared in manuscript.

Place	Date	Hour	Summary of Events and Information	Remarks and references to Appendices
OSHOTT				
SINDRIS	8/9/19		Riding School & classes of instruction as usual.	AA&QMG
"	9/9/19		Riding School etc. Victory Medal Authorized. Capt. J. C. Humphry	AA&QMG
			M.C. rejoins Regt. from Lancers Machine Gun Squadron.	AA&QMG
			London Gazette – Following 2nd Lieuts to be Lieuts – 2nd Lt. G.D. Proctor	AA&QMG
			W.R. Lineman (seine unique) A.E.G. Steele.	AA&QMG
"	10/9/19		Riding School & classes of Instruction	AA&QMG
"	11/9/19		Mess Meeting. Capt. J.H. Brooke elected Mess President.	AA&QMG
"	12/9/19		Riding School etc. as usual.	AA&QMG
"	13/9/19		" " " "	AA&QMG

Army Form C. 2118.

WAR DIARY
or
INTELLIGENCE SUMMARY
(Erase heading not required.)

Instructions regarding War Diaries and Intelligence Summaries are contained in F. S. Regs., Part II. and the Staff Manual respectively. Title pages will be prepared in manuscript.

Place	Date	Hour	Summary of Events and Information	Remarks and references to Appendices
SINDORF	14.9.19		Riding School etc. Chose 6 12th Lancer Barracks cancelled	RNSTL
"	15/9/19		Riding School etc as usual	RNSTL
"	16.9.19		" " " "	RNSTL
"	17.9.19		Foot drill as usual. Reagles went out this morning and had a good hunt. Large draft arrived from England 42 NCOs + OR.	JHu Pt
"	18.9.19		Riding School etc as usual	JBO Lt
"	19.9.19		" "	JBa Pt
"	20.9.19		Training as usual. Cologne races	JHu Pt.
"	21.9.19		Sunday	JBO Schl.
"	22.9.19		Training as usual school etc.	JBO Capt
"	25.9.19		Training as usual. Guard of honour with Standard under Capt Fleury - Teulon left for Cologne.	
"	24.9.19		No training on account of rain. The guard of honour was complimented by the Divisional Commander on its smart appearance	JHu Capt.
"	25.9.19		Preparing for move to Cologne	JBO Capt
"	26.9.19		Moved to Dans Barracks, Cologne	JBa Capt
"	27.9.19		No training. Squadron cleaned up and settled into Barracks	Ja Lt Pt

Army Form C. 2118.

WAR DIARY
or
INTELLIGENCE SUMMARY.
(Erase heading not required.)

Instructions regarding War Diaries and Intelligence Summaries are contained in F. S. Regs., Part II. and the Staff Manual respectively. Title pages will be prepared in manuscript.

Place	Date	Hour	Summary of Events and Information	Remarks and references to Appendices
Cologne	Sept 28th		Sunday	J L Wright Lieut Capt
"	29th		Recruits training etc	" Capt
"	30th		"	" Capt
"	October 1st		"	" Capt
"	2nd		"	" Capt
"	3rd		"	" Capt
"	4th		"	" Capt
"	5th		Sunday	" Capt

Original.
/ Dragoon [?]
√ (E)

Confidential

War Diary

of

INNISKILLING DRAGOONS

From Nov. 1st 1914. To Nov 30th 1914.

Army Form C. 2118.

WAR DIARY
or
INTELLIGENCE SUMMARY.
(Erase heading not required.)

Instructions regarding War Diaries and Intelligence Summaries are contained in F. S. Regs., Part II. and the Staff Manual respectively. Title pages will be prepared in manuscript.

Place	Date	Hour	Summary of Events and Information	Remarks and references to Appendices
COLOGNE	1.XI.19		Riding School before breakfast.	RWR 71
"	2.XI.19		Sunday.	RWR 71
"	3.XI.19		Recruit parade as usual	RWR 71
"	4.XI.19		" " " "	RWR 71
"	5.XI.19		" " " " Horses of "B" Sqd inspected by the C.O.	RWR 71
"	6.XI.19		Recruit parade as usual. Horses of "C" Sqd inspected by the C.O.	RWR 71
"	7.XI.19		" " " " Horses of Transport inspected by the C.O.	RWR 71
"	8.XI.19		Change of programme in work.	RWR 71
"	9.XI.19		Sunday.	RWR 71
"	10.XI.19		Recruit parades as return. No riding school before breakfast. Riding School daily but no recruit to do more than three rides a week.	RWR 71
"	11.XI.19		Anniversary of the Armistice. All Ranks to stand to attention for two minutes at 11 o'clock. Guard to turn out & trumpeter to sound the last post.	RWR 71

(A5001) D. D. & L., London, E.C. 750,000 5/17 Sch. 52 Forms/C2118/14 Wt. W14721/M2031

Army Form C. 2118.

WAR DIARY
or
INTELLIGENCE SUMMARY.
(Erase heading not required.)

Instructions regarding War Diaries and Intelligence Summaries are contained in F. S. Regs., Part II. and the Staff Manual respectively. Title pages will be prepared in manuscript.

Place	Date	Hour	Summary of Events and Information	Remarks and references to Appendices
COLOGNE	12-XI-19		Recruits as usual. If weather is bad recruits parade in the Riding School in two parts.	Attch
"	13-XI-19		08.30 hours & 09.30 hours. Recruits parade as usual	Attch Attch
"	14-XI-19		Lecture by the Medical Officer.	Attch
"	15-XI-19		Riding School for recruits in the morning of Flanks.	Attch
"	16-XI-19		Sunday. "A" Sqdn attended divine service. R.Q.M.S Chapman died of double pneumonia at No.4 General Hospital. Cologne.	Attch Attch
"	17-XI-19		No riding school for recruits.	Attch
"	18-XI-19		The funeral of R.Q.M.S Chapman D.C.M took place at SUD-FRIEDHOF CEMETRY at 14.30 hours	Attch Attch
"	19-XI-19		Recruits parade as usual	Attch
"	20-XI-19		Extract London Gazette:- Capt + RT Lt. Col R.G. Pitron to be Major (July 2nd)	Attch

Army Form C. 2118.

WAR DIARY
or
INTELLIGENCE SUMMARY.
(Erase heading not required.)

Instructions regarding War Diaries and Intelligence Summaries are contained in F. S. Regs., Part II. and the Staff Manual respectively. Title pages will be prepared in manuscript.

Place	Date	Hour	Summary of Events and Information	Remarks and references to Appendices
COLOGNE	20.XI.19		Continued:- Capt. & R⁰ Major G.L.R Reunkaer attire & granted rank of Major	AA&QMG
"	21.XI.19		Riding School as usual & foot drill	AA&QMG
"	22.XI.19		Riding School before breakfast	AA&QMG
"	23.XI.19		Sunday	AA&QMG
"	24.XI.19		Recruits parade as usual	AA&QMG
"	25.XI.19		" " "	AA&QMG
"	26.XI.19		" " " Officers mess meeting	AA&QMG
"	27.XI.19		Recruit parade as usual	AA&QMG
"	28.11.19		" " "	Gen. Capt.
"	29.11.19		Riding School suspended owing to shortage of men. Corps Commander walked around barracks Stables etc.	Gen. Capt.
"	30.11.19		Sunday	Gen. Capt.

DUPLICATE.

CONFIDENTIAL.

WAR DIARY

of the

Inniskilling Dragoons.

From 1/12/19 to 31/12/19.

WAR DIARY
INTELLIGENCE SUMMARY
(Erase heading not required.)

Army Form C. 2118.

Instructions regarding War Diaries and Intelligence Summaries are contained in F. S. Regs., Part II. and the Staff Manual respectively. Title pages will be prepared in manuscript.

Place	Date	Hour	Summary of Events and Information	Remarks and references to Appendices
COLOGNE	1st Dec	—	Training of Recruits morning and afternoon. Dinner held in Cologne at 7.30 pm in commemoration of the action at VILLERS-GUISLAIN on Dec 1st 1917, attended by all Officers, Warrant Officers, non commissioned Officers and men who took part in the action and were still serving with the Regiment on Dec 1st 1919.	
"	2nd 3rd	—	Training of Recruits. Regtl orders published that riding school would be suspended for recruits until further orders: (owing to shortage of men).	
"	4th	—	Inspection of Band & Transport horses by C.O. at 12.30 hrs. Educational school for recruits commenced at 11.00 hrs. under Capt J. Rickard-Brown, Lt. J. Leslie and Schoolmaster Reed, all attached for educational training. 2Lts Earle & Kitching dismissed Riding School by Comdg Officer. Regtl Order published to the effect that Major J.B. Nixon rel'd 30th Nov 1919 on retired pay (Adm Gaz).	
"	5th	—	First issue of Clothing Belts made to Draft Majors & Sergeants for parades Tuesday Out.	
"	7th	—	Church parade for "A" Squadron under Mr Revd Johnson at 10.00 hrs.	
"	8th	—	Officers' Ride opens to non cos in Aut Order. "A"Sqn bathing parade at 14.00 hrs. 5735/5 Pte J. Roe, Inniskillings on Trial by F.G.C.M.. Deutz Barracks, Cologne	

WAR DIARY
or
INTELLIGENCE SUMMARY.

(Erase heading not required.)

Army Form C. 2118.

Place	Date	Hour	Summary of Events and Information	Remarks and references to Appendices
Cologne	Dec 8th	-	Regtl Order 334(1) states that "Captain C.A. Hewis Tuton to be Major Nov 30th" (San Faz).	M
"	10th	-	Commander-in-Chief's Inspection of Regiment:— Dismounted parade in drill order with rifles. Officers' Sergeants in the Swords. Regt formed up in Mass march-past for Inspection. 0930 hrs 10.00 hrs Officers' Ride under Lt Col. GP Burpet DSO 10.15 hrs Recruits Ride under Lt M.M. Wilder 11.30 hrs B Sqn horses inspected 10.45 hrs A Sqn " " 11.00 hrs B Sqn stables visited 11.15 hrs Officers' Sergeants' Messes visited	M
"	11th	-	Second Day of C-in-Chief's Inspection of Regt. 0930 hrs Senior NCOs Ride under the Adjutant 0945 hrs Recruits Ride under Lt Elliot 10.00 hrs C Sqn horses inspected 10.10 hrs Band & Transport horses inspected 10.20 hrs C Sqn stables visited 10.30 hrs Baths, Cookhouses, Canteen, Mess & Barrack Rooms inspected	M
"	12th	-	Owing to lack of horse accommodation, all B Sqn horses removed to stabling recently occupied by Polish Government horses, in vicinity of Barracks. Corpl. Mess opened in Deutz Barracks, Cologne. Lt Rimington took over duties of Capt J.J. Waters as A/Adjt during leave. Orders issued for respirators to be taken on recruit parades that have be used for respirator drill under Rhine Garrison Gas Officer & NCO.	M
"	14th	-	Church Parade for B Sqn 10.00 hrs. Followed by The Communion. Rev _____ G. Tuson Officiating.	M

Army Form C. 2118.

WAR DIARY
or
INTELLIGENCE SUMMARY.
(Erase heading not required.)

Instructions regarding War Diaries and Intelligence Summaries are contained in F. S. Regs., Part II. and the Staff Manual respectively. Title pages will be prepared in manuscript.

Place	Date	Hour	Summary of Events and Information	Remarks and references to Appendices
Cologne	15th	—	Board of Officers assembled to examine Pte Jones, who applies to determine as to their fitness for service in the Cavalry. Pres. Lt. Col. Garrott DSO.	MM
—	16th	—	Quarter Dress Football Team beat 51st N'land Fusiliers 3 goals to nil (selected by Lyn leaders) under the Riding School for the young N.C.O.'s per Sqn. at 0815 hrs., and for 16 senior NCOs at 0945 hrs. Adjutant at 0815 hrs.	MM
—	—	—	Messing subscription ordered, for all Opls & Privates, of 2d per diem for the purpose of improving the messing.	MM
—	17th	—	Revolver practice for all Officers at 1400 hrs on regimental range near the "White City" Cologne - Deutz.	MM
—	—	—	Football match against 44st Bn W.S.C. (Draw: 1-1). 8 reinforcements joined. (vs Round Cologne League)	MM
—	18th	—	Junior N.C.O's Ride at 0900 hrs under the Adjutant.	MM
—	—	—	Exercise under Squadron arrangements.	MM
—	20th	—	Lt. R.Webber commenced Regimental Course at Wilthurst under the Trans Auth 1 Officer 1 W.O.(ii) 2 Sgts. 35 Pte Jones from Euf. Corps.	MM
—	21st Sunday	—	Church Parade for C.Sqn. as 1000 hrs under Revd. Johnson	MM
—	22nd	—	Educational School closed until 5th Jan. 1920 (for Army School Regs.)	MM
—	24th	—	Sto Gilles. Inniskilling Dragoons tried by F.G.C.M. (acquitted Three sickness / accident)	MM
—	25th	—	XMAS DAY. Divine Service for the Regt. conducted by Revd Johnson took Round 9 Officers walked round their dinners at 1300 hrs.	MM
—	26th	—	BOXING DAY No Parades	MM

WAR DIARY
INTELLIGENCE SUMMARY

Army Form C. 2118.

Place	Date	Hour	Summary of Events and Information	Remarks and references to Appendices
Cologne	28th (Sunday)	-	Church Parade for "A" Sqn. At 1000 hrs, followed by Holy Communion. Revd. Johnson officiated.	MM
	29th	-	R.O. 351(2):- Extract from Gen. Gaz: "Lt. G.R. Lipton returns on return from (Dec 20) and is granted rank of Captain". "Major E.A. Fitzgerald Capt. R.D. Snigden MC joined from Newport. (posted to "C" Sqn) NCOs' Recruits Rides as before.	MM
	30th 31st	-	Leave for O.Rks. throughout the month, at the rate of 6 per day, equally divided between Old soldiers and recruits as they became eligible. 24 NCOs' + men struck off the strength of the Regiment during month, for reasons of evacuations, sick, demobilization etc. Increase during month of 40 ORks.	MM MM

Original

CONFIDENTIAL

War Diary
of
THE INNISKILLING DRAGOONS.
from
Feb 1st 1920
to
Feb. 29 1920

Army Form C. 2118.

WAR DIARY
or
INTELLIGENCE SUMMARY.
(Erase heading not required.)

Instructions regarding War Diaries and Intelligence Summaries are contained in F. S. Regs., Part II. and the Staff Manual respectively. Title pages will be prepared in manuscript.

Place	Date	Hour	Summary of Events and Information	Remarks and references to Appendices
DEUTZ BK. COLOGNE.	Feb 2nd to Feb 9		A) Recruits Rides every week day from 0900 hrs to 1100 hours. B) Senior N.C.O. Rides every Tuesday at 1400 hours. C) Foot Drill, & Preliminary Musketry, & School every day at 1400 hrs D) Revolver Practice for all Officers every Thursday at 1400 hrs E) Divine Service every Sunday. One Squadron each Sunday. F) Medical Inspection for all men every Saturday at 0900 hrs.	JHA left
"	Feb 3rd		London Gazette Feb. 2nd "Lieut: W.R. Donald, Inniskilling Dragoons, resigns his commission (Jan. 31st) & retains rank of Lieutenant.	JHA left
	Feb 5		Course of Instruction. 2Lt. J. P. S. Kitching & No. D/10901 Cpl. R. E. Jackson selected to attend a Course of Hotchkiss Rifle assembling at JHYTHE on the 16" inst.	JHA left
	Feb 5th		London Gazette Feb. 4th 2Lt A. M. Niall, Inniskilling Dragoons, to be Lieutenant (Jan 24th 1918).	JHA left
	Feb 9		London Gazette Feb. 7th Cavalry School (Netheravon) Lt. Col. & B. Col. E. Paterson, D.S.O. from half pay dist & to be Temporary Col. whilst so employed. vice Col. A.F.W. Herman C.B, D.S.O.	JHA left

Army Form C. 2118.

WAR DIARY
or
INTELLIGENCE SUMMARY.
(Erase heading not required.)

Instructions regarding War Diaries and Intelligence Summaries are contained in F. S. Regs., Part II. and the Staff Manual respectively. Title pages will be prepared in manuscript.

Place	Date	Hour	Summary of Events and Information	Remarks and references to Appendices
DEOTD BKS COLOGNE.	Feb 14th		London Gazette Feb 1/15. Lieut. C.V.R. Buchanan, Inniskilling Dragoons is seconded for service with the R.A.F. (Jan 23rd)	JM Cuff
	Feb 19th		Obituary. The commanding officer regrets to announce the death of S.S.M. J.R. Mellor "B" Squadron which occurred this afternoon.	JM Cuff
			London Gazette. Feb 18th. 2/Lieut. R.I.P. Earle to be Lieutenant. (Oct 24th 1917).	JM Cuff
	Feb 20th		In honour of the visit of General Degoutte, Commanding in Chief, Armies of the Rhine, the Regiment furnished a Guard of Honour on the Cathedral Square, Cologne, composed of 3 Officers, 1 S.S.M. 9 16 men a Squadron. The Standard & the Band dismounted.	
			London Gazette Feb 19th Lieut. J.M. Graham M.C. restored to the establishment Sept 20 1918	JM Cuff
	Feb 23rd		Musketry lecture for Officers & N.C.O's at 14:30 hr.	JM Cuff
	Feb 24th		Musketry Parade at 14:30 hr for all men who have not fired general musketry course or Recruits Course.	JM Cuff
	Feb 27th		London Gazette Feb 23rd. Inniskilling Dragoons, 2/Lieutenants to be Lieutenants; J.P.S. Kitching, H.J. Byrne, A.J.D. Crawford.	JM Cuff
			Band Mounted Practice at 0.800 hr.	

BEF
CAV. DIV.
DRAGOON. BDE.

MACHINE GUN SQN

1919 APR to 1919 AUG

FROM 1 CAN DIV 1 BDE
Box 1108

1st M.G. Squadron

Army Form C. 2118.

WAR DIARY
or
INTELLIGENCE SUMMARY
(Erase heading not required.)

Vol. 40

1st MACHINE GUN SQUADRON
1st CAVALRY BRIGADE

Instructions regarding War Diaries and Intelligence Summaries are contained in F. S. Regs., Part II. and the Staff Manual respectively. Title pages will be prepared in manuscript.

Place	Date	Hour	Summary of Events and Information	Remarks and references to Appendices
Beauvois	Aug. 1		Lt. J.S. Lunt on leave to U.K.	
	2		Lt. H.O. Seaton in leave to U.K.	
	3		Lt. R.S. Painter M.G.C. on 7/Lt. W.G. Cain to U.K. for demobilization.	
	4		2/Lt. H.G. Taylor to leave.	
	5		Horses from Remount Squadron. R. M.G.D. - 259 - killed + isolated.	
	7		Inspected by Brigade Commander.	
	20		Lt. J.S. Lunt from leave	
	23		Lt. H.B. Bruce + Lt. H.O. Seaton from leave. Lt. R.C. Hunter to leave.	
	24		Lt. J.S. Lunt on special duty to Cologne	
	25		Parade of all ranks for special duty + inspection by G.O.C.	
	26		Lt. Col. A.T. No. Wilson joined	
	31		Cases clothed. 2/Lt. C.L. Banks on leave	

W. Major
O. Cdy 1 M.G. Sqn

Confidential.

"War Diary"
of
1st Machine Gun Squadron.

From 1st to 31st May, 1919

Army Form C. 2118.

WAR DIARY
or
INTELLIGENCE SUMMARY.
(Erase heading not required.)

"A" M.G. Sqdn

Instructions regarding War Diaries and Intelligence Summaries are contained in F. S. Regs., Part II. and the Staff Manual respectively. Title pages will be prepared in manuscript.

Place	Date MAY	Hour	Summary of Events and Information	Remarks and references to Appendices
BERRENDORF	2nd		Lt. Col. A. Helwood Milne assumed Command of the Squadron	A/L
			Major J. McBrel. & Lt. McGreevey to U.K. for demobilisation	A/L
	6th		Horses inspected by A.D.V.S. Brig. Gen. Harman present	A/L
	7th		"Duty Coln." paraded for inspection by the C.O.	
			Lt. H. Neklo leave to U.K.	
			Lt. R.C. Hollis & 1 O.R. to U.K. for dispersal	
			Lt. C.E. Bowles to Home Establishment	
			2 O.R. struck off strength	
	8th		Church Parade. 1 O.R. + 2 horses arrived & taken on strength	A/L
	11th		3 O.R's taken on strength.	A/L
	14th		Extract from Lieven Gazette. 2/Lt. H.D. Peake to be Lieut. dates April 28th 1919.	A/L
	15th		2 horses evacuated	A/L
	17th		1 O.R. to U.K. for dispersal	A/L
	18		21 O.R's attended lectures on Palestinians at Horrem	A/L
	23		Armourer Staff Sgt. Bull joined	A/L
	24		Lt. J. Forsyth Grant struck off strength	A/L
	25		Sports meeting held in the afternoon.	A/L

Contd

Army Form C. 2118.

1st Mo. G. Sqdn

WAR DIARY
or
INTELLIGENCE SUMMARY.
(Erase heading not required.)

Instructions regarding War Diaries and Intelligence Summaries are contained in F. S. Regs., Part II. and the Staff Manual respectively. Title pages will be prepared in manuscript.

Place	Date MAY	Hour	Summary of Events and Information	Remarks and references to Appendices
BERRENDORF	26		The Officers & men of the Germs attached to this unit, being replaced by 1 Officer & 26 O.R's of another platoon.	Hs
	28		"Duty Section" was inspected by the G.O.C Brigade at 10.30 hrs at THORR	Hs
	29		Lecture on Education at 14.30 hrs. 2 horses evacuated to No. 24 Vet Hospital, Cologne	Hy
	31		Horses inspected by the C.O. at 09.00 hrs. During this month, Equitation and other training has had to be almost entirely suspended, owing to the shortage of men	Hs

H Woodallam

Lt. Col
Comdg 1st Mo. G. Sqdn

V (F)

Confidential
War Diary
of
Dragoon Machine Gun Squadron.
Period 1st to 30th June 1919
Volume XIX

Army Form C. 2118.

Dragoon M.G. Sqdn.

WAR DIARY
or
INTELLIGENCE SUMMARY.
(Erase heading not required.)

Instructions regarding War Diaries and Intelligence Summaries are contained in F.S. Regs., Part II. and the Staff Manual respectively. Title pages will be prepared in manuscript.

Place	Date 1919 JUNE	Hour	Summary of Events and Information	Remarks and references to Appendices
BERRENDORF	5		Lt. Col. A. J. McWilson on leave to France. Capt. B.C. King assumed command of the Squadron.	
			L.S. McWakefield in London Gazette for D.C.M.	
	8		Church Parade with rest of Royal Dragoons.	
	10		Lieut. Cpt. One Joined from 5th M.G. Squadron.	
	11		1 O.R. M.G.C. (Cav.), & 18 O.R. Labour Corps. joined	
	12		2/Lt. M.G. McMurray on leave to U.K. 2 horses evacuated.	
	13		Riding School Class of 12 men commenced & continued daily until 17th inst.	
	14		1 O.R. Farrier Ogden	
	17		Orders received at 05.00 hrs for Duty Section to proceed to COLOGNE. Left at 10.15 hrs & were inspected en route at ICHENDORF by G.O.C. Cavalry Division at 12.00 hrs. Reached DEUTZ Barracks COLOGNE at 16.15 hrs & stayed there over night. Capt. King, Q.O.M. Wakefield, 2 O.R's, Lt. Lucian, & 45 O.R's, 62 horses with Duty Section.	
			Lt. M.G. Ogden, Lt. Hicks, Lt. Lucian, & 45 O.R's, 62 horses with Duty Section.	
			20 O.R's Labour Corps. joined.	
			Lt. M.G.D. Smith assumed command.	
	18		Duty Section joined Dragoon Mobile Squadron, moving off at 05.30 hrs and proceeded to BONN	(Contd.)

Army Form C. 2118.

WAR DIARY
or
INTELLIGENCE SUMMARY.
(Erase heading not required.)

Dragoons No G. Agdn

Instructions regarding War Diaries and Intelligence Summaries are contained in F. S. Regs., Part II. and the Staff Manual respectively. Title pages will be prepared in manuscript.

Place	Date 1915 JUNE	Hour	Summary of Events and Information	Remarks and references to Appendices
BERRENDORF	19.		Orders received that an extension of time had been granted for the signing of the Peace terms. Section remained in camp at BORN	
	20.		Lt. W. D. Little No. 6 struck off strength from 1.3.19	
	21.		Lt. A. H. Stafford joined from 5th No G. Agdn. G.O.C. Cavalry Division inspected squadron at 10.30 hrs. Lt. Col. Wilson rejoined from leave.	
	22		Peace having been signed, the Cavalry Section received orders to return to COLOGNE	
	29		Left billets at 09.30 hrs. arrived COLOGNE 12.30 hrs., & billetted in DEUTZ barracks. The section had excellent billets during its stay at BORN. Country good for grazing, and on fine or dine fine mornings, the time was spent in training	
	30.		Weather on the whole was bad, with much rain.	

Howard Capt
Lieu Lt. Col
Cmdg Dragoons No. G. Agdn

Confidential

"War Diary"

of

Dragoons Machine Gun Squadron.

From 1st to 31st July, 1919

Dragoon 76. G. Ogden

Army Form C. 2118.

WAR DIARY
or
INTELLIGENCE SUMMARY.
(Erase heading not required.)

Instructions regarding War Diaries and Intelligence Summaries are contained in F. S. Regs., Part II. and the Staff Manual respectively. Title pages will be prepared in manuscript.

Place	Date 1919. JULY	Hour	Summary of Events and Information	Remarks and references to Appendices
BERRENDORF	1		Duty Section left DEUTZ Barracks COLOGNE at 07.45 hrs. & regimental depot at BERRENDORF at midday.	
	3.		Riding School & dismounted classes for 76 C.O's re-commenced	
	7.		24 O.R's from Labour Corps joined. G.O.C. Brigade inspected Squadron. All those were mallein-ed. 13 O.R's Labour Corps joined.	
	8		Observed as a holiday in commemoration of Peace.	
	10.		G.O.C. IV Corps inspected Squadron Billets, horses	
	11		G.O.C. Div. Dis. inspected Equitation & Sawing Classes at 11.0 hrs, & afterwards held horse show.	
	14		Preliminary classification of horses commenced	
	25.		Lt. H.C.O. Luxton on leave to U.K.	
	29.		Shot detail left for COLOGNE under Lt. Weekes to compete in Cav. Bde. Cross Shoot	
	30.		Preliminary classification of horses completed by Capt. Ogden R.A.V.C.	

A.H. Stafford Lieut. for O.C.
Dragoon 76. G. Ogden

Confidential
War Diary
of
The Dragoon Machine Gun Squadron.
from
1st to 31st August, 1919.

Army Form C. 2118.

Dragoon No. 9 Sqn

WAR DIARY
or
INTELLIGENCE SUMMARY.
(Erase heading not required.)

Instructions regarding War Diaries and Intelligence Summaries are contained in F. S. Regs., Part II. and the Staff Manual respectively. Title pages will be prepared in manuscript.

Place	Date 1919 AUGUST	Hour	Summary of Events and Information	Remarks and references to Appendices
BERRENDORF GERMANY	4		40 men per day attend Cavalry Division Horse Show at COLOGNE	JH
	9			JH
	10.		All horses classified by Classification Board. Brig. Gen. J.A. Tyres was present	JH
	12.		Capt. F.C. King having resigned his commission, proceeded to England. 3 Horses evacuated	JH
	14.		2 O.R's Labour Corps transferred to 'E' Battery R.H.A.	JH
	16.		6 Horses taken on strength from Royal Dragoons	JH
	21		2/Lt. J. Wood proceeded to DUREN to rejoin his unit (83rd Govonno)	JH
	24.		Church Parade	JH
	25.		Lecture at Elsdorf on War Savings Certificates. 10 men attended	JH
	27		F.O. inspected 76. Section horses	JH
	29.		Lt. 96. Walker on leave to U.K.	JH
	30.		Farewell dinner to Machine Gunner of unit.	JH
	31		Equipment in charge of Lt. Sutton 1 Sgt. + 6 O.R's left for Antwerp. Church Parade	JH

J.H. Attwood Lt Col
Comdg Dragoon No 9 Sqn

BEF
Cav. Div

Hussar Bde H.Q

1919 - 1919
APR   JULY

Confidential.

War Diary
of
Headquarters Hussar Brigade
Late 9th Cavalry Bde.

April 1919
Volume No. 1

HEADQUARTERS,
HUSSAR-BDE.

Army Form C. 2118.

WAR DIARY
INTELLIGENCE SUMMARY.
(Erase heading not required.)

Instructions regarding War Diaries and Intelligence Summaries are contained in F. S. Regs., Part II. and the Staff Manual respectively. Title pages will be prepared in manuscript.

Headquarters.,
HUSSAR BRIGADE.
APRIL, 1919. Volume. No. 1.

Place	Date	Hour	Summary of Events and Information	Remarks and references to Appendices
HARFF	1st.	18.00	Lecture at BEDBURG by the Rev. Stanley BLUNT on EGYPT.	Reference Maps GERMANY 1/100,000. Sheets.1.L and 1.K.
			Snow during the morning.	
"	2nd.	12.00	New nomenclature of Brigades taken into use. 9th Cavalry Brigade becomes Hussar Brigade.	
"	3rd.	18.00	Lecture at KONIGSHOVEN by the Rev. Stanley BLUNT on EGYPT.	
			Three companies of Infantry joined the Brigade to help in grooming, etc. Posted to Units as under :-	
			"B" Company 4th Gordon Highlanders to 3rd Hussars.	
			"D" " " " " to 10th Hussars.	
			Composite Company of 5th Argyll and Sutherland Highlanders to 15th Hussars.	
			A fine day.	
"	4th.		One platoon "B" Coy. 4th Gordon Highlanders to 9th Machine Gun Squadron.	
			One platoon "D" Coy. 4th Gordon Highlanders to SINDORF for Cavalry Corps Bridging Park.	
			Received warning order from Division - the Brigade will probably move to an area about KERPEN on the 8th instant.	
		15.00	Conference at Brigade Headquarters to discuss - Employment of attached Infantrymen. Formation of a Mobile Striking Force - The forthcoming move. C.O's of all Units attended.	

Army Form C. 2118.

WAR DIARY
or
INTELLIGENCE SUMMARY.
(Erase heading not required.)

Instructions regarding War Diaries and Intelligence Summaries are contained in F. S. Regs., Part II. and the Staff Manual respectively. Title pages will be prepared in manuscript.

Place	Date	Hour	Summary of Events and Information	Remarks and references to Appendices
HARFF.	4th (Contd).		A fine day.	
	5th.	08.30	Received orders from Division for the Brigade (less 3rd Hussars and "O" and "Y" Batteries) to move to the KERPEN area on the 7th inst.	
		10.30	Issued Hussar Brigade Order No.1.	Appendix.1.
			A fine day.	
	6th.		"Y" Batty R.H.A. marches to HORREM tomorrow under orders of C.R.H.A. and ceases to form part of this Brigade.	
	7th.		Brigade marched in accordance with Hussar Brigade Order No.1. Move completed 15.00 hours.	
			Units of Brigade situated as follows :-	
BERGERHAUSEN.			Brigade H.Q. & Signals. BERGERHAUSEN. "O" Batty RHA. MILLENDORF.	
			3rd Hussars:- KIRCHHERTEN. 9th M.G.Sqdn. BLATZHEIM.	
			10th Hussars:- TURNICH, BALKHAUSEN, BRUGGEN. 9th Cav.Fld.Amb.) BOLHEIM.	
			15th Hussars:- KERPEN. and)	
				39th M.V. Section.)	
			15th Hussars and 9th M.G.Sqdn will be comfortable. 10th Hussars are very scattered.	
			9th C.F.A. a little scattered but good billets and a good rest station.	
			Brigade H.Q. accommodation for men very limited. A fine day.	

Army Form C. 2118.

WAR DIARY
or
INTELLIGENCE SUMMARY.
(Erase heading not required.)

Instructions regarding War Diaries and Intelligence Summaries are contained in F. S. Regs., Part II. and the Staff Manual respectively. Title pages will be prepared in manuscript.

Place	Date	Hour	Summary of Events and Information	Remarks and references to Appendices
BERGERHAUSEN.	8th.		Brigadier and Brigade Major rode round the area. There is a lot of grass land between KERPEN and BRUGGEN on both sides of the river. It is intersected by large and small dykes but there are several stretches where a Regiment could be drilled at the gallop.	
	9th.		G.O.C., IV Corps visited Brigade Headquarters, 10th Hussars, 15th Hussars and 9th M.G.Sqdn. He inspected a few billets and stables of each Unit. A fine day.	
	11th.		"O" Battery RHA marched under Divisional Orders from MILLENDORF to NORVENICH and HOCHKIRCHEN. Good billets for Officers, men and horses.	
	14th.		Brigadier General "T.T.PITMAN, C.B. C.M.G. arrived to take over command of the Brigade. Brigadier General D'A.LEGARD, C.M.G. D.S.O. visited units to say goodbye. Brigadier General T.T.PITMAN. C.B. C.M.G. assumed command of the Brigade. Capt.R.H.O.HANBURY, 15th Hussars, relinquished the duties of Acting Staff Captain. Duties assumed by Brigade Major.	
	16th & 17th.		Rain.	
	18th.		Inspection of Unit's Veterinary Equipment by O.C.39th M.V.Section. A fine day.	

Army Form C. 2118.

WAR DIARY
or
INTELLIGENCE SUMMARY.
(Erase heading not required.)

Instructions regarding War Diaries and Intelligence Summaries are contained in F. S. Regs., Part II. and the Staff Manual respectively. Title pages will be prepared in manuscript.

Place	Date	Hour	Summary of Events and Information	Remarks and references to Appendices
BERGERHAUSEN	19th	14.30	Conference at Brigade Headquarters. All C.O's attended.	
			Party of 5th Argyll and Sutherland Highlanders attached to 15th Hussars relieved by similar number (3 Officers and 100 O.R's) of 52nd Gordon Highlanders.	
			Capt.A.R.W.CURTIS. M.C. 11th Hussars, joined the Brigade and assumed the duties of Staff Captain.	
			A fine day.	
	22nd.		Brigadier visited 10th Hussars and inspected horses and billets.	
			A fine day.	
	23rd.		3 platoons of 4th Gordon Highlanders attached 3rd Hussars relieved by 2 platoons 52nd Gordon Highlanders.	
			3 platoons of 4th Gordon Highlanders attached 10th Hussars relieved by 3 platoons of 52nd Gordon Highlanders.	
			1 platoon of 4th Gordon Highlanders attached 9th M.G.Sqdn relieved by 1 platoon 52nd Gordon Highlanders.	
			Received orders for the move of the 3rd Hussars to DUREN on Saturday April 26th.	
			A fine day.	
			Issued Hussar Brigade Order No.2.	Appendix.2.

(A9753) Wt. W2458/P360 600,000 12/17 D. D. & L. Sch. 53a. Forms/C2118/13.

Army Form C. 2118.

WAR DIARY
or
INTELLIGENCE SUMMARY.
(Erase heading not required.)

Instructions regarding War Diaries and Intelligence
Summaries are contained in F. S. Regs., Part II.
and the Staff Manual respectively. Title pages
will be prepared in manuscript.

Place	Date	Hour	Summary of Events and Information	Remarks and references to Appendices
BERGERHAUSEN.	24th.	14.00.	Conference of Brigade Commanders and C.R.H.A. at Divisional Headquarters.	
			Some rain.	
	25th.		Brigadier visited 15th Hussars and inspected horses at a watering order parade and saw the billets, stables, etc.	
	26th.		Army Commander visited units as under and saw a few billets and stables of each :-	
			10th Hussars :- 10.00. 15th Hussars :- 10.30. 9th M.G.Sqdn :- 11.00.	
			3rd Hussars moved to DUREN and took over barracks vacated by 9th Lancers. Move completed at 15.30 hours.	
			Some rain.	
	29th.	10.30.	Parade of composite Regiment found by this Brigade for Mobile Striking Force.	
			Composition :- Headquarters and 3 Squadrons and 1 Section Machine Guns.	
			Each Regiment of Brigade finds one Sqn of 4 Officers & 69 O.Rs.	
			(3 troops only).	
		11.30.	Brigadier visited "O" Batty R.H.A. and saw billets, stables, etc.	
			Some rain.	

Army Form C. 2118.

WAR DIARY
or
INTELLIGENCE SUMMARY.
(Erase heading not required.)

Instructions regarding War Diaries and Intelligence Summaries are contained in F. S. Regs., Part II. and the Staff Manual respectively. Title pages will be prepared in manuscript.

Place	Date	Hour	Summary of Events and Information	Remarks and references to Appendices
BERGERHAUSEN	30th	10.00	Brigadier visited 9th Cavalry Field Ambulance and 39th Mobile Vety Section and saw billets, Stables, etc.	
		11.30	Brigadier visited 9th Machine Gun Squadron and saw billets, stables, etc.	
			Some rain.	
			Demobilization of Regiments of the Brigade has been practically completed during the month; very few reinforcements have been received and all Units are very weak in men still. The attached Infantry are of the greatest assistance.	
			There has been a great deal of rain during the month.	

[signature], Captain.,
Brigade Major., Hussar Brigade.

APPENDIX. 1

SECRET.   Copy No....

                    Hussar Brigade   Order No.1.
          -*-*-*-*-*-*-*-*-*-*-*-*-*-*-*-*-*-*-*-

Reference Maps:- 1.K. and 1.L. 1/100,000.   5th April, 1919.

1. The Brigade (less 3rd Hussars and "Q" abd "V" Batteries R.H.A.) will move on the 7th instant to an area about KERPEN in accordance with the attached March Table.

2. The move of the 3rd Hussars to EUPEN will not take place for the present.

3. Lorries to convey billeting parties will report at Unit Headquarters at 07.00 hours on the 6th instant :-

        10th Hussars   :-   1 lorry.
        15th Hussars   :-   1 lorry.
        Hussar M.G.S.   :-   1 lorry.

4. Lorries to convey personnel and kit will report at Unit Headquarters as under :-

	05.00 hours 7th inst.	17.00 hours 6th inst. (will not proceed to new area till 7th inst).
10th Hussars :-	9	9
15th Hussars :-	9	9
Hussar M.G.S. :-	3	4
Hussar O.F.A. :-	-	1
Brigade H.Q. & Signal Troop. :-	-	1

5. Details re personnel to assist in this move will be issued later.

6. Acknowledge.

                                              (signed)
                                                      Captain.,
                                    Brigade Major., Hussar Brigade

Issued at 10.30. hours.

Operation Order Distribution.

March Table. (Issued with Hussar Brigade Order No.1.)

"A"	"B"	"C"	"D"	"E"
Serial No. Unit.	Starting Point.	Time.	Route.	Destination.
1. 15th Hussars.	S exit of BLATZHEIM.	09.00.	THORR - IPPENDORF - SINDORF	KERPEN.
2. Hussar M.G. Sqdn.	S exit of KASTER.	09.00.	BEDBURG - LIVERICH - ELSDORF - BUIR.	BLATZHEIM.
3. Brigade H.Q. & Signal Troop.	First E of HARFF.	09.00.	As for serial 1.	BERGERHAUSEN.
4. Hussar C.F.A. & Hussar M.V.S.	First E of HARFF.	09.05.	As for serial 2.	BOLHEIM.
5. 10th Hussars.	First E of HARFF.	09.30.	BEDBURG - BERGHEIM - HORREM.	ZUFFICH - BALIKHAUSEN - BRUGGEN.

APPENDIX 2

SECRET.   Copy No.

Hussar Brigade Order No.2.

23rd April 1919.

1. 3rd Hussars will move to DUREN on Saturday April 26th and take over the Barracks vacated by 9th Lancers.

2. 3rd Hussars will be clear of present billets by 11.00 hours, otherwise no restrictions as to time of start or route, but this Office will be notified of both.

3. 3rd Hussars will notify this office by 24th inst., what extra personnel and what motor transport they require to assist them to move.

4. Completion of move to be wired to this office.

5. Acknowledge (3rd Hussars only).

Captain,

Brigade Major, Hussar Brigade.

Operation Order Distribution.

HUSSAR BRIGADE.

EFFECTIVE STRENGTH in Hussar Brigade for week ending 26/4/19.

UNIT.	Offrs.	O.R.	Rdg.	Dght.	Pack.	Mules.
Headquarters.	6	29	21	15	-	-
3rd Hussars.	44	320	469	60	24	-
10th Hussars.	29	255	494	61	24	-
15th Hussars.	35	352	478	61	25	-
9th M.G.Sqdn.	10	123	177	71	41	-
"O" Batty.RHA.	6	163	102	130	-	-
9th C.F.Amb.	4	82	19	42	-	-
9th Sig. Trp.	1	22	14	4	1	-
TOTAL.	135	1346	1774	444	115	-

WANTING TO COMPLETE on same date.

UNIT.	Offrs.	O.R.	Rdg.	Dght.	Pack.	Mules.
Headquarters.	3	12	1	1	-	-
3rd Hussars.	-	174	18	1	-	-
10th Hussars.	-	239	-	-	-	-
15th Hussars.	-	158	13	-	-	-
9th M.G.Sqdn.	-	124	26	-	1	-
"O" Batty.RHA.	-	40	-	1	-	-
9th C.F.Amb.	2	32	-	2	-	-
9th Sig. Trp.	-	2	-	-	-	-
TOTAL.	5	781	58	5	1	-

ARRIVALS during week.

    Capt. A.FRASER. R.A.M.C.   22/4/19   From No.5 C.F.A.

DEPARTURES during week.

    Lieut-Col.F.H.D.C.WHITMORE.   14/4/19   Demobilized in U.K.
        C.M.G.,D.S.O.
    Major A.BUXTON. D.S.O.   22/4/19   To Demob.
    Lieut.E.P.AWDRY. M.C.   23/4/19   " "

HUSSAR BRIGADE.

EFFECTIVE STRENGTH in Hussar Brigade for week ending 19/4/19.

UNIT.	Offrs.	O.R.	Rdg.	Dght.	Pack.	Mules.
Headquarters.	5	34	20	15	-	-
3rd Hussars.	44	332	471	60	24	-
10th Hussars.	32	255	496	61	25	-
15th Hussars.	40	485	450	61	25	-
9th M.G.Sqdn.	11	166	178	71	41	-
"O" Batty.RHA.	6	161	103	131	-	-
9th C.F.Amb.	3	90	18	42	-	-
9th Sig. Trp.	1	22	14	4	1	-
TOTAL.	142	1545	1749	445	116	-

WANTING TO COMPLETE on same date.

UNIT.	Offrs.	O.R.	Rdg.	Dght.	Pack.	Mules.
Headquarters.	4	7	2	1	-	-
3rd Hussars.	-	162	16	1	-	-
10th Hussars.	-	239	-	-	-	-
15th Hussars.	-	25	41	-	-	-
9th M.G.Sqdn.	-	105	25	-	1	-
"O" Batty.RHA.	-	42	-	-	-	-
9th C.F.Amb.	3	25	-	2	-	-
9th Sig. Trp.	-	-	-	-	-	-
TOTAL.	7	605	84	4	1	-

ARRIVALS during week.

Major (Bt.Lt.Col.) P.J.V. KELLY,C.M.G.,D.S.O.	13/4/19	From U.K.
Lieut. D.H.WILLIAMS.	16/4/19	" Oxford Hussars.
Capt. T.C.STOREY,M.C., R.A.M.C.	11/4/19	Joined for duty, from Base
Lieut.R.H.E.ABDY.	15/4/19	" " " " "
Major J.BIGGAM,M.C,, R.A.M.C.	14/4/19	Posted from Div.H.Q.

DEPARTURES during week.

Lieut. R.C.MARSH.	18/4/19	To U.K. Demob.
Capt. A.W.FORREST, R.A?M.C.	12/4/19	" " "
Capt. G.F.ASHTON, R.A.V.C.	12/4/19	" R.A.V.C., Base.
Lieut.R.W.HOWE,M.C.	15/4/19	"No. 2 Traffic Control Sqdn, NAMUR.
Lieut. R.C.SHELTON.	17/4/19	" U.K. Demob.
Capt. R.C.AITCHISON. R.A.M.C.	14/4/19	" U.K.

HUSSAR BRIGADE

EFFECTIVE STRENGTH in Hussar Brigade for week ending 12/4/1919.

UNIT.	Offrs.	O.R.	Rdg.	Dght.	Pack.	Mules.
Headquarters.	4	33	16	14	-	-
3rd Hussars.	48	334	479	59	24	-
10th Hussars.	33	264	499	61	25	-
15th Hussars.	39	489	457	61	25	-
9th M.G.Sqdn.	11	167	175	69	40	-
"Y" Batty.RHA.	5	196	-	90	-	-
"O" Batty.RHA.	6	134	102	131	-	-
9th C.F.Amb.	3	90	19	43	-	-
9th Sig. Trp.	1	22	14	4	1	-
T O T A L.	150	1729	1761	532	115	-

WANTING TO COMPLETE on same date.

UNIT.	Offrs.	O.R.	Rdg.	Dght.	Pack.	Mules.
Headquarters.	5	8	8	2	-	-
3rd Hussars.	-	160	8	2	-	-
10th Hussars.	-	230	-	-	-	-
15th Hussars.	-	21	32	-	-	-
9th M.G.Sqdn.	-	104	28	2	2	-
"Y" Batty.RHA.	-	-	42	-	-	-
"O" Batty.RHA.	-	69	-	-	-	-
9th C.F.Amb.	3	25	-	1	-	-
9th Sig. Trp.	-	2	-	-	-	-
T O T A L.	8	619	118	7	2	-

ARRIVALS during week.

Lieut. J.K. HARVIE.	6/4/19	From U.K.
2/Lt. L.E.R. FISHER? M.C.	6/4/19	" "
2/Lt. W.B. SHOOK, M.M.	19/3/19	" 4th M.G.Sqdn.
" R.H. FRENCH.	24/3/19	" " " "
" C.P.W. STROUD.	27/3/19	" 7th " "
Lieut-Col. A.N.R. mc.NEILL, D.S.O.	9/4/19	" 7th C.F.Amb.
Capt. R.H. THOMPSON.	9/4/19	" " " "

DEPARTURES during week.

Lieut. C. EADE, M.C.	2/4/19	To U.K. for Demob.
" S.J. PINKER.	24/3/19	Transferred to 3rd M.G.Sqd
Capt. J.J. MAGNER. R.A.M.C.	5/4/19	To duty, N.Russia.
" C.W. SPARKS, M.C., R.A.M.C.	5/4/19	" " " "
" J.A. O'DRISCOLL.	9/4/19	Rejoined 1st C.F.A.

HUSSAR BRIGADE

EFFECTIVE STRENGTH in Hussar Brigade for week ending 5/4/1919.

UNIT.	Offrs.	O.R.	Rdg.	Dght.	Pack.	Mules.
Headquarters.	4	33	30	14	-	-
3rd Hussars.	46	334	477	61	24	-
10th Hussars.	33	268	504	61	25	-
15th Hussars.	39	489	499	61	25	-
Hussar M.G.Sqdn.	11	238	191	70	42	-
"Y" Batty.R.H.A.	5	204	13	167	-	-
"O" Batty.R.H.A.	6	122	102	131	-	-
Hussar C.F.Amb.	3	88	12	43	-	-
Hussar Sig.Trp.	1	22	14	4	1	-
TOTAL.	148	1798	1842	612	117	-

WANTING to COMPLETE on same date.

UNIT	Offrs.	O.R.	Rdg.	Dght.	Pack.	Mules.
Headquarters.	5	8	-	2	-	-
3rd Hussars.	-	160	10	-	-	-
10th Hussars.	-	226	-	-	-	-
15th Hussars.	-	21	-	-	-	-
Hussar M.G.Sqdn.	-	33	12	1	-	-
"Y" Batty.R.H.A.	-	-	29	-	-	-
"O" Batty.R.H.A.	-	81	-	-	-	-
Hussar C.F.Amb.	3	26	-	1	-	-
Hussar Sig.Trp.	-	2	-	-	-	-
TOTAL.	8	557	51	4	-	-

ARRIVALS during week.

Capt. E.W.A.K. HUTCHISON. R.A.S.C.	3/4/19	From 2nd Cav. Div.
Capt. A.W. KEITH-FALCONER.	1/4/19	" Ox. Hussars.
" H. GORING.	1/4/19	" 4th Cav. Bde.
Lieut.J. WALL, D.C.M.	1/4/19	" 8th Hussars.
" ? WILLIAMS.	1/4/19	" Ox. Hussars.
Lt. C.H. PARR	29/3/19	" 12th Lancers.
Lieut.B.C. LESTER.	30/3/19	" "N" By. R.H.A.
" W.P. LASSETER.	30/3/19	" " " "
Capt. R.C. AITCHISON. R.A.M.C.	2/4/19	" No. 47 Gen.Hosptl.

DEPARTURES during week.

Capt. V. LINDEMERE. R.A.S.C.	1/4/19	To Demobilization.
" W. SHAKESPEARE.	3/4/19	" Pool of Quartermasters CALAIS.
Lieut.C.H. PARR.	30/3/19	" Demobilization.
2/Lt. F.A. CONSTABLE.	15/3/19	" "
Lieut.W.A. GREENSLADE.	3/4/19	" "

CONFIDENTIAL.

WAR DIARY.

of

HUSSAR BRIGADE HEADQUARTERS.

MAY, 1919.

Volume. No. 2.

Army Form C. 2118.

WAR DIARY
INTELLIGENCE SUMMARY

HEADQUARTERS., HUSSAR BRIGADE.

MAY 1919. Volume No. 2.

(Erase heading not required.)

Instructions regarding War Diaries and Intelligence Summaries are contained in F. S. Regs., Part II. and the Staff Manual respectively. Title pages will be prepared in manuscript.

Place	Date	Hour	Summary of Events and Information	Remarks and references to Appendices
BERGERHAUSEN.	1st.		Nothing to report.	(a)
	2nd.		Cavalry Memorial Service, BERGHEIM.	(a)
	3rd.		Nothing to report.	
	4th.		Nothing to report.	
	5th.		Brigadier inspected Brigade Signal Troop and Brigade Headquarters.	(a)
	6th.		G.O.C. IV Corps inspected 3rd Hussars Barracks and stables. Brigadier attended.	(a)
	7th.		Nothing to report.	
	8th.		Brigadier as Acting Divisional Commander accompanied H.R.H. The Duke of Connaught on his visit to 17th Lancers at COLOGNE.	(a)
	9th.		Lecture on Ancient Romans at KERPEN.	
	10th.		Nothing to report.	
	11th.		Nothing to report.	
	12th.		Brigadier attended Tactical Exercise of 3rd Hussars.	(a)
	13th.		Nothing to report.	

Army Form C. 2118.

WAR DIARY.
or
INTELLIGENCE SUMMARY.
(Erase heading not required.)

Instructions regarding War Diaries and Intelligence Summaries are contained in F. S. Regs., Part II. and the Staff Manual respectively. Title pages will be prepared in manuscript.

Place	Date	Hour	Summary of Events and Information	Remarks and references to Appendices
BERGHAUSEN.	14th.		Brigadier attended Tactical Exercise of 10th Hussars.	a
	15th.		Commander-in-Chief held review of DUREN Garrison. 3rd Hussars found Squadron of 100 strong.	a
			C-in-C inspected 3rd Hussars Barracks after.	a
			Lecture on State Control of Drink at KERPEN.	
	16th.		Brigadier attended Tactical Exercise of 15th Hussars.	a
	17th.		Nothing to report.	
	18th.		Nothing to report.	
	19th.		Brigadier, D.A.A.&Q.M.G., Cavalry Division and O.C., 1st Field Squadron R.E. inspected stable sites of 10th and 15th Hussars and 9th M.G.Squadron.	a
	20th.		Brigadier, D.A.A.&.M.M.G., Cavalry Division and O.C., 1st Field Squadron R.E. inspected stable sites of 3rd Hussars, "Q" Batty. R.H.A. and 39th M.V.Section.	a
	21st.		Nothing to report.	
	22nd.		Divisional Commander held conference at Brigade H.Qrs. of Commanding Officers and Squadron Leaders, and discussed the military situation, training and routine.	
	23rd.		Lecture on Bolshevism at HORREM.	a

Army Form C. 2118.

WAR DIARY
or
INTELLIGENCE SUMMARY.
(Erase heading not required.)

Instructions regarding War Diaries and Intelligence Summaries are contained in F. S. Regs., Part II. and the Staff Manual respectively. Title pages will be prepared in manuscript.

Place	Date	Hour	Summary of Events and Information	Remarks and references to Appendices
BERGERHAUSEN.	23rd (cont).		Organization of Cavalry Division Composite Regiment in event of possible advance.	Cav Dn Order No.1 (a)
			Composition of Hussar Brigade Squadron for a possible advance. G.P.2/15 and 16.	Appendix.1. (a)
	24th.		Supplementary to G.P.2/15. Hotchkiss Rifle Detachment.	" 11. (a)
	25th.		Nothing to report.	
	26th.		Warning Order that J - 3 day would probably be 27th.	(a)
			Brigadier received orders to move to Cavalry Division H.Q. whilst Acting Divisional Commander.	(a)
			G.O.C., Cavalry Division (Acting IV Corps Commander) inspected 3rd Hussars. Brigadier attended.	(a)
	27th.		Brigadier assumed Command of Cavalry Division at 12.00 hours and moved to QUADRATH.	(a)
	28th.		Nothing to report.	
	29th.		Nothing to report.	
	30th.		Supplementary to G.P.2/15 and 17. G.P.2/18 issued.	Appendix.111. (a)
	31st.		Lieut.Col.W.WILLCOX.C.M.G. 3rd Hussars assumed command of the Brigade. Brigadier General., T.T.PITMAN. C.M.G. C.B. proceeded to U.K. on leave.	(a)

Christie
Captain.,

Brigade Major., "HUSSAR" Brigade.

HUSSAR BRIGADE.

EFFECTIVE STRENGTH in Hussar Brigade for week ending 3/5/19.

UNIT.	Offrs.	O.Rs.	Rdg.	Dght.	Pack.	Mules.
Headquarters.	6	27	22	15	-	-
3rd Hussars.	41	379	459	61	24	-
10th Hussars.	29	273	490	61	24	-
15th Hussars.	33	327	465	61	25	-
9th M.G.Sqdn.	10	116	173	71	40	-
"O"Batty.RHA.	6	169	102	131	-	-
9th C.F.Amb.	4	80	17	42	-	-
9th Sig. Trp.	1	22	14	4	1	-
TOTAL.	130	1393	1742	446	114	-

WANTING TO COMPLETE on same date.

UNIT.	Offrs.	O.Rs.	Rdg.	Dght.	Pack.	Mules.
Headquarters.	3	14	-	1	-	-
3rd Hussars.	-	115	28	-	-	-
10th Hussars.	-	221	-	-	-	-
15th Hussars.	5	183	26	-	-	-
9th M.G.Sqdn.	-	131	30	-	2	-
"O"Batty.RHA.	-	34	-	-	-	-
9th C.F.Amb.	2	34	-	2	-	-
9th Sig. Trp.	-	2	-	-	-	-
TOTAL.	10	734	84	3	2	-

ARRIVALS during week.

NIL.

DEPARTURES during week.

Brig-Genl.D'A. LEGARD. C.M.G.,D.S.O. 30/4/19   To U.K.
Capt. H.GORING.   To Staff Capt. Dragoon Bde. Authy. A.G.7896/12 (O)

Lieut.J.B.F.AUSTIN.   26/3/19   Transfer to U.K.
" R.C.SHELTON.   18/4/19   To U.K. for Demob.
" N.W.LEAF.   10/3/19   To U.K. from Cav. Corps Equit. Sch.
" C.EADE. M.C.   2/4/19   To U.K. for Demob.

HUSSAR BRIGADE.

EFFECTIVE STRENGTH in Hussar Brigade for week ending 10/5/1919.

UNIT.	Offrs.	O.Rs.	Rdg.	Dght.	Pack.	Mules.
Headquarters.	6	27	22	15	-	-
3rd Hussars.	41	367	444	61	24	-
10th Hussars.	36	295	473	58	24	-
15th Hussars.	33	357	452	60	25	-
9th M.G.Sqdn.	10	112	170	69	38	-
"O" Batty RHA.	6	196	102	131	-	-
9th C.F.Amb,.	4	79	14	42	-	-
9th Sig Troop.	1	22	14	4	1	-
T O T A L.	137	1455	1691	440	112	-

WANTING TO COMPLETE on same date.

UNIT.	Offrs.	O.Rs.	Rdg.	Dght.	Pack.	Mules.
Headquarters.	3	14	-	1	-	-
3rd Hussars.	-	127	43	-	-	-
10th Hussars.	-	199	14	3	-	-
15th Hussars.	5	153	39	1	-	-
9th M.G.Sqdn.	-	135	33	2	4	-
"O" Batty RHA.	-	7	-	-	-	-
9th C.F.Amb,.	2	35	-	2	-	-
9th Sig Troop.	-	2	-	-	-	-
T O T A L.	10	672	129	9	4	-

ARRIVALS during week.

N I L.

DEPARTURE during week.

N I L.

HUSSAR BRIGADE.

EFFECTIVE STRENGTH in "HUSSAR" Brigade for week ending 17/5/1919.

UNIT.	Offrs.	O.R's.	Rdg.	Dght.	Pack.	Mules.
Headquarters.	6	31	20	15	-	-
3rd Hussars.	40	356	457	61	24	-
10th Hussars.	29	279	474	58	24	-
15th Hussars.	33	275	458	60	24	-
9th M.G.Sqdn,.	9	108	177	67	37	-
"O" Batty RHA.	6	197	102	130	-	-
9th C.F.Amb,.	4	75	11	41	-	-
9th Sig.Troop,	1	8	14	4	1	-
TOTAL.	128	1329	1713	436	110	-

WANTING TO COMPLETE on same date.

UNIT.	Offrs.	O.R's.	Rdg.	Dght.	Pack.	Mules.
Headquarters?	3	13	-	1	-	-
3rd Hussars.	-	138	30	-	-	-
10th Hussars.	-	215	17	3	-	-
15th Hussars.	-	219	29	1	-	-
9th M.G.Sqdn,.	-	139	26	4	5	-
"O" Batty RHA.	-	4	-	1	-	-
9th C.F.Amb,.	2	37	-	3	-	-
9th Sig.Troop,	-	15	-	2	-	-
TOTAL.	5	780	102	15	5	-

ARRIVALS during week.

    N I L .

DEPARTURES during week.

    Captain, C.J.RYAN. R.A.V.C. to 10th M.V.Section.
      ,, G.V.NICHOLAS.R.A.V.C. to U.K.
    Lieut. R.C.MARSH. 3rd Hussars. to U.K.
    Captain, R.P.NICOL. 9th M.G.Sqdn. to U.K.
      ,, R.C.AITCHISON. 9th C.F.Amb. to U.K.

HUSSAR BRIGADE.

EFFECTIVE STRENGTH in "HUSSAR" Brigade for week ending 24th May, 1919.

UNIT.	Offrs.	O.R's.	Rdg.	Dght.	Pack.	Mules:
Headquarters.	6	29	20	15	-	-
3rd Hussars.	40	357	456	61	24	-
10th Hussars.	29	274	474	58	24	-
15th Hussars.	33	268	453	61	24	-
9th M.G.Sqdn.	9	108	176	66	37	-
"O" Batty RHA	6	196	102	130	-	-
9th C.F.Amb,.	4	74	11	41	-	-
9th Sig.Troop	1	8	13	4	1	-
TOTAL.	128	1314	1705	436	110	-

WANTING TO COMPLETE on same date.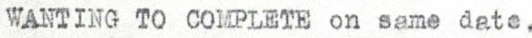

UNIT.	Offrs.	O.R's.	Rdg.	Dght.	Pack.	Mules.
Headquarters.	3	15	-	1	-	-
3rd Hussars.	-	137	31	-	-	-
10th Hussars.	-	220	13	3	-	-
15th Hussars.	-	226	34	-	-	-
9th M.G.Sqdn.	-	139	27	5	5	-
"O" Batty RHA	-	5	-	1	-	-
9th C.F.Amb,.	2	38	-	3	-	-
9th Sig.Troop.	-	15	-	-	-	-
TOTAL.	5	795	105	13	5	-

ARRIVALS during week.

    Lieut. P.DONNER. 11th Hussars.from U.K. A.D.C.to G.O.C.,"Hussar" Brigade.
    "   R.W.HOWE. M.C. 10th Hussars from No.2, Traffic Control Sqdn,.
    "   A.C.STRAKER. 15th Hussars. from G.H.Q. 3rd Echelon.

DEPARTURES during week.

    Lieut. Hon.G.E.D.C.GLYN.10th Hussars. to Demob.
    "   H.J.JOEL, 15th Hussars. to Demob.
    Maj. Rev. J.S.D.RYDER,M.C. to Demob.
    Capt. R.P.NICOL 9th M.G.Sqdn,. Transferred to Home Establishment.

HUSSAR BRIGADE.

EFFECTIVE STRENGTH in "HUSSAR" Brigade for week ending 31st May, 1919.

UNIT.	Offrs.	O.R's.	Rdg.	Dght.	Pack.	Mules.
Headquarters.	6	30	20	15	-	-
3rd Hussars.	40	355	454	61	24	-
10th Hussars.	29	276	471	58	24	-
15th Hussars.	33	277	430	61	24	-
9th M. G. S.	9	107	172	61	36	-
"O" Batty RHA.	6	197	102	131	-	-
9th C. F. A.	1	70	11	41	-	-
9th Sig. Troop.	1	7	14	4	1	-
TOTAL.	125	1319	1674	432	109	-

WANTING TO COMPLETE on same date.

UNIT.	Offrs.	O.R's.	Rdg.	Dght.	Pack.	Mules.
Headquarters.	3	14	-	1	-	-
3rd Hussars.	-	139	33	-	-	-
10th Hussars.	-	218	16	3	-	-
15th Hussars.	-	217	57	-	-	-
9th M. G. S.	-	140	31	10	6	-
"O" Batty RHA.	-	4	-	-	-	-
9th C. F. A.	5	42	-	3	-	-
9th Sig. Troop.	-	16	-	-	-	-
TOTAL.	8	790	137	17	6	-

ARRIVALS during week.

    Lieut. B.J.L.BANKS. 15th Hussars. from U.K.

DEPARTURES during week.

    Lieut A. IRELAND. 15th Hussars. to Demob.
    A/Major. J.BIGGAM, M.C. 9th C.F.A., to Cavalry Division, H.Q.
    Capt. A.N.R.McNEIL, D.S.O., 9th C.F.A. to No.1. C.F.A.
    ,, A.H.THOMSON. 9th C.F.A. to No.1. C.F.A.

APPENDIX III

SECRET.

G.P.2/18.   30/5/19.

HEADQUARTERS, HUSSAR BDE.

MOBILE STRIKING FORCE.

In addition to the Establishment laid down for Regtl Troops in G.P.2/15 and G.P.2/17.

(a). The 3rd Hussars and the 10th Hussars will each find one mounted signaller, who will report for attachment to Composite Regimental Headquarters on J - 2 day, i.e. the day after the concentration in COLOGNE.

(b). The 3rd Hussars and the 15th Hussars will each find one cyclist, who will report for attachment to Composite Regimental Headquarters on J - 3 day, after the concentration of the Composite Regiment in COLOGNE.

Acknowledge.

Operation Order Distribution.

APPENDIX II.

SECRET.

HEADQUARTERS,
HUSSAR
BRIGADE.

No..........
Date.........

G.P.2/17.   24/5/19.

MOBILE STRIKING FORCE.

Supplementary to G.P.2/15.

Each Troop of the Hussar Brigade Squadron will find a Hotchkiss Rifle Detachment consisting of :-

    4 O.R's.   4 Riding horses.
    1 Hotchkiss Gun Pack.
    1 Hotchkiss Rifle Ammunition Pack.

Detail of equipment will be as laid down in Cavalry Division Organization Table.3.

A.K.W.Curtis

Captain.,
Brigade Major., HUSSAR Brigade.

Operation Order Distribution.

APPENDIX. 1.

SECRET.

G.P.2/16.   23/5/19.

HEADQUARTERS, HUSSAR BDE.
No.........

MOBILE STRIKING FORCE.

1. Hussar Brigade No.G.P.2/9 is cancelled and the attached letter No.G.P.2/15 is substituted.

2. Names of officers to be detailed will be wired to this office as soon as possible. No Officer other than troop leaders and Second-in-Command M.G. Section will be changed without reference to this office.

3. Acknowledge.

[signature]

Captain.,

Brigade Major., Hussar Brigade.

Operation Order Distribution.

SECRET.

G.P.2/15.   23/5/19.

MOBILE STRIKING FORCE.

1.   If an advance is ordered, the Infantry is to advance with Advanced Guards in lorries.
   A Mobile Cavalry Force, composed as under, is to be attached to VI Corps and would be concentrated in COLOGNE. The Cavalry mission would probably be to keep touch between the Advanced Guards in lorries, which would advance about 30 miles a day, and the main body.
   The earliest date on which the advance may be ordered (called J day hereafter) is 26th May.

2.   The Cavalry Force will be as follows :-

Under the command of a Lt.Col. & Regt Staff found by Dragoon Brigade
{
A Composite Regiment - formed from 1 Sqdn. per Cav.Bde., each Regt. finding a strong troop,
"G" Battery R.H.A.
1 Composite M.G.Sqdn - Formed of 1 section of each M.G.Sqdn.
}

3. (a). The Squadron found by the HUSSAR Brigade will be composed as follows :-

   Sqdn Leader - Capt.H.F.BRACE. DSO. MC. 15th Hussars.
   Second-in-Command to be detailed by 10th Hussars.
   1 S.S.M. to be detailed by 15th Hussars.
   1 S.Q.M.S. to be detailed by 10th Hussars.
   3 Troops (one from each Regt) composed of
         2 Subalterns.
       + 70 Other Ranks.

TOTAL Strength 8 Officers, 212 Other Ranks.

              + 2 Shoeing smiths and 1 cyclist will be included in this number.
              15th Hussars will find a cook for the Officers Mess.

   (b). 9th M.G.Sqdn will find one section for the composite M.G.Sqdn, consisting of :-

         2 Officers.
         47 Other Ranks.
         4 Machine Guns.

4.   The HUSSAR Brigade Force would rendezvous in the Grass Field West of MODRATH on J - 3 days and billet in Lancer Brigade Area in COLOGNE.   The HUSSAR Brigade Squadron would be billetted in the Artillery Barracks with accommodation from 12th Lancers.   The 9th M.G. Section in the Cavalry Barracks with accommodation from 2nd M.G.Sqdn.

                                             5. Transport.

5. **Transport.**

   "A" Echelon.
   1 L.G.S. wagon per Troop.
   (Load as in para.2. of Appendix "A" issued
   with Hussar Brigade G.P.2/9).
   1 Mess Cart found by 15th Hussars.
   (Officers of other Regiments will bring Mess
   equipment on their L.G.S. wagon to be
   transferred later).
   3 L.G.S. wagons for 9th M.G.Section.
   (Load as in para.3. of Appendix"A" issued
   with Hussar Brigade G.P.2/9).

   "B" Echelon.
   Will be taken up to the Concentration Area
   in COLOGNE and left there to be sent up if required.

   1 G.S. wagon per Cavalry Regiment.

6. **Dress.**

   Marching order as laid down in Cavalry Division
   Organization Table.1.

7. 2 boxes of horse shoes will be carried in "A"
Echelons L.G.S. wagons.

8. A.A.&Q.M.G., is to issue 1 iron ration forthwith. These will not be issued to troops until a move
is ordered.

9. 1/200,000 maps are to be issued by the Division.
All map reference will be made to these.

10. A Code Message "HUN" will be the Warning Order
to Units for the moves involved by these orders.

                                        Captain.,
                        Brigade Major, "HUSSAR" Brigade.

Operation Order Distribution.

CONFIDENTIAL.

WAR DIARY

of

HUSSAR BRIGADE HEADQUARTERS.

JUNE, 1919.

VOLUME. No.3.

WAR DIARY
or
INTELLIGENCE SUMMARY

(Erase heading not required.)

Army Form C. 2118.

"HUSSAR" BRIGADE HEADQUARTERS.

JUNE, 1919.

VOLUME No. 3.

Instructions regarding War Diaries and Intelligence Summaries are contained in F. S. Regs., Part II. and the Staff Manual respectively. Title pages will be prepared in manuscript.

Place	Date	Hour	Summary of Events and Information	Remarks and references to Appendices
BERGERHAUSEN.	1st.		Situation unchanged.	
	4th.		Some rain during the night.	
	8th.		Brig-General.T.T.PITMAN. C.B., C.M.G., Captain.R.G.P.WOOD. M.C., Brigade Major and Lieut.P.J. DONNER A.D.C. rejoined from leave in U.K.	
	9th.		Inspection of Small Box Respirators of Mobile Squadron at KERPEN. Conference at Divisional Headquarters on Cavalry Division Horse Show.	
	11th.		Brigadier inspected cook-houses and messing arrangements of 10th and 15th Hussars.	
	15th.	21.30	Received Warning Order "J" Day will probably be Friday June 17th ("J" - 3 day is therefore Tuesday 14th). Units warned by telephone.	
	16th.	10.00	Divisional Commander inspected 3rd Hussars in Equitation - Foot-drill - Musketry and Physical Training.	
	17th.	04.00	Notified that "J" Day will be Friday - consequently the Mobile Striking Force will concentrate in COLOGNE today. See G.P.2/15, 2/16, 2/17 and 2/18 in appendix to War Diary for May.	
		04.20	Orders issued by wire and telephone.	
		12.00	Mobile Striking Force Sqdn and Section of M.G's concentrated in Meadows West of MODRATH and marched to COLOGNE. The Squadron billets in 12th Lancers Barracks (Artillery Barracks) and	

Army Form C. 2118.

WAR DIARY
or
INTELLIGENCE SUMMARY.

(Erase heading not required.)

Instructions regarding War Diaries and Intelligence Summaries are contained in F. S. Regs., Part II. and the Staff Manual respectively. Title pages will be prepared in manuscript.

Place	Date	Hour	Summary of Events and Information	Remarks and references to Appendices
BERGERHAUSEN.	17th (Contd)		the Machine Gun Section in 1st Machine Gun Sqdn Barracks (Cavalry Barracks). Issued G.P. 2/23 and 2/25 to 9th M.G. Sqdn re protection of bridges in the event of an advance or civil disturbances.	Appendix. 1.
	18th.	09.30.	Divisional Commander inspected 15th Hussars in Equitation, Foot-drill and Physical Training.	
	19th.		Notified that "J" Day is postponed. Mobile Striking Force remains in readiness for action.	
	21st.		Divisional Commander inspected billets, stables, etc, of 9th M.G. Sqdn.	
	24th - 27th		Continual heavy showers of rain.	
	27th.		9th M.G. Sqdn, 9th Signal Troop and 9th Cav. Field Ambulance become Hussar M.G. Sqdn, Hussar Signal Troop and Hussar Field Ambulance.	
	28th.	20.00	Notified that Peace had been signed.	
			During the month the 10th Hussars have been made up to strength with young recruits from England, the 3rd Hussars have received 50 recruits and 15th Hussars about 100.	

B.P.... , Captain.,

Brigade Major., "HUSSAR" Brigade.

HUSSAR BRIGADE.

EFFECTIVE STRENGTH in "HUSSAR" Brigade for week ending 24th May, 1919.

UNIT.	Offrs.	O.R's.	Rdg.	Dght.	Pack.	Mules.
Headquarters.	6	29	20	15	-	-
3rd Hussars.	40	357	456	61	24	-
10th Hussars.	29	274	474	58	24	-
15th Hussars.	33	268	453	61	24	-
9th M.G.Sqdn.	9	108	176	66	37	-
"O" Batty RHA	6	196	102	130	-	-
9th C.F.Amb,.	4	74	11	41	-	-
9th Sig.Troop	1	8	13	4	1	-
TOTAL.	128	1314	1705	436	110	-

WANTING TO COMPLETE on same date.

UNIT.	Offrs.	O.R's.	Rdg.	Dght.	Pack.	Mules.
Headquarters.	3	15	-	1	-	-
3rd Hussars.	-	137	31	-	-	-
10th Hussars.	-	220	13	3	-	-
15th Hussars.	-	226	34	-	-	-
9th M.G.Sqdn.	-	139	27	5	5	-
"O" Batty RHA	-	5	-	1	-	-
9th C.F.Amb,.	2	38	-	3	-	-
9th Sig.Troop.	-	15	-	-	-	-
TOTAL.	5	795	105	13	5	-

ARRIVALS during week.

    Lieut. P.DONNER. 11th Hussars,from U.K. A.D.C.to G.O.C.,"Hussar" Brigade.
    " R.W.HOWE. M.C. 10th Hussars from No.2. Traffic Control Sqdn,.
    " A.C.STRAKER. 15th Hussars. from G.H.Q. 3rd Echelon.

DEPARTURES during week.

    Lieut. Hon.G.E.D.C.GLYN.10th Hussars. to Demob.
    " H.J.JOEL, 15th Hussars. to Demob.
    Maj. Rev. J.S.D.RYDER,M.C. to Demob.
    Capt. R.P.NICOL 9th M.G.Sqdn,. Transferred to Home Establishment.

SECRET.

9th M.G. Squadron.

G.P.2/23.   17/3/19.

1. In the event of a General Advance, the 9th M.G. Squadron, may be called upon to find and man 2 machine guns to assist the C.R.A.S.C. who is responsible for mounting guards at the following bridges :-

    Kilo. 20. 2.   Sheet.1.L.   M.E. 84.98.
    ,,   20. 0.   ,,   M.2. 89.01.
    ,,   19. 5.   ,,   M.2. 97.07.

2. In the event of civil disturbances one Section 9th M.G. Sqdn will "stand to" in billets ready to turn out at half an hours notice.

3. ACKNOWLEDGE.

(sd) R.G.P.WOOD., Captain.,
Brigade Major., "HUSSAR" Brigade.

HUSSAR BRIGADE.

EFFECTIVE STRENGTH in Hussar Brigade for Week Ending, 8th June, 1919.

UNIT.	Offrs.	O.R.S.	Rdg.	Dght.	Pack.	MULES.
Headquarters.	6	32	20	15	-	-
3rd Hussars.	40	341	447	61	24	-
10th Hussars.	23	251	472	58	24	-
15th Hussars.	33	279	420	61	24	-
9th M.G.S.	9	107	172	60	35	-
"O" Batty RHA.	7	199	102	131	-	-
9th Signal Troop.	1	8	14	4	1	-
TOTAL.	124	1217	1647	390	108	-

WANTING TO COMPLETE on same date.

UNIT.	Offrs.	O.Rs.	Rdg.	Dght.	Pack.	Mules.
Headquarters.	3	12	-	1	-	-
3rd Hussars.	-	153	40	-	-	-
10th Hussars.	-	243	15	3	-	-
15th Hussars.	-	215	67	-	-	-
9th M.G.S.	-	140	31	11	7	-
"O" Batty RHA	-	2	-	-	-	-
9th Signal Troop.	-	15	-	-	-	-
TOTAL.	3	780	153	15	7	-

ARRIVALS during week.

    Capt. W.A.DICKINSON. R.A.V.C
      " R.H.TOWELL. M.C., "O" Batty RHA.
      " W.A.KELLETT. R.A.V.C.

DEPARTURES during week.

    ... NIL ...

HUSSAR BRIGADE.

EFFECTIVE STRENGTH in Hussar Brigade for Week Ending, 14th June, 1919.

UNIT.	Offrs.	O.R's.	Rdg.	Dght.	Pack.	Mules.
HEADQUARTERS.	8	20	20	15	-	-
3rd HUSSARS.	41	337	445	61	24	-
10th HUSSARS.	28	256	472	58	24	-
15th HUSSARS.	33	274	419	61	24	-
9th M. G. S.	9	107	173	61	35	-
"O" Batty RHA.	6	196	102	131	-	-
9th Signal TROOP.	1	9	14	4	1	-
TOTAL.	126	1199	1645	391	108	-

WANTING TO COMPLETE on same date.

UNIT.	Offrs.	O.R's.	Rdg.	Dght.	Pack.	Mules.
HEADQUARTERS.	1	16	-	1	-	-
3rd HUSSARS.	-	157	42	-	-	-
10th HUSSARS.	-	238	15	3	-	-
15th HUSSARS.	-	220	68	-	-	-
9th M. G. S.	-	140	30	10	7	-
"O" BATTY RHA.	-	5	-	-	-	-
9th SIGNAL TROOP.	-	14	-	-	-	-
TOTAL.	1	790	155	14	7	-

ARRIVALS during week.

    Lieut. W.G. PETHERICK, 3rd Hussars, from U.K. 8/6/19.

DEPARTURES during week.

    Lieut. W.P. LASSETTER, "O" Btty R.H.A. to U.K. 12/6/19.

HUSSAR BRIGADE.

EFFECTIVE STRENGTH in Hussar Brigade for week ending 21st June 1919.

UNIT.	Offrs.	O.R's.	Rdg.	Dght.	Pack.	Mules.
Headquarters.	9	30	22	15	-	-
3rd Hussars.	41	339	444	61	24	-
10th Hussars.	28	493	464	58	24	-
15th Hussars.	33	333	428	61	24	-
9th M.G.S.	9	106	174	62	35	-
"O" Batty RHA.	6	208	102	130	-	-
9th Sig. Troop.	1	13	9	4	1	-
TOTAL.	127	1522	1643	391	108	-

WANTING TO COMPLETE on same date.

UNIT.	Offrs.	O.R's.	Rdg.	Dght.	Pack.	Mules.
Headquarters.	-	14	-	1	-	-
3rd Hussars.	-	155	43	-	-	-
10th Hussars.	-	1	23	3	-	-
15th Hussars.	-	161	59	-	-	-
9th M.G.S.	-	141	29	9	7	-
"O" Batty RHA.	-	-	-	1	-	-
9th Sig. Troop.	-	11	5	-	-	-
TOTAL.	-	483	159	14	7	-

ARRIVALS during week :-

    Lieut. G.E.BOOTH, to 9th M.G.Sqdn, (from leave) 7th M.G.Sqdn.

DEPARTURES during week :-

    2/Lieut. F.TWIST, MC. MM., 9th M.G.Sqdn., to Demob.

HUSSAR BRIGADE

EFFECTIVE STRENGTH in Hussar Brigade for Week ending 28th June 1919.

UNIT	Offrs.	O.R's.	Rdg.	Dght.	Pack.	Mules.
Headquarters.	9	28	22	15	-	-
3rd Hussars	41	381	444	61	24	-
10th Hussars	27	515	463	58	24	-
15th Hussars	31	369	415	61	24	-
Hussar M.G.S.	9	105	175	65	35	-
"O" Battery RHA	6	206	102	129	-	-
Hussar Signal Troop	1	15	9	4	1	-
TOTAL.	124	1619	1630	393	108	-

WANTING TO COMPLETE on same date.

UNIT	Offrs.	O.R'S;	Rdg.	Dght.	Pack.	Mules.
Headquarters	-	16	-	1	-	-
3rd Hussars	-	113	43	-	-	-
10th Hussars	-	-	24	3	-	-
15th Hussars	-	125	72	-	-	-
Hussar M.G.S.	-	142	28	6	7	-
"O" Battery RHA	-	-	-	2	-	-
Hussar Sig. Troop	-	9	5	-	-	-
TOTAL	-	405	172	12	7	-

ARRIVALS during week :-

       NIL.

DEPARTURES during week :-

    Lieut. R.B.HARVIE 15th Hussars to U.K.
    Lieut. G.A.WINDSOR 15th Hussars to A.P.M. Staff, PARIS.
    Capt. E.W.E.PALMES,M.C. 10th Hussars to U.K.

CONFIDENTIAL.

WAR DIARY

of

HUSSAR BRIGADE HEADQUARTERS.

JULY, 1919.

VOLUME. No. 4.

Army Form C. 2118.

WAR DIARY
INTELLIGENCE SUMMARY

(Erase heading not required.)

Headquarters., HUSSAR BRIGADE.

JULY, 1919.

Instructions regarding War Diaries and Intelligence Summaries are contained in F. S. Regs., Part II. and the Staff Manual respectively. Title pages will be prepared in manuscript.

Place	Date	Hour	Summary of Events and Information	Remarks and references to Appendices
BERGERHAUSEN.	1st.		Mobile Striking Force rejoins Units.	
	3rd.		The Divisional Commander inspected the 3rd Hussars.	
	7th.	09.30.	The Divisional Commander inspected the 10th Hussars.	
	8th.		Peace Celebrations. Holiday.	
			The following party for PARIS Victory March proceed to COLOGNE :-	
			Major.F.J.DuPRE. D.S.O. 3rd Hussars. 6 Other Ranks per Regiment.	
	18th.		The PARIS Victory March party rejoins Units.	
	19th.		PEACE Day. Holiday.	
	28th.		Commander-in-Chief inspected the 10th Hussars and 15th Hussars and saw recruits at Foot-drill and Riding School.	

P.R.....

Captain.,

Brigade Major., "HUSSAR" Brigade.

HUSSAR BRIGADE

EFFECTIVE STRENGTH in Hussar Brigade for Week ending 5th July 1919

UNIT	Offrs	O.Rs	Rdg.	Dght.	Pack	Mules
Headquarters	9	28	23	15	-	-
3rd Hussars	41	380	441	61	25	
10th Hussars	25	519	463	58	24	
15th Hussars	30	367	414	61	25	
Hussar M.G.S.	9	105	175	65	35	
"O" Battery RHA	7	207	102	129	-	
Hussar Signal Troop	1	15	9	4	1	
TOTAL	125	1621	1632	393	110	-

WANTING TO COMPLETE on same date.

UNIT	Offrs	O.Rs	Rdg.	Dght	Pack	Mules
Headquarters	-	16	-	1	-	-
3rd Hussars	-	114	41	-	-	-
10th Hussars	-	-	24	3	-	-
15th Hussars	-	127	73	-	-	-
Hussar M.G.S.	-	142	28	6	7	-
"O" Battery	-	-	-	2	-	-
Hussar Signal Troop	-	9	5	-	-	-
TOTAL	-	408	166	12	7	-

ARRIVALS during week :-

    Lieut-Col H. MAIN   from U.K. 2.7.19

DEPARTURES during week :-

    Lieut. D.P. TENNENT   15th Hussars   To Demob.

HUSSAR BRIGADE

EFFECTIVE STRENGTH in Hussar Brigade for Week ending 12th July 1919

UNIT	Offrs	O.R'S	Rdg.	Dght.	Pack	Mules
Headquarters	8	27	23	15	-	-
3rd Hussars	41	378	447	61	25	-
10th Hussars	28	519	463	58	24	-
15th Hussars	29	365	414	61	25	-
Hussar M.G.S.	9	104	175	65	35	-
"O" Battery RHA	7	206	102	130	-	-
Hussar Signal Troop	1	15	10	4	1	-
TOTAL	123	1614	1634	394	110	-

WANTING TO COMPLETE on same date

UNIT	Offrs	O.R's	Rdg.	Dght	Pack	Mules
Headquarters	1	17	-	1	-	-
3rd Hussars	-	116	40	-	-	-
10th Hussars	-	-	24	3	-	-
15th Hussars	-	129	73	-	-	-
Hussar M.G.S.	-	143	28	6	7	-
"O" Battery RHA	-	-	-	1	-	-
Hussar Signal Troop	-	9	4	-	-	-
TWO TAL	1	414	169	11	7	-

ARRIVALS during week :-   N I L.

DEPARTURES during week :-   N I L.

HUSSAR BRIGADE.

EFFECTIVE STRENGTH in "HUSSAR" Brigade for week ending 19th July, 1919.

UNIT.	Offrs.	O.R's.	Rdg.	Dght.	Pack.	Mules.
Headquarters.	8	28	22	16	-	-
3rd Hussars.	40	377	447	61	25	-
10th Hussars.	27	518	463	58	24	-
15th Hussars.	30	364	414	61	25	-
Hussar M.G.S.	9	104	174	65	35	-
"O" Batty RHA	6	206	101	130	-	-
Hussar Sig.Troop.	1	15	10	4	1	-
TOTAL.	121	1612	1651	395	110	-

WANTING TO COMPLETE on same date.

UNIT.	Offrs.	O.R's.	Rdg.	Dght.	Pack.	Mules.
Headquarters.	1	16	-	-	-	-
3rd Hussars.	-	120	40	-	-	-
10th Hussars.	-	-	24	3	-	-
15th Hussars.	-	130	73	-	-	-
Hussar M.G.S.	-	143	29	6	7	-
"O" Batty RHA	-	-	1	1	-	-
Hussar Sig.Troop.	-	9	4	-	-	-
TOTAL.	1	418	171	10	7	-

ARRIVALS during week :-

    Lieut H.H.S.T.TUFTON. 15th Hussars from U.K.

DEPARTURES during week :-

    Lieut G.L.L.FOSTER. Beds Yeo attd 3rd Hrs to U.K.sick 7.7.19.
    " A.E.LOWTHER 10th Hrs. to A.D.C. Cof G.S. EGYPT. W.O.letter 9/7/19
  2/ " W.G.BAIN. 10th Hussars to U.K. 7.7.1919.
    Lieut.E.J.BODINGTON. 10th Hussars. to Demob.26.4.1919.
    Major. R.R.COPELAND "O" Batty RHA. to U.K. 14.7.1919.

HUSSAR BRIGADE.

EFFECTIVE STRENGTH in "HUSSAR" Brigade for week ending 26th JULY, 1919.

UNIT.	Offrs.	O.R.'S.	Rdg.	Dght.	Pack.	Mules.
Headquarters.	8	29	22	16	-	-
3rd Hussars.	39	377	446	61	25	-
10th Hussars.	28	516	460	57	25	-
15th Hussars.	30	365	409	60	25	-
Hussar M.G.S.	9	104	171	65	35	-
"O" Batty RHA	6	207	101	130	-	-
Hussar Sig.Troop.	1	15	10	4	1	-
TOTAL.	121	1613	1619	393	111	-

WANTING TO COMPLETE on same date.

UNIT.	Offrs.	O.R.'S.	Rdg.	Dght.	Pack.	Mules.
Headquarters.	1	15	-	-	-	-
3rd Hussars.	-	130	41	-	-	-
10th Hussars.	-	-	27	4	-	-
15th Hussars.	-	129	78	1	-	-
Hussar M.G.Sqdn,.	-	143	32	6	7	-
"O" Batty RHA.	-	-	1	1	-	-
Hussar Sig.Troop.	-	9	4	-	-	-
TOTAL.	1	416	183	12	7	-

ARRIVALS during week :-

    Major.W.P.LITTLEWOOD, 10th Hussars, from U.K. 23.7.1919.

DEPARTURES during week :-

    2/Lieut.L.E.R.FISHER, MC. resigned 24.5.1919.

WAR DIARY

of

HEADQUARTERS, HUSSAR BRIGADE.

AUGUST, 1919.

VOLUME No. 5.

Army Form C. 2118.

WAR DIARY
of
INTELLIGENCE SUMMARY.

(Erase heading not required.)

Headquarters,
HUSSAR BRIGADE.

August, 1919.   Volume No. 5.

Instructions regarding War Diaries and Intelligence Summaries are contained in F.S. Regs., Part II. and the Staff Manual respectively. Title pages will be prepared in manuscript.

Place	Date	Hour	Summary of Events and Information	Remarks and references to Appendices
Bergerhausen.	6th		Received orders to find a Composite Regiment of three Composite Squadrons, for a ceremonial parade to be held at COLOGNE, on August 12th. Composition of Regiment :- Commanding Officer. Lt.Col. A. SEYMOUR, D.S.O., 10th Hussars. Adjutant. Lieut. S.P.L.A. LITHGOW. 15th Hussars. 1 Trumpeter. 1 Regimental Sergeant Major. 6 Officers and 80 Other Ranks from each Regiment.	
- do -	7th		Parade at COLOGNE postponed. Brigadier General, T.T.PITMAN, C.B., C.M.G., proceeded on leave. Bt.Lt.Col P.V. KELLY, C.M.G., D.S.O., 3rd Hussars assumed command of the Brigade.	
- do -	8th	10.00	Parade of composite Squadrons from 10th Hussars and 15th Hussars on Brigade Sports Ground to practice ceremonial parade for the COLOGNE Review which was to have taken place on the 12th.	2
- do -	9th		COLOGNE Review will probably take place on 18th instant.	
- do -	12th		Wire received from Division - 3rd Hussars will not take part in Ceremonial Parade at COLOGNE on 18th instant.	2
- do -	13th		Received warning order to effect that this Division will entrain for ENGLAND early in September.	3

Army Form C. 2118.

WAR DIARY
or
INTELLIGENCE SUMMARY.
(Erase heading not required.)

Instructions regarding War Diaries and Intelligence Summaries are contained in F. S. Regs., Part II. and the Staff Manual respectively. Title pages will be prepared in manuscript.

Place	Date	Hour	Summary of Events and Information	Remarks and references to Appendices
Bergerhausen.	14th		Lieut. D.H.H. CLERKE, 15th Hussars, Brigade Intelligence Officer admitted Hospital with a damaged eye.	
			Orders received appointing Lieut. J.A. PATON, Brigade Signalling Officer to be Staff Captain Dragoon Brigade.	
			Received Orders that 15th Hussars will entrain before the rest of the Brigade - probably as follows :-	
			Equipment ...... 24th August.	
			Personnel ...... 28th August.	
			Horses .... 28th & 30th August.	
- do -	15th		Composite Squadrons of 10th & 15th Hussars marched to COLOGNE.	
			Composition of Brigade attachment :-	
			Commanding Officer :- Lt. Col. A. SEYMOUR, D.S.O., 10th Hussars.	
			Adjutant. :- Lieut. S.P.L.A. LITHGOW. 15th Hussars.	
			14 Officer. (including C.O., and Adjt,.)	
			164 Other Ranks.	
			182 Horses.	
			2 G.S. wagons with 2 men and 4 horses each.	
- do -	18th	11.00	Ceremonial Parade in COLOGNE. 15th Hussars Squadron rejoined Unit after the parade.	
			Received definite table of Horse Trains. (See appendix).	

Army Form C. 2118.

WAR DIARY
or
INTELLIGENCE SUMMARY.
(Erase heading not required.)

Instructions regarding War Diaries and Intelligence Summaries are contained in F. S. Regs., Part II. and the Staff Manual respectively. Title pages will be prepared in manuscript.

Place	Date	Hour	Summary of Events and Information	Remarks and references to Appendices
Bergerhausen.	19th		10th Hussars composite Squadron rejoined its Unit.	(a)
- do -	21st		Received table of Personnel and Equipment train (See appendix).	(a)
- do -	25th		Brigadier General T.T.PITMAN, C.B., C.M.G., rejoined from leave.	(a)
- do -	28th		Captain R.G.P.WOOD, M.C., Brigade Major proceeded to CALAIS for duty in connection with detrainment of Division.	(a)
- do -	29th		Equipment of the 15th Hussars and Hussar M.G.Sqdn., entrained at DUREN.	

- do -	30th		Equipment of the following Units entrained at DUREN :-
			
			  3rd Hussars.
			  10th Hussars.
			  "O" Battery R.H.A.
			  Hussar M.V.Sect.
			  Hussar Signal Troop.
			  Hussar Brigade H.Qrs.
				(a)

A.W.Curtis

Captain,
Brigade Major, "HUSSAR" Brigade.

APPENDIX 1.

Detail of Personnel, Horse and Equipment trains.

PERSONNEL.

UNIT.	STRENGTH.			Entraining Station.	Date.	Remarks.
	Offrs.	W.O's & Serts.	O.R's.			
15th Hussars.	8	36	103	B U I R .	Sept. 2nd.	
Hussar M.G.S.	4	3	40	B U I R .	Sept. 2nd.	
10th Hussars.	8	12	230	H O R R E M .	Probable date Sept. 13th.	
3rd Hussars.	8	29	122	D U R E N .	,,	Sept. 20th.
"O" Btty R.H.A.	2	3	51	D U R E N .	,,	Sept. 20th.
Hussar M.V.S.	1	-	8	D U R E N .	,,	Sept. 20th.
Hussar Sig.Trp.	-	1	11	D U R E N .	,,	Sept. 20th.
Hussar Bde H.Qrs.	2	1	11	D U R E N .	,,	Sept. 20th.

HORSES.

UNIT.	STRENGTH.			Entraining Station.	Date.	Remarks.
	Offrs.	O.R's.	Horses.			
Hussar M.G.S.	2	56	238	D U R E N .	Sept. 3rd.	
15th Hussars.	3	182	334	H O R R E M .	Sept. 5th.	
15th Hussars.	2	80	145	H O R R E M .	Sept. 6th.	
3rd Hussars.	3	182	334	D U R E N .	Sept. 17th.	
10th Hussars.	3	182	334	H O R R E M .	Sept. 18th.	
10th Hussars.	2	85	149	H O R R E M .	Sept. 19th.	
"O" Btty. RHA.	2	121	221	D U R E N .	Sept. 20th.	
Hussar Bde.H.Qrs.	1	-	36	D U R E N .	Sept. 20th.	
Hussar Sig.Trp.	-	28	15	D U R E N .	Sept. 20th.	
Hussar M.V.S.	1	15	28	D U R E N .	Sept. 20th.	
3rd Hussars.	1	18	146	D U R E N .	Sept. 25th.	

EQUIPMENT.

UNIT.	Strength. Axles.	Entraining Station.	Date.	Remarks.
15th Hussars.	27	DUREN	Aug. 29th.	
Hussar M.G.S.	34	DUREN	Aug. 29th.	
3rd Hussars.	27	DUREN	Aug. 30th.	
10th Hussars.	27	DUREN	Aug. 30th.	
"O" Btty RHA	43	DUREN	Aug. 30th.	
Hussar M.V.S.	5	DUREN	Aug. 30th.	
Hussar Sig.Trp.	2	DUREN	Aug. 30th.	
Hussar Bde.H.Qrs.	8	DUREN	Aug. 30th.	

HUSSAR BRIGADE.

EFFECTIVE STRENGTH in 'HUSSAR' Brigade for week ending 2nd August, 1919.

UNIT.	Offrs.	O.R.'s.	Rdg.	Dght.	Pack.	Mules.
Headquarters.	8	27	20	16	-	-
3rd Hussars.	39	377	447	61	25	-
10th Hussars.	26	511	460	56	25	-
15th Hussars.	29	365	419	60	25	-
Hussar M.G.S.	9	106	167	66	35	-
'O' Batty RHA	7	208	101	130	-	-
Hussar Sig.Troop.	1	15	10	4	1	-
TOTAL.	119	1609	1624	393	111	-

WANTING TO COMPLETE on same date.

UNIT.	Offrs.	O.R.'s.	Rdg.	Dght.	Pack.	Mules.
Headquarters.	1	17	-	-	-	-
3rd Hussars.	-	123	40	-	-	-
10th Hussars.	-	-	27	5	-	-
15th Hussars.	-	132	68	1	-	-
Hussar M.G.S.	-	141	36	5	7	-
'O' Batty RHA	-	-	1	1	-	-
Hussar Sig Trp.	-	9	4	-	-	-
TOTAL.	1	422	176	12	7	-

ARRIVALS during week :-

    Lieut.Col. A.G. SEYMOUR. DSO. 10th Hussars. from U.K. 26.7.1919.
    Lieut. D.M. ABEL. 'O' Battery RHA. from U.K. 27.7.1919.

DEPARTURES during week :-

    Lieut. C.S. CAMPBELL. 10th Hussars. to U.K. 30.7.1919.
    2/Lieut. E.R. KIMBELL. 14th Hussars. to U.K. 31.7.1919.
    Lieut. F.A. TILSLEY. 15th Hussars. to U.K. 31.7.1919.

HUSSAR BRIGADE

EFFECTIVE STRENGTH in 'HUSSAR' Brigade for week ending 9th August 1916.

UNIT	Offrs	O.R's	Rdg.	Dsmt.	Pack.	Mules.
Headquarters.	8	27	20	16	-	-
3rd Hussars	32	387	447	61	25	-
10th Hussars	25	410	460	56	25	-
15th Hussars	28	371	418	60	25	-
Hussar M.G.S.	9	106	137	66	36	-
'O' Battery RHA	8	203	102	130	-	-
Hussar Sig. Troop	1	15	12	4	1	-
T O T A L	116	1624	1626	393	111	-

WANTING TO COMPLETE on same date

UNIT	Offrs	O.R's	Rdg.	Dsmt.	Pack.	Mules.
Headquarters.	1	17	-	-	-	-
3rd Hussars	-	110	40	-	1	-
10th Hussars	-	-	27	5	2	-
15th Hussars	-	128	39	1	-	-
Hussar M.G.S.	-	141	56	5	7	-
'O' Battery RHA	-	-	-	1	-	-
Hussar Sig. Tp.	-	8	2	-	-	-
T O T A L	1	403	174	12	3	-

ARRIVALS during week :-

        N I L

DEPARTURES during week :-

    Lieut. W.J.BRISLEY 10th Hussars to U.K. 8-8-16.
    Capt. C.H.LIDDELL 15th Hussars to U.K. 8-8-16.

HUSSAR BRIGADE

HUSSAR BRIGADE

EFFECTIVE STRENGTH in "HUSSAR" Brigade for week ending 16th August 1919.

UNIT	Offrs.	O.R's.	Rdg.	Dght.	Pack.	Mules.
Headquarters.	8	27	20	16	-	-
3rd Hussars	28	374	447	61	25	-
10th Hussars	24	507	460	56	25	-
15th Hussars	28	371	416	60	25	-
Hussar M.G.S.	9	106	167	66	35	-
"O" Battery RHA	5	207	102	129	-	-
Hussar Sig.Tp.	1	15	13	4	1	-
TOTAL	103	1607	1625	392	111	-

WANTING TO COMPLETE on same date.

UNIT	Offrs	O.R's	Rdg.	Dght	Pack	Mules.
Headquarters.	1	17	-	-	-	-
3rd Hussars	-	123	40	-	-	-
10th Hussars	-	-	27	5	-	-
15th Hussars	-	126	71	1	-	-
Hussar M.G.S.	-	141	36	5	7	-
"O" Battery RHA	-	-	-	2	-	-
Hussar Sig. Tp.	-	9	1	-	-	-
TOTAL.	1	412	175	13	7	-

ARRIVALS during week:- NIL.

DEPARTURES during week:-

Lieut.	P.A.WATERLOW	3rd Hussars	Struck off stength	10/7/19.
T/Lieut.	J.WALL DCM	do	do	12/8/19.
Major	H.W.CLINCH	do	do	8/8/19.
Lieut.	H.I.L.CHILDE-PEMBERTON		do	7/8/19.
T/Lieut.	R.D.K.NINNIS	do	do	do
T/2nd Lieut.	H.E.CRAIG	do	do	do
2nd Lieut.	E.E.LLOYD	do	do	do
T/2nd Lieut.	B.E.HERMAN	do	do	do
2nd Lieut.	A.M.LENEY	do	do	do
Lieut.	H.R.BARTON, M.C.	do	do	9/8/19.
Lieut.	G.GG. NICHOLSON, M.C.	"O" Battery RHA.	To U.K.	9/8/19.

HUSSAR BRIGADE

EFFECTIVE STRENGTH in "HUSSAR" Brigade for week ending August 23rd 1919

UNIT	Offrs.	O.R's	Rdg.	Dght.	Pack	Mules
Headquarters	8	29	20	16	-	-
3rd Hussars	30	376	432	61	25	-
10th Hussars	24	505	455	53	25	-
15th Hussars	28	359	397	50	25	-
Hussar M.G.S.	9	89	166	66	35	-
'O' Battery RHA	6	207	102	128	-	-
Hussar Sig. Tp.	-	14	7	4	1	-
TOTAL	105	1579	1579	388	111	-

WANTING TO COMPLETE on same date.

UNIT	Offrs.	O.R.'s	Rdg.	Dght.	Pack.	Mules.
Headquarters.	1	19	-	-	-	-
3rd Hussars	-	121	55	-	-	-
10th Hussars	-	-	30	8	-	-
15th Hussars	-	138	90	1	-	-
Hussar M.G.S.	-	158	37	5	7	-
'O' Battery RHA	-	-	-	3	-	-
Hussar Signal Tp.	1	10	-	-	-	-
TOTAL	2	442	212	17	7	-

ARRIVALS during week :-

    Lieut. W.H. NAPIER,   "O" Battery R.H.A.   Joined 21/8/19.

DEPARTURES during week :-

    N I L.

HUSSAR BRIGADE.

EFFECTIVE STRENGTH in "HUSSAR" Brigade for week ending 30th August, 1919.

UNIT.	Offrs.	O.R's.	Rdg.	Dght.	Pack.	Mules.
Headquarters.	8	28	14	16	-	-
3rd Hussars.	30	370	432	61	25	-
10th Hussars.	24	498	441	53	25	-
15th Hussars.	28	359	394	59	25	-
Hussar M.G.S.	8	118	157	51	32	-
"O" Btty. RHA.	6	205	102	117	-	-
Hussar Sig. Tp.	-	14	7	4	1	-
TOTAL.	104	1592	1547	361	108	-

WANTING TO COMPLETE on same date.

UNIT.	Offrs.	O.R's.	Rdg.	Dght.	Pack.	Mules.
Headquarters.	1	16	11	-	-	-
3rd Hussars.	-	127	55	-	-	-
10th Hussars.	-	-	46	8	-	-
15th Hussars.	-	138	93	2	-	-
Hussar M.G.S.	1	129	46	20	10	-
"O" Btty. RHA.	-	-	-	14	-	-
Hussar Sig Tp.	1	10	7	-	-	-
TOTAL.	3	420	258	44	10	-

ARRIVALS during week :-

... NIL ...

DEPARTURES during week :-

Lieut. H.C. MOUNT, M.C.   Hussar M.G.S.   25.8.1919.

BEF

CAV DIV

HUSSAR Bde

3 K.O HUSSARS

1919 - 1919
APR   AUG

FROM 2 CAV DIV 4 CAV BDE
BOX 1136

WAR DIARY

of
3rd King's Own Hussars

from 1st April 1919 to 30th April 1919.

Volume LVI.

Confidential

Army Form C. 2118.

WAR DIARY of 3rd K.O. Hussars.
INTELLIGENCE SUMMARY.
The Hussar Brigade. Cavalry Division of the Army of the Rhine.

(Erase heading not required.)

Place	Date	Hour	Summary of Events and Information	Remarks and references to Appendices
GROTTEN-HIRTEN.	1919 April 1		The Regiment in same billets:— H.Q., Signal Troop & Band in GROTTENHIRTEN. 'A' Squadron " " 'B' & 'C' Squadrons " KIRCHHERTEN. The 1st Cavalry Division is now called The Cavalry Division of the Rhine commanded by Gen. W.E. PEYTON KCB. KCVO. DSO. The Division consists of Three Brigades. The Hussar Brigade. Brig. Genl. T.T.PITMAN CB. DSO. The Lancer Brigade, consisting of 9', 12' & 17' Lancers. The Dragoon Brigade, " - 6' D.G., 1st and 6' Dragoons.	A.T.P. A 2nd Cav. Div. Circular.
	2		The Regiment being so short of men and up to war strength in horses, 150 men of the 4 Bn. Gordon Highlanders are attached. They are armed ar with trenches mortars. The Highlanders have no experience of	W.T.W. W.T.W.

WAR DIARY of 3rd K.O. Hussars Hussar Brigade.

or

INTELLIGENCE SUMMARY.

Army Form C. 2118.

(2)

Place	Date	Hour	Summary of Events and Information	Remarks and references to Appendices
GROTTEN-HERTEN	1919 April 2		horses but their desperate keenness and good humour by their useful men in the stables, and many of them volunteering to learn to ride were put through a course of riding school. They soon became	App. B. Mobile Force.
	4		The Regt was warned to march to DUREN on the 7th, but the orders were subsequently cancelled. The Brigade HQ, 10th & 15th Hussars & the other units left the Kerf area and marched to the KERPEN area, & leaving the 3rd Hussars behind. The 3rd H. was detailed for DUREN but there was no room there for them.	WD
	25		The men detached from the A. Bn. Gordon Highlanders rejoined their battalion, being relieved by a similar number of the 52nd Bn. Gordon Highlanders.	WD
DUREN.	26		The Regt. marched via LICH to DUREN and was quartered in the Cavalry Barracks vacated by the 9th Lancers who marched to COLOGNE. A mobile force from the Brigade is organized as in App. B. to deal with any riots.	WD

WAR DIARY

INTELLIGENCE SUMMARY

of 3 Hussars, Neesan Raigh.

Army Form C. 2118.

Instructions regarding War Diaries and Intelligence Summaries are contained in F. S. Regs., Part II. and the Staff Manual respectively. Title pages will be prepared in manuscript.

(Erase heading not required.)

Place	Date	Hour	Summary of Events and Information			Remarks and references to Appendices
DUREN	1919 April 31		Casualties during the month.	Officers	Other Ranks	App. C.
				Nones	Nones	Roll of Officers
			Joined Major (B⁺/L⁺Col) P.J.V.KELLY C.M.G., D.S.O. as 2 i Command.		4	app. D
			L⁺ J.R. HARVIE (from wounds)			Strength of Reg⁺
			2⁻L⁺ L.E.R.FISHER M.C.	5		app. E
			T/L⁺ K.E.DUNN.		1	
			T/ L⁺ J.W. IRONS.	1		
						Secret
					5	Others
			Struck off strength			
			Evacuated sick		5	
			Demobilized		1	
			Destroyed			
			On Strength	5	4	
			Off "	2	10	W⁺Tel
						W.T.Wilkinson,
						Colonel,
						Comdg. 3 K.O. Hussars.

TO ALL RANKS

of the

SECOND CAVALRY DIVISION

✼✼✼✼✼✼

Now that the Division is about to be broken up after a period of 4 1/2 years since its formation, I wish to offer each one of you my heartfelt thanks for your services both individually and collectively. I do so, not only in my own name but in the names of the Divisional Commanders who preceded me.

While some of you enter into civil life, others remain at the helm, but wherever you may go, I would like you to keep with you a remembrance of the great part which has been played by your Division in the greatest of all wars. The Division has come through 4 1/2 years of war without a stain on its character or a single regrettable incident, and as you will see by the account of its doings overleaf, it has come to the rescue of the Army at many a critical moment.

I hope that each one of you will always remember the good feeling which has kept us together during these years and carry the same into home life in England. Let us do this in memory of those we have unfortunately been compelled to leave behind ; may their names never be forgotten.

Thomas. T. Pitman

MAJOR GENERAL,
Commanding 2nd Cavalry Division.

11th March 1919.

1914

The Second Cavalry Division was formed on 16th September 1914 on the Aisne. It originally consisted of the 3rd and 5th Cavalry Brigades under command of Major General H. de la P. Gough, C. B. The 4th Brigade joined the Division shortly after the capture of the Mont des Cats. This brilliant operation by the combined action of the 3rd and 5th Brigades first brought the Division to a prominent position as a fighting unit.

The units in the Division have remained the same throughout the war with the exception of the Composite Household Cavalry Regiment in the 4th Cavalry Brigade who were replaced by the Queen's Own Oxfordshire Hussars on 19th November 1914.

The Division distinguished themselves in a contest against overwhelming numbers on the Wytschaete – Messines line from October 20th to November 1st and later in the vicinity of Wulverghem until the end of the First Battle of Ypres.

1915

In January and February 1915 the Division had their first experience of regular trench warfare in the Ypres salient, the first big mine of the war exploding under one of the trenches held by them.

In March they were in support at the Battle of Neuve Chapelle, the 5th Cavalry Brigade making the 1st attempt of Cavalry to break through the enemy's trench system.

Shortly after returning to billets the Division was again hurried up to the Salient to take part in the Second Battle of Ypres where the enemy launched poisoned gasses against us.

On 15th April, Major General C. T. McM. Kavanagh, C.V.O., D.S.O., took over command.

Throughout the summer of 1915 large working parties were found for constructing defences in the vicinity of Kemmel.

On the 15th July, Major General Sir P. W. Chetwode, Bart. C.M.G., D.S.O., took over command.

In September and October the Division was in support at the Battle of Loos.

1916

The Division spent the first two months of the year in the trenches et VERMELLES when mining and countermining were of almost nightly occurrence.

From June to September they were in support of the Second Army which had been considerably weakened to find troops for the Battle of the Somme.

In September the Division moved South to the Somme where they remained in vicinity of Dernancourt until the beginning of November.

On 16th November, Major General W. H. Greenly, C.M.G., D.S.O., took over command of the Division.

1917

Early in the year the Division furnished strong working parties for railway construction, and in the beginning of April took part in the Battle of Arras under very trying conditions for the horses.

From there they went into the trenches in front of Ronssoy. A most successful raid was carried out at Gillemont Farm and a few days later, a stubborn defence was put up when the Germans counter-raided the same position.

On November 16th after a short spell in billets, the Division moved East to take part in the Battle of Cambrai. The mounted scheme having failed to materialise, a dismounted Brigade was formed which had very heavy fighting in the defence of Bourlon Wood.

On the 30th November when the Germans made their big counter-attack the Second Cavalry Division assisted the Guards in restoring the situation.

They ended up the year by going once again into the trenches near Hargicourt.

1918

There they remained until the end of January and afterwards moved into the area round Athies.

In March, in order to meet the threatened German attack, the Division moved to vicinity of Grandrue in support of the IIIrd Corps.

When the attack came on 21st March, the Division was immediately sent up in motor lorries to try and restore the situation. All units of the Division were engaged in very heavy fighting especially on the Jussy canal, suffering heavy casualties.

On March 25th, the mounted Division was again reformed under command of Brigadier General Pitman.

On the 26th they made a combined mounted and dismounted attack on the Bois des Essarts. This attack succeeded in holding up the Germans until the arrival of large French reinforcements.

From there the Division, to which was attached the Canadian Cavalry Brigade, made a forced march to Montdidier to support a reported break in the French line, and thence by another forced march to vicinity of Amiens where the situation of the Fifth Army was critical.

On the 30th March, the British line having broken, the Canadian Cavalry Brigade and 3rd Cavalry Brigade made a mounted attack at Moreuil Wood and restored the situation.

On the 1st April, the line having again broken, the whole Division carried out a brilliant dismounted attack on Rifle Wood under cover of their own artillery and machine gun barrage. The objectives were gained and the line restored, heavy casualties being inflicted on the enemy.

The losses of the Division from 21st March to 1st April were 70 officers and 2.000 other ranks.

The appointment of Brigadier General T. T. Pitman, C. B., C. M. G., to command the Division with the temporary rank of Major General was confirmed (dated March 29th).

From Amiens the Division was moved North to vicinity of Blaringhem and Flêtre to support the Second Army.

On 9th and 10th August the Second Cavalry Division took part in the successful operations in front of Amiens which started the final battle of the war.

As soon as the war of movement commenced, there was a general outcry for Cavalry, and the Division was split up on a front of three Armies. Playing a prominent part throughout the final operations they had the satisfaction of knowing that nearly every squadron of the Division was well in front when the cease fire sounded on November 11th; one regiment taking part in the final attack on Mons, entered the town at the head of the Canadian Corps.

During the advance through Belgium after the armistice was signed, the Second Cavalry Division acted as Advanced Guard to the Fourth Army.

App. C.

3rd (K.O) Hussars.

ROLL OF OFFICERS BY SQUADRONS.

HEADQUARTERS.

        Lieut Colonel W.T.Willcox, C.M.G.
        Major, (Bt.Lt.Col) P.J.V. Kelly, C.M.G., D.S.O.
        ,, H.W. Clinch,   (Cav Corps Con Camp)
        ,, F.J. Du Pre, D.S.O.
        Captain and Adjutant H.T.Bromley
        Lieut and Q.M. J.R. Furnell
T/   ,, H.V. Hart, (2nd R.C.R)
        Captain A.V. Nicholas, (R.A.V.C) attd 10th Hussars.
        ,, G.S. Douglas, (R.A.M.C)

"A" SQUADRON.

        Captain R.A.Bagnell,   Leave.
        Lieut J.H.Eliot, M.C.
        ,, G.H.Eastwood, (S.R)   ,,
        ,, W.G.N.H. Dalrymple,   ,,
T/   ,, N.V. Cannon, (2nd R.C.R)
,,   ,, R.D.K. Ninnis, (2nd R.C.R) Cav Base Depot.
        ,, G.S.L. Foster, (Beds Yeo) Leave
        ,, H.J. Soames, (Oxford Hussars) ,,
        ,, H.Hodgson,   ,,

"B" SQUADRON.

        Captain S.F. Clarke.
        Lieut C.L. Huggins,   Leave.
        ,, H.R. Barton, M.C.   ,,
        ,, P.A. Waterlow,
        ,, J.E. Blumenfeld,
T/ 2nd ,, P. Kirkus, (6th R.C.R)
,, ,, ,, H.E. Craig, (2nd R.C.R) Cav Base Depot.
,, ,, ,, E.E. Lloyd, (3rd Co. of Lon Yeo)
,, ,, ,, J.C. Giles.

"C" SQUADRON.

        Captain Hon. D.S.P. Howard.
        Lieut H.M. Naylor.
        ,, J.K. Harvie
        ,, F. Craig, M.C.   H.Q. 2nd Cavalry Division.
        ,, P.C. Marsh, (S.R)   To U.K. Pending Demob.
        ,, J.B.F. Austin,   Hospital.
        ,, H.S.W. Fields-Clarke, (Beds Yeo)
        ,, A.J.A. Booth,   Leave.
        ,, D.H. Williams, (Q.O.O.H) ,,
   2nd ,, L.E.R. Fisher, M.C.
    ,,   ,, H.F.A. Cossentine, (S.R) Area Commandant, VERVIERS.
T/ ,,   ,, B.E. Herman, (2nd R.C.R) Cav Base Depot.
  ,,   ,, A.M. Leney.   Leave.

UNATTACHED.

        Captain A.W. Keith-Falconer, (Q.O.O.H) Armistice Comm'n.
T/   ,, H. Goring, (4th Cav Bde)
        ,, R.I.L. Childe-Pemberton, (18th Hrs, S.R)
,,   Lieut J.Wall, D.C.M. (Special List, Res. Cav)(5 Rem.Base)
   2nd ,, J. Deeks, (Lin.Yeo)

3rd (K.O) HUSSARS.

App. D.

Strength and distribution of Regiment on 30th April.

	Officers	O.R.s	Horses.
With Regiment	20	216	541
At various stations etc.	24	103	15
Total	44	319	556

Wanting to complete:-

Other Ranks,	175
Horses,	16

Surplus:-

Officers,	20

Details of Detached.

	Officers.	O.R.s	Horses.
Leave,	10	51	
Sick,	1	9	
Courses,	1	4	
Outside Army Area,	11	18	4
Inside Army Area,	1	21	11
	24	103	15

Details of Attached.

	Officers.	O.R.s	Horses.
Band,	-	23	-
R.A.M.C.	-	2	-
Interpreter,	-	1	-
17th Lancers,	-	1	-
52nd Battalion Gordon Highlanders,	3	101	-
	3	128	-

Army of the Rhine G.I. 43/14.
IV Corps No. 16/26 (G)

App E
Secret Order

SECRET.

IV Corps.

1. It has been reported from what is stated to be a sure source that at a recent meeting held in unoccupied GERMANY, the proposal to kill on one night all British and French Officers in Occupied Territory was accepted in principle.

2. There is no information as to how far the necessary measures of organization have been carried out, though it has been ascertained that the proposal has been discussed amongst the workmen of certain factories in the area of the Army of the Rhine.

                          Sd. E. BEDDINGTON, Lt. Col.
                        for Major General, General Staff.
9th April, 1919.   Army of the Rhine.

Cavalry Division.

    Reference above letter.
    The Corps Commander wishes to remind all Officers that they are in an enemy's country. Although he does not propose at present to order Officers to carry revolvers at all times, he wishes that Commanding Officers will ensure that all Officers are in possession of revolver ammunition, and that they keep their revolvers readily available when in their billets.
    All motor cars when in use will carry a rifle and 50 rounds of ammunition.

                        Sd. H.L. MONTGOMERY. Lt. Col. for
27th April, 1919.   B.G. G.S. IV Corps.

S.G. 68.   28.4.19.

    Reference above.

1. Os.C. Units will arrange forthwith that all Officers are made acquainted with this order, and that they are possession of sufficient revolver ammunition.

2. Os.C. Units concerned will also arrange that motor cars will carry rifles and 50 rounds of ammunition.
    A similar procedure will be adopted regarding lorries and box cars.

3. All motor D.Rs will in future carry revolvers and ammunition.

4. Instructions regarding the drawing of any ammunition that may be required are attached herewith.

                        Sd. T. BRACKNELL, Lt. Col.
                           A.A. & Q.M.G.
                           Cavalry Division.

APPENDIX "B".

MOBILE STRIKING FORCE.

1. In the event of a mobile force being required suddenly, a composite brigade will be formed from out of the Division and will rendezvous at one of the concentration points as laid down below.

2. Each Brigade will furnish a composite Regiment of <u>Headquarters and 3 Squadrons</u>, strength approximately 19 Officers and 220 O.R.s, exclusive of transport personnel. (No Hotchkiss or tool packs will be taken)

3. The composition of the Regiment found by this Brigade will be as follows:-
    (a) <u>Headquarters</u> :-

        Commanding Officer. Lt. Colonel W.T.Willcox,C.M.G., 3rd Hussars.
        2nd-in-Command. Capt.E.W.E.Palmes,M.C., 10th Hussars.
        Adjutant, Capt.H.T.Bromley, 3rd Hussars.
        Quartermaster, Lt. H.Jordison, D.C.M. 15th Hrs
        R.S.M. R.S.M. Smith, D.C.M. 3rd Hussars
        R.Q.M.S. To be detailed by O.C. 3rd Hrs
        Clerk, ,, ,, ,,15th Hrs.
        Medical Officer. ,, ,, ,,9th C.F.A
        Veterinary Officer. ,, ,, ,,39th M.V.S

    <u>Signals:-</u>

    Officer to be detailed by 3rd Hussars.
    (b) <u>Three Squadrons.</u> (One from each Regiment)

        Composition of Squadron:-
            1 Squadron Leader.
            1 S.S.M.
            1 S.Q.M.S.
            1 S.S.
            3 Troops each of 1 Offr and 22 O.R.s½

4. Rendezvous will be as follows:-
    Rendezvous North :- Grass field 300 yards South of LORSFELD Schloss, (N. of KERPEN).

    Rendezvous East :- Grass meadows West of HODRATH.

    Rendezvous West :- Grass meadow South of BLATZHEIM

5. <u>Transport.</u>

    1 L.G.S. wagon for R.H.Q.
    1 Mess cart for R.H.Q.
    1 L.G.S. wagon for each Squadron.
    1 Mess cart for each Squadron.

War Diary

of

3rd (King's Own) Hussars.

From 1st May 1919 to 31st May 1919.

Volume LVII.

Confidential

Army Form C. 2118.

WAR DIARY
or
INTELLIGENCE SUMMARY
(Erase heading not required.)

of 3 K.O. Hussars,
Mhow Brigade,
Army of the Rhine.

Instructions regarding War Diaries and Intelligence Summaries are contained in F.S. Regs., Part II. and the Staff Manual respectively. Title Pages will be prepared in manuscript.

Place	Date	Hour	Summary of Events and Information	Remarks and references to Appendices
DUREN	1919 May 1		The Regiment quartered in the German barracks. Two squadrons (A & E) in good stables with 'B' Sqdn. picketed in the riding school. Owing to the shortage of men 2 officers and 94 men of the 1/5 52nd Batt Gordon Highlanders remain attached to the Regiment for stable & other duties.	MW
"	5		The C. in C., Army of the Rhine, Gen. Sir Wm. Robertson G.C.B. inspected the Duren garrison.	WDR
"	22		100 horses turned out to graze in requisitioned fields a couple of miles west of Duren.	
"	26		The Regiment is warned of the probability of a forward move by the Army in the event of the Germans refusing to sign the Peace Terms. The Cavalry Division is forming a force as in Appendix A. All horses stopped.	App. A Mobile Force. WDR

WAR DIARY

INTELLIGENCE SUMMARY of 3 K.O. Hussars

Army Form C. 2118.

Place	Date 1919	Hour	Summary of Events and Information	Remarks and references to Appendices
DUREN	May 31		**Strength of Regiment.**	
			Officers Other Ranks Horses	
			With Regiment 23 282 522	App. B Regt'l Orders
			Detached etc. 17 97 17	App. C Detached Personnel
			40 379 539	
			Attached 52 Gordon High'rs & R.A.M.C. 2 95 1	
			Surplus to Strength 16 — 33	
			Wanting to complete — 140 —	
			Casualties during month.	
			Joined Departs.	
			Officers — — Struck off str.	
			Other Ranks 42 22 T/Capt. H. Goring	Evacuated 1
			Horses 14 — Lieut. J.R.F. Austin	1
			3	—
			Health of the men during the month very good. W.Thinnot L/Colonel	24 W.Dr
			Comdg. 3 Hussars.	

App. A.

MOBILE STRIKING FORCE.

1. If an advance is ordered, the infantry is to advance with advanced guards in lorries.
    A Mobile Cavalry Force, composed as under, is to be attached to VI Corps and would be concentrated in COLOGNE. The Cavalry Mission would probably be to keep touch between the advanced guards in lorries which would advance about 30 miles a day, and the main body.
    The earliest date on which the advance may be ordered (called J day hereafter) is 26th May.

2. The Cavalry Force will be as follows:-

    Under the command of a Lt. Col and Regtl. Staff found by Dragoon Brigade.
    - A Composite Regiment - formed from 1 Sqdn per Cav. Bde. each Regt. finding a strong troop.
    - "G" Battery R.H.A.
    - 1 Composite M.G.Sqdn. - formed of 1 Section of each M.G.Sqdn.

3. The Squadron found by the Hussar Brigade will be composed as follows:-

Squadron Leader	-	Capt. H.F.Brace.D.S.O.,M.C. 15th Hrs.
2nd in Command	-	From 10th Hussars.
6 Subalterns.	-	2 from each Regiment.
72 Other ranks.	-	3rd Hussars.
72 ,, ,,	-	10th ,,
72 ,, ,,	-	15th ,,

    Each Troop to contain in addition to the above numbers a Hotchkiss Gun Detachment consisting of:- 4 Other ranks and 6 horses.

    Transport.
    1. L.G.S.Wagon per Troop.
    1. Mess Cart.
    3. L.G.S.Wagons from 9th M.G.Section.
    1. G.S.Wagon per Regiment.

4. The Code Message "HUN" will be the warning Order to Units for the moves involved by these orders.

===========================

The composition of the 3rd (K.O.) Hussars' Troop is as follows:-

Troop Officer........Lieut P.A.Waterlow.
2nd in Command.;......... ,, A.J.A.Booth.

"A" Sqdn.	"B" Sqdn.	"C" Sqdn.
1 Sergt.	1 Corpl.	1 Sergt.
1 L.Cpl.	1 L.Cpl.	1 L.Cpl.
23 men.	1 S.Smith.	1 S.Smith.
1 cyclist.	21 men	20 men.
	1 batman.	1 batman.
		1 cyclist.

Transport:-   2 men, 4 L.D.Horses & 1.L.G.S.Wagon.
              2 ,, 4   ,,   & 1.G.S.Wagon.

SUMMARY.

Officers.	Other ranks.	Horses.			Vehicles.
		R.	LD.	P.	
2	80	76	8	2	2

App. B.

3rd (K.O) Hussars.

ROLL OF OFFICERS BY SQUADRONS.

HEADQUARTERS.

         Lieut Colonel W.T.Willcox, C.M.G.
         Maj.(Bt.Lt.Col) P.J.V.Kelly, C.M.G., D.S.O., (F).
         ,, H.W.Clinch,   Cav Corps Con Camp.
         ,, F.J.Du Pre, D.S.O.
         Capt & Adjt.H.T.Bromley,   Leave.
         Lieut & Q.M. J.R.Furnell.
T/   ,, H.V.Hart,
         Captain G.S.Douglas, R.A.M.C.

"A" SQUADRON.

         Captain R.A.Bagnell.
         Lieut J.H.Eliot, M.C.   Cav.School, Netheravon.
         ,, G.H.Eastwood, (S.R)
         ,, W.G.N.H.Dalrymple,
T/   ,, N.V.Cannon,   Leave.
,,   ,, R.D.K.Ninnis,   Cav Base Depot.
      ,, G.S.L.Foster,(Beds Y) Attached Bde H.Q.
      ,, H.J.Soames,(Ox.Hrs)
      ,, H.Hodgson,   ,,   Reconnaisance. (Attd)

"B" SQUADRON.

         Captain C.F.Clarke,
         Lieut C.L.Huggins,
      ,, H.R.Barton, M.C.   Reconnaisance.
      ,, P.A.Waterlow,
      ,, J.E.Blumenfeld,
T/   ,, P.Kirkus,
,, 2nd ,, H.E.Craig,   Cav Base Depot.
   ,,   ,, E.E.Lloyd,(3rd Co.of L.Y)   ,,
   ,,   ,, J.C.Giles,

"C" SQUADRON.

         Captain Hon.D.S.P.Howard,
         Lieut H.M.Naylor,
      ,, J.K.Harvie,
      ,, F.Craig, M.C.   2nd Cav Div., Claims.
      ,, H.S.W.Fields-Clarke,(Beds Y)
      ,, A.J.A.Booth,
      ,, D.H.Williams, (Ox.Hrs)
    2nd ,, L.E.R.Fisher, M.C.
    ,,   ,, H.E.A.Cossentine,(S.R) Area Commandant, VERVIERS.
T/ ,,   ,, B.E.Herman,   Cav Base Depot.
   ,,   ,, A.M.Leney,   Leave.

UNATTACHED.

         Captain A.W.Keith-Falconer,(Ox.Hrs) Armistice Com'n, SPA
         Lieut R.I.L.Childe-Pemberton,(S.R)(18th Hrs) Leave.
T/   ,, J.Wall, D.C.M.,(Special List R.C) 5th Remount B.D.
   2nd ,, J.Deeks,(Lin.Yeo)   2nd Army Agricultural College
                                         BONN.

W.T.Willcox
Lt.Col.

3rd (K.O) Hussars.

App. C.

DETAILS OF DETACHED PERSONNEL.

	Offrs.	O.R.s	Horses.
Leave...............................	4	23	
Sick...............................	-	22	
G.H.Q.Wireless School, ABBEVILLE..		2	
Agricultural College, BONN........	1	1	
Army P.T.School, ALDERSHOT,......		1	
Cavalry School, NETHERAVON,.......	1	2	
Cavalry Corps Concentration Camp.	1	1	
Armistice Commision, SPA..........	1		
2nd Cavalry Division Claims......	1	1	
G.R.B.Depot......................	4	1	
No.5 Remount Base Dept...........	1		
Area Commandant, VERVIERS,.........	1	1	2
3rd Military Prison, LE HAVRE....		2	
5th Cyclist Regt., N.I.H..........		2	
Cadre 2nd Cavalry Division,......		1	
Animal Collecting Camp...........		2	
124 Infantry Brigade.............		1	
4th Division,....................		1	
4th M.G.Squadron.................		2	
6th S.L.I........................		1	
Oxford Hussars...................		2	
Reconnaisance, Army Area.........	1	3	4
Hussar Brigade...................	1	6	6
D.A.P.M., Cavalry Division,.......		2	
H.Q.Cavalry Division,............		8	
Dragoon Bde......................		1	
3rd C.F.A........................		1	
H.Q.Army of the Rhine,...........		3	
15th Hussars.....................		1	
IV Corps.........................		1	
R.A.S.C.........................		1	2
Highland Division,...............			2
59th Squadron, R.A.F.............			1
8th Infantry Brigade.............		1	
	17	97	17

War Diary.

of

3rd (King's Own) Hussars.

1st June 1919 to 31st June 1919.

Volume LVIII.

Confidential

Army Form C. 2118.

WAR DIARY
or
INTELLIGENCE SUMMARY

(Erase heading not required.)

Instructions regarding War Diaries and Intelligence Summaries are contained in F.S. Regs., Part II. and the Staff Manual respectively. Title Pages will be prepared in manuscript.

of 3rd R.O. Hussars
Johnson Rupert
Army of the Rhine

(1)

Place	Date	Hour	Summary of Events and Information	Remarks and references to Appendices
DUREN	1918 June 10	-	The Regiment in the DUREN transfers with 100 horses out of grass. Gordon Highlanders attached to the Regiment as last month.	WD
"	16		The Mobile Force as described last month left for MODRATH and COLOGNE; to win the frown detailed to empower the Peace terms	WD
"	28		Peace signed	WD
"	30		Strength & distribution of Regiment	

			Officers. Other Ranks. Horses
			With Regiment 22 259 438
			Detached 18 152 91
			            Total 40 411 529
			            Passed — 30
			                    40 441 529
			Wanting to complete to establishment, 113 O.R., 43 horses — 16 officers.	

WAR DIARY

INTELLIGENCE SUMMARY of 32nd R.O. Armrs (2)

Army Form C. 2118.

Place	Date	Hour	Summary of Events and Information	Remarks and references to Appendices
DUREN	1919 June 30		Casualties during month.	
			Period. To Hospital from Hosp U. Evacuations Remaining n.	
			Officers - Lt Parkin etc. 1st Greenish 24 (then Gunnery)	
			(from wounds)	
			Other Ranks 61 14 7 —	
			Horses 2 — 1 6	
			Detail of Re-infts. rec^d during month.	
			Date From Unit N^o.	
			17 June 2 Reserve Cav Reg^t 6	
			" " 13 Hussars 5	
			20 " 7 Hussars 2	
			23 " 30 Labour Corps 40	
			25 " 11 Hussars 90	
			25 " " " 48	
			26 " 30 Labour Corps 49	
			Total 61 Hussars;	
			179 Labour Corp.	

WTh

Army Form C. 2118.

WAR DIARY
INTELLIGENCE SUMMARY of 3 K.O. Hussars

(Erase heading not required.)

Place	Date	Hour	Summary of Events and Information	Remarks and references to Appendices
DUREN	1919 June 30		The Training of the Regiment during the month consisted of instruction with a view to the recruits becoming efficient in the Regiment proper. W.Willcox Lt Colonel Comdg. 3 Hussars	App. A detail of drafts App. B. Return of Officers

3rd (K.O) Hussars.

DETAILS OF ATTACHED.

	Offrs.	O.R.s	Horses.
52nd Bn. Gordon Highlanders.....	2	93	1
51st ,, ,, ,, ...		2	
1/4th ,, ,, ,, ...		1	
1/5th ,, ,, ,, ...		2	
30th Labour Company,.............		176	
771st Divisional Employment Co...		3	
17th Lancers.....................		1	
R.A.M.C..........................		1	
Interpreter......................		1	
	2	280	1

DETAILS OF DETACHED.

	Offrs.	O.R.s	Horses.
Mobile Striking Force,...........	2	80	86
Leave	5	28	
Hospital.........................	1	16	
Courses..........................	2	6	
Armistice Commision, SPA.........	1	2	
2nd Cavalry Division, Claims	1		
General Reinforcements Base Depot. (inc. Cav Base Depot)	4		
No.5 Remount Base Depot,.........	1		
3rd Military Prison, LE HAVRE....		1	
10th ,, ,, DUNKIRK.....		1	
124th Infantry Bde...............		1	
H.Q. 4th Division,...............		1	
4th Machine Gun Sqdn.............		2	
H.Q. Hussar Brigade..............	1	6	4
D.A.P.M. Cavalry Division,.......		2	
H.Q. Cavalry Division,...........		3	
H.Q. Army of the Rhine,..........		1	
59th Squadron R.A.F..............			1
Area Sub-Commandant, LUXEMBOURG...		1	
Signals, Cavalry Division,.......		1	
	18	152	91

3rd (K.O) Hussars.

ROLL OF OFFICERS BY SQUADRONS.

HEADQUARTERS.

Lieut Colonel W.T. Willcox, C.M.G.
Maj.(Bt.Lt.Col) P.J.V. Kelly, C.M.G., D.S.O.
,, F.J. Du Pre, D.S.O.
Captain & Adjutant H.T. Bromley,
Lieut & Q.M. J.R. Furnell,   (Leave)
T/ ,, H.V. Hart,
Captain G.S. Douglas, R.A.M.C.

"A" SQUADRON.

Captain R.A. Bagnell,
Lieut J.H. Eliot, M.C.   (Cavalry School,
  ,, G.H. Eastwood, (S.R)   Netheravon)
  ,, W.G.N.H. Dalrymple,
T/ ,, N.V. Cannon,
 ,, ,, R.D.K. Ninnis,   (Cav. Base Depot)
  ,, G.L.L. Foster, (Beds Yeo)   (Attached Hussar Bde)
  ,, H.J. Soame, (Oxford Hussars)
  ,, H. Hodgson, (,,   ,,)   (Not posted to Regt)
                                    (Leave)

"B" SQUADRON.

Captain C.F. Clarke,
Lieut C.L. Huggins, M.C.
  ,, H.R. Barton, M.C.
  ,, P.A. Waterlow,   (Mobile Force.)
  ,, J.E. Blumenfeld,   (Leave)
T/ ,, P. Kirkus,
,, 2nd ,, H.E. Craig,   (Cavalry Base Depot)
,, ,, E.E. Lloyd,(3rd Co.of L.Yeo)   ,,   ,,   ,,
,, ,, J.C. Giles.

"C" SQUADRON.

Captain Hon. D.S.P. Howard,
Lieut H.M. Naylor,
  ,, J.K. Harvie,   (Leave)
  ,, F. Craig, M.C.   (2nd Cav Div. Claims)
  ,, H.V.W. Fields-Clarke, (Beds Yeo)
  ,, A.J.A. Booth,   (Mobile Force)
  ,, D.H. Williams, (Oxford Hussars)
  2nd ,, L.E.R. Fisher, M.C.   (Leave)
  ,, ,, H.E.A. Cossentine, (S.R)   (Hospital)
T/ ,, ,, B.E. Herman,   (Cavalry Base Depot)
  ,, ,, A.M. Leney,   (Leave)
  ,, W.G. Petherick,

UNATTACHED.

Captain A.W. Keith-Falconer, (Oxford Hrs)(Armistice Com'n)
Lieut R.I.L. Childe-Pemberton, (S.R)(18th Hrs)(Leave)
T/ ,, J. Wall, D.C.M. (Special List,Res,Cav)(No.5 Rem.B.D)
  2nd ,, J. Deeks, (Lin.Yeo)   (Army Agricultural Col)

War Diary.

3rd King's Own Hussars.

from:— 1st July, 1919
to:— 31st July, 1919.

Volume LIX.

Confidential.

Army Form C. 2118.

WAR DIARY
3rd (King's Own) Hussars.
Hussar Brigade,
Cavalry Division,
Army of the Rhine.

(Erase heading not required.)

Place	Date 1919.	Hour	Summary of Events and Information	Remarks and references to Appendices
DUREN.	JULY. 1st		The Regiment quartered in HINDENBURG Barracks.	W/JP
,,	5th		The following Officers and Other Ranks mentioned in F.M. C. in C. Sir Douglas Haig's Despatches of March 1919:- WILLCOX. Lieut. Colonel, W.T.; C.M.G. COMBE. Major.(Actg.Lieut.Col.) H.,D.S.O. Commanding 15th The King's Hussars. PETHERICK. Capt.(Temp.Lieut.Col.) J.C.,M.C. attd M.G.Corps. DALRYMPLE,Lieut. W.G.N.H. GORING. Lieut.(Temp.Capt.) H. HICKS. H/45042. a/S.Q.M.S.,C. BURTON. H/2066. Sergt., C.H.C. EDGINGTON. H/45.Saddler Corpl., E. CHITTY. H/45076. Pte., E.	W/JP
,,	7th		A party consisting of Major F.J.DuPre.D.S.O., R.S.M.H.Smith,D.C.M.,S.S.M.Elliott,D.C.M,Saddler- Corpl.W.Townsend., Corpl.M.Dady,M.M. and Lance Corpl.H.Peers,M.M.together with 4 batmen and 15 horses proceeded to COLOGNE to join the detachment of the Cavalry Division which went with a Detachment from the Army of the Rhine to represent the British Army in the procession of the Allied Armies in PARIS on the 14th July, in celebration of the Peace. Major DuPre was in command of the British Cavalry Detachment. The party returned on the 17th July.	W/JP
,,	9th		The Company of the 52nd Gordon Highlanders left to rejoin their Battalion. These were supplanted by 179 Other Ranks of the 30th Labour Company, Labour Corps who arrived from COLOGNE to Well Durchin the routine of the Regiment.	W/JP

Army Form C. 2118.

WAR DIARY of 3rd (K.O.) Hussars..... CONTINUED.

INTELLIGENCE—SUMMARY.

(Erase heading not required.)

Place	Date 1919 JULY.	Hour	Summary of Events and Information	Remarks and references to Appendices
DUREN.	18th.		All horses of Regimental Headquarters, Signal Troop, "A" and "C" Squadrons were classified by the Commanding Officer.	
,,	20th.		All horses of "B" Squadron and Transport were classified by the Commanding Officer.	
,,	28th.		All horses of the Regiment were inspected by the Re-Classification Committee and divided into the various Classes as under :-	
			T Retained for Cavalry.	
			T- Unsuitable for Cavalry but retained for other units.	
			E Suitable for sale in England.	
			S. To be sold to the Germans.	
			Casualties to Officers during Month:- Lieut. L.E.R.Fisher resigned his commission. 10.7.19.	
			Lieut. G.L.L.Foster. Invalided to England. 7.7.19.	

Commanding 3rd (K.O.) Hussars.

App. A. Roll of Officers.

App. B. Strength.

App. A

3rd (K.O.) Hussars.

ROLL OF OFFICERS BY SQUADRONS.

HEADQUARTERS.
Lieut. Colonel W.T.Willcox.C.M.G. (Leave).
Major (Bt.Lt.Col).P.J.V.Kelly.C.M.G.,D.S.O.
,, H.W.Clinch. (Cav. Corps. Conctn. Camp)
,, F.J.DuPre.D.S.O.
Captain & Adjutant H.T.Bromley.
Lieut. & Qr.Mr.J.R.Furnell.
T/ ,, H.V.Hart.
Captain G.S.Douglas. R.A.M.C.

"A" SQUADRON.
Captain R.A.Bagnell.(F)
Lieut. J.H.Eliot.M.C.
,, G.H.Eastwood.(S.R.)
,, W.G.N.H.Dalrymple.
T/ ,, N.V.Cannon.
,, R.D.K.Ninnis. (Gen Reinfcts Base Depot.)
Lieut. H.J.Soame. (1/1st Q.O.O.H.).
,, H.Hodgson. ,, ,,

"B" SQUADRON.
Captain C.F.Clarke.(F)   (Leave).
Lieut. C.L.Huggins.M.C.   (Hospital).
,, H.R.Barton,M.C.   (Leave).
,, P.A.Waterlow.   (H.Q. Northern Division).
,, J.E.Blumenfeld.
T/ ,, P.Kirkus.
T/ 2nd. H.E.Craig.   (Gen. Reinfcts.Base Depot).
,, E.E.Lloyd. (3rd C.of London Yeo.) ,, ,,
,, J.C.Giles.

"C" SQUADRON.
Captain Hon.D.S.P.Howard.   (Leave).
Lieut. H.M.Naylor.   (Leave).
,, J.K.Harvie.
,, F.Craig,M.C.   Claims, 2nd Cav. Divn.
,, H.V.W.Fields-Clarke. (Beds.Yeo).
,, A.J.A.Booth.
,, D.H.Williams.(1/1st Q.O.O.H.)
2nd ,, H.E.A.Cossentine.(S.R.)
T/ ,, ,, B.E.Herman.   (Gen. Reinfcts Base Depot).
,, ,, A.M.Leney.
Lieut. W.G.Petherick.

UNATTACHED.
Captain A.W.Keith-Falconer,(1/1st Q.O.O.H.). Armn Commn.
Lieut. R.I.L.Childe-Pemberton,(S.R.). (Leave).
T/ ,, J.Wall. D.C.M. (Spec.List R.Cav.).(S R.B.Depot)
2nd. ,, J.Deeks..(Lincs. Yeo).

App. B.

STRENGTH and DISTRIBUTION of REGIMENT on 31st July, 1919.

	Officers.	Other Ranks.	Horses.
With Regiment.	19	264	504
On leave.	8	78	-
Sick (in hospital).	1	29	-
At various Stations.	11	39	29
Total strength of Regiment.	39	410	533

Details of Attached.

	Other Ranks.
30th Labour Company.	177
Interpreter.	1
1/4th Gordons.	1
52nd Gordons.	2
?71st Divisional Employment Coy.	3
Total......	184

Confidential

War Diary.
of 3rd (K.O.) Hussars.

From:- 1st August, 1919.
To:- 31st August, 1919.

Volume LX.

WAR DIARY of 3rd K.O. Hussars Hindenburg Cavalry Division of the Rhine

INTELLIGENCE SUMMARY.

Army Form C. 2118.

(Erase heading not required.)

Place	Date	Hour	Summary of Events and Information	Remarks and references to Appendices
	1919			
DUREN.	1st Aug:		Regiment quartered in the Hindenburg Barracks.	WT
	8th		All Privates serving on Normal Attestations, with 2 years or more to do on 1st March, 1919, and who will be 19 years of age on 1st October, 1919, ordered home to the 7th Hussars.	WT
	13th		Orders received for Regiment to make preparations to return home early in September.	WT
	15th		All Leave stopped pending return home.	
NIDEGGEN.	17th		Band proceeded to COLOGNE to play in Review by the Army Council.	WT
DUREN.	20th		Officers' Chargers classified. 30 chosen to be post-war chargers, and marked "O" with a special number.	WT
	25th		Details as follows received as to move home:- (i) Mobilization Store Table Equipment to be sent by train on 30th August, to AINTREE. (ii) First train load of horses to go on 16th September. (iii) Personnel train on 20th September. (iv) Remainder of horses, with Officers' Chargers, on 24th September.	WT
	26th		News received that the Regiment will be quartered in ALDERSHOT.	WT
	29th		All "S" Horses sent to IV Corps Animal Collecting Camp, DUREN, for sale.	WT
	30th		All Mobilization Store Table Equipment despatched from DUREN Station for AINTREE.	

W Trimmer
Lt Colonel
Comdg. 3rd Hussars

3rd (K.O) HUSSARS.

ROLL OF OFFICERS BY SQUADRONS.

HEADQUARTERS.
  Lieut Colonel W.T. Willcox, C.M.G.
  Maj.(Bt.Lt.Col) P.J.V.Kelly, C.M.G., D.S.O., (F)
  Major F.J. Du Pre, D.S.O.
  Captain and Adjutant H.T.Bromley.
  Lieut & Q.M. J.R. Furnell.
 T/ Lieut. H.V. Hart.   Leave.
  Captain G.S.Douglas, (R.A.M.C.)

... ...

"A" SQUADRON.
  Captain R.A.Bagnell, (F)
  Lieut J.H.Eliot, M.C.,   Cavalry School.
  ,, G.H.Eastwood, (S.R)
  ,, W.G.N.H.Dalrymple,
 T/ ,, N.V.Cannon,   Leave.
 ,, ,, R.D.K.Ninnis,
  ,, H.J.Soame, (Oxford Hussars)   Leave.
  ,, H.Hodgson, (,, ,,)

... ...

"B" SQUADRON.
  Captain C.F.Clarke, (F)
  Lieut C.L.Huggins, M.C.,   Leave.
  ,, J.T.Blumenfeld,
 T/ ,, P.Kirkus,
 2nd ,, J.C.Giles,

... ...

"C" SQUADRON.
  Captain Hon. D.S.P.Howard, (F), Leave pending Resig-
  Lieut. H.M.Naylor,   (nation.
  ,, J.K.Harvie,
  ,, F.Craig, M.C.,   Claims, Lux: Area.
  ,, H.V.W.Fields-Clarke, (Beds Yeo) To U.K. for
  ,, A.J.A.Booth,   (interview.
  ,, D.H.Williams, (Oxford Hussars) Leave.
  ,, W.G.Petherick,
 2nd ,, H.T.A.Cossentine, (S.R)   Gas Course, U.K.

... ...

UNATTACHED.
  Captain A.W.Keith-Falconer, (Oxford Hussars)
    (Armistice Commission, COLOGNE)
 2nd Lieut. J.Deeks, (Lincoln: Yeo) Army Science College,
               BONN.

... ...

3rd (K.O) HUSSARS.

DETAILS OF ATTACHED.

	Offrs.	O.R.s	Horses.
Q.O. Oxford Hussars..................	1	–	–
1/5th Gordon Highlanders,..........		1	–
51st ,, ,, ...		1	–
R.A.S.C.............................		4	–
30th Labour Company,...............		153	–
	1	159	–

Away from Regiment.(Leave and Hospital)
1/4th Gordon Highlanders......		1	–
30th Labour Company...........		20	–
	1	180	–

DETAILS OF DETACHED.

Unit to which attached, &c.	Offrs.	O.R.s	Horses.
Leave................................	10	2	–
Hospital.............................		21	6
Hussar Brigade.......................	1	9	–
Lancer Brigade.......................		1	–
18th Hussars.........................		1	–
D.A.P.M. Cavalry Division,...........		2	–
Cavalry School, Netheravon,.........	1	2	–
3rd Military Prison, Le Havre,......		1	–
10th ,, ,, , Dunkirk,......		1	–
A.P.M. IV Corps,.....................		1	–
Cavalry Division, H.Q.,..............		2	–
Signals, Cavalry Division,...........		1	–
2nd South Infantry Brigade, H.Q.....		1	–
Armistice Commission, Cologne,......	1	1	–
G.H.Q. Wireless School, Abbeville,..		1	–
Army Science College, Bonn,.........	1	–	–
Claims, Luxembourg,..................	1	–	–
Gas School, Aldershot,...............	1	–	–
Equipment conducting Party, Antwerp,	1	3	–
TOTAL,......	17	50	6

3rd (K.O) HUSSARS.

CASUALTIES DURING AUGUST.

	Joined.	Demobilized &c.	Struck off. (To U.K. & transf'd)	To Hospital	From Hospital.
OFFICERS.	Lt.R.D.K.Ninnis, from Base, 16.8.19.		Major H.W.Clinch, Lt.R.I.L.Childe-Pemberton, 2nd Lt.E.E.Lloyd, T/2/Lt.H.E.Craig, B.E.Herman 2/Lt.A.M.Leney, Lt.P.A.Waterlow, H.R.Barton,MC T/Lt.J.Wall,DCM. All above struck off on Authy.Rhine Army "A", 12.8.19.		
OTHER RANKS.	14	10	2	23	33
HORSES.	5	-	1 (died)	49	4

App. D.

3rd (K.O) Hussars.

Strength and distribution of Regiment on the last day of the month.

	Offrs.	O.R.s,	Horses.
With Regiment,	13	356	472
At various stations etc.,	17	50	6
	30	406	478

	Offrs.	O.R.s,	Horses.
Surplus,	6	-	-
Wanting to complete,	-	124	95

BEF

Cav Div

Hussar Bde

10 Hussars

1919 to 1919
APR   AUG

From 3 Cav Div 6 Bde
Box 1153

CONFIDENTIAL.

F. Johnstone Bph
20/5/5

WAR DIARY
of
10th (P.W.O.) ROYAL HUSSARS.
for
APRIL 1919.
Volume No. 471

APRIL 1919

WAR DIARY

INTELLIGENCE SUMMARY.

(Erase heading not required.)

Copy 1 Sheet No 1 10th (PWO) Royal Hussars

Place	Date	Hour	Summary of Events and Information	Remarks and references to Appendices
KONIGSHOVEN	1st to 6th April 1919		Squadrons under their Leaders. Young Officers to Foot Drill	
"	7th		The Regiment paraded at 0900 hours, and marched to new area. Headquarters at TURNICH, 'A' & 'C' Squadrons at BRUGGEN, + 'B' Sqdn at BALKHAUSEN.	
TURNICH	8th to 30th		Squadrons under their Leaders. Young Officers to Foot Drill. The Regiment found a Squadron of 4 Officers & 75 Other Ranks from 22nd April for a Mobile Striking Force for use in case of emergency. The following Officers left during the month:— Capt W Shakespeare to Pool of Quartermasters on 3rd April. Lieut R W Howe, M.C. to No 2 Traffic Control Sqdn, NAMUR on 15th April. Lieut Colonel F.N.D.C. Whitmore, C.M.G, D.S.O., T.D., to demobilization 16th April 1919	

APRIL 1919

WAR DIARY
or
INTELLIGENCE SUMMARY.

Army Form C. 2118.

TENTH ROYAL HUSSARS.
MAY 2 1919
MODDERLY ROOM

Sheet 2. Copy 1. 10th (PWO) Royal Hussars

Instructions regarding War Diaries and Intelligence Summaries are contained in F. S. Regs., Part II. and the Staff Manual respectively. Title pages will be prepared in manuscript.

Place	Date	Hour	Summary of Events and Information	Remarks and references to Appendices
TURNICH	APRIL (continued)		Lieut. E P Awdry M.C. to demobilization 23rd April 1919	

A Whitmore Major
O.C. 10th (PWO) Royal Hussars

MAY 1919

VOLUME 42

Army Form C. 2118.

WAR DIARY
or
INTELLIGENCE SUMMARY.
(Erase heading not required.)

10ᵗʰ (PWO) Royal Hussars

Sheet No 1

Place	Date	Hour	Summary of Events and Information	Remarks and references to Appendices
TURNICH	1ˢᵗ to 12ᵗʰ May 1919		Squadrons under their leaders. Subaltern Officers to Foot Drill. 2/Lieut P.J. Matthews joined Regt. 1ˢᵗ May. M.C. Lieut H Drewett to demobilization 2ⁿᵈ May.	
	13ᵗʰ to 31ˢᵗ May		Squadrons under their leaders. Subaltern Officers to Foot Drill. Lieut R.W. Howe, M.C. joined Regt 21ˢᵗ May. Lieut Hon G & D C Glyn to ENGLAND 22ⁿᵈ May. During the month the Regiment continued to supply a Squadron for a Mobile Striking Force for use in case of emergency.	

A Andrews
Major
Commanding 10ᵗʰ (PWO) Royal Hussars

CONFIDENTIAL

WAR DIARY
of
107 (PWO) ROYAL HUSSARS.
JUNE 1944.
VOLUME No 3.

Army Form C. 2118.

WAR DIARY
INTELLIGENCE SUMMARY.
(Erase heading not required.)

VOLUME 43

JUNE 1919

SHEET No 1 Copy 1

10th (P.W.O) Royal Hussars

Place	Date	Hour	Summary of Events and Information	Remarks and references to Appendices
TURNICH	1st to 7th June.		Squadrons under their Leaders. Officers, NCO's & Band to Riding School	
	8th June.		This day being the King's Birthday was observed as a holiday	
	9th to 12th June.		Squadrons under their Leaders. Officers, N.C.O's & Band to Riding School	
	13th June.		A Memorial Service was held in the grounds of SCHLOSS, TURNICH, for the late Lieut-Colonel P.E. Hardwick, D.S.O. (Colonel of the Regiment) who died at his residence in LONDON on the 9th inst	
	14th to 16th June.		Squadrons under their Leaders. Officers, NCO's & Band to Riding School.	
	17th June.		The Mobile Striking Force consisting of 4 Officers, 81 Other Ranks & 89 Horses proceeded to COLOGNE for use in case of emergency.	
	18th to 21st June.		Squadrons under their Leaders. Officers, NCO's & Band to Riding School. Recruits to Physical Drill	

CONTINUED.

JUNE 1919.

VOLUME 43.

Army Form C. 2118.

WAR DIARY
or
INTELLIGENCE SUMMARY.
(Erase heading not required.)

SHEET No 2 Copy 1

10ᵗʰ (PWO) Royal Hussars

Place	Date	Hour	Summary of Events and Information	Remarks and references to Appendices
TURNICH.	28ᵗʰ June 1919.		PEACE signed.	
	29ᵗʰ to 30ᵗʰ June		Squadrons under their leaders. Officers, NCO's & Band to Riding School. Recruits to Physical Drill. During the month 255 Reinforcements joined the Regiment.	

B. Wilmour, Major,
Commanding. 10ᵗʰ (PWO) Royal Hussars.

CONFIDENTIAL.

WAR DIARY

of

10th (P.W.O) Royal HUSSARS.

JULY, 1919.

VOLUME. No. 44.

July 1919.   Volume 44   War Diary.   *In lieu of*
                                          Army Form C.2118.

10th (P.W.O) Royal Hussars

Sheet No 1 Copy 1

Place.	Date.	Hour	Summary of Events and Information.	Remarks and references to Appendices
TURNICH	1st to 5th	July.	Riding School for Officers, NCO's & Infantry transfers. Physical Drill for recruits.	
	6th	July.	Thanksgiving Service for Peace at KERPEN, at 10.00 hours	
	7th	July.	Inspection by G.O.C. Division of methods of training in Regiment	
	8th	July.	Observed as a holiday. Peace Sports held at BRUGGEN	
	9th	July.	Riding School for Officers, Infantry transfers & recruits. Physical Drill at 08.00 hours & Foot Drill at 12.00 hours for Recruits	
	10th	July.	Inspection by IV Corps Commander.	
	11th	July.	Tho mounted parades.	
	12th	July.	Riding School for Officers, Infantry transfers & recruits. Physical Drill at 08.00 hours & Foot Drill at 12.00 hours for Recruits	
	13th to 18th	July.		
	19th	July.	G.O. Inspected Horses of Regiment for Re-classification	

July 1919   VOLUME 44   WAR DIARY.   In lieu of Army Form C 2118.

10ᵗʰ (P.W.O) Royal Hussars

SHEET No 2 COPY 1

PLACE.	DATE.	HOUR.	SUMMARY OF EVENTS AND INFORMATION.	Remarks and references to Appendices.
TURNICH	20ᵗʰ to 26ᵗʰ July		Riding School for Officers. Infantry transfer & recruits Physical Drill at 0800 hours & Foot Drill at 1200 hours for Recruits.	
	27ᵗʰ July		Church Parade at BALKHAUSEN	
	28ᵗʰ July		Commander-in-Chief inspected Recruits at Riding School	
	29ᵗʰ July		Riding School for Officers. Horses of Regiment classified by Remount Board	
	30ᵗʰ July			
	31ˢᵗ July		Riding School for Officers. Infantry transfer & recruits.	

During this month the following Officers have joined Regiment from U.K. –
    Captain E.A. Feilden. M.C – 3/7/19
    Major W.P. Littlewood. – 23/7/19.
    Lt. Col. A.J. Seymour D.S.O – 28/7/19

Lieut. E.S Campbell proceeded for demobilisation 30/7/19

W. [signature] Lt. Col.
Commanding 10ᵗʰ (P.W.O) Royal Hussars

In lieu of
Army Form C 2118.

WAR DIARY.

AUGUST 1919. VOLUME 45

10th (P.W.O) Royal Hussars

PLACE.	DATE.	HOUR.	SUMMARY OF EVENTS AND INFORMATION. Sheet 1 Copy	Remarks and references to Appendices
TURNICH.	1st to August.		Riding School for Officers, Infantry transfers & recruits at 08.15 hours. Physical Drill for Recruits at 08.00 hours.	
	7th August.		Composite Squadron for Review at COLOGNE paraded at 10.00 hours, for rehearsal.	
	8th August.		Riding School for Officers, Infantry transfers & recruits at 08.15 hours. Physical Drill for Recruits at 08.00 hours.	
	9th August.		Composite Sqdn for Review at COLOGNE paraded at 10.00 hours.	
	12th to August.		Riding School at 08.15 hours.	
	13th August.		Riding School for Officers, Infantry transfers & recruits at 08.15 hours. Foot Drill for undermanned recruits at 14.00 hours.	
	14th to August.		Riding School for Officers, Infantry transfers & recruits at 08.15 hours. Foot Drill for undermanned recruits at 14.00 hours	
	16th August.			
	17th to August.		Riding School for Officers, Infantry transfers & recruits at 08.15 hours. Physical Drill at 08.00 hours.	
	24th August.		Riding School for Officers, Infantry transfers & recruits at 08.15 hours. Foot Drill for undermanned recruits at 14.00 hours	
	25th to August.			
	31st August.		During this month the undermentioned Officers have proceeded to U.K. & are struck off the strength:- Lieut W.J. Busley - 6/8/19. Lieut B.G. Bearman 9/8/19 2/Lieut J.D. Wrangham 2/8/19	

W Weirdham Lt-Col.
Commanding 10th (P.W.O) Royal Hussars.

BAEF

CAV DIV

HUSSAR Bde

~~10~~ 15 HUSSARS

1919 to 1919
APR   AUG

FROM 1 CAV DIV 9 BDE
BOX 1114

WAR DIARY

OF

15TH "THE KING'S" HUSSARS.

FOR

APRIL, 1919.

VOLUME XLIX.

CONFIDENTIAL.

Army Form C. 2118.

WAR DIARY
or
INTELLIGENCE SUMMARY.

VOL. XLIX.

from 1.4.19.
to 30.4.19.

15th "The King's" Hussars.

(Erase heading not required.)

Place	Date	Hour	Summary of Events and Information	Remarks and references to Appendices
BEDBURG	1st	18.00	Lecture by Rev. Stanley Blunt, Chaplain to the British Embassy in PARIS, in Cinema Hall BEDBURG. Subject:- "Egypt".	WC
—	2nd	12.00	Parade of horses proposed for casting. In College Square.	WC
			Equitation Course for Subaltern Officers commenced.	
			4 other ranks proceed to the U.K. for demobilization.	
—	3rd		3 Officers, 100 other ranks of 1/15th Argyll & Sutherland Highlanders joined Regt. for duty and taken on attached strength.	WC
			(Lieut. R.F.E. Rhodes, M.C. proceeded on leave to the U.K.	
			4 other ranks proceeded to the U.K. for demobilization. 2 other ranks returned from Course at 2nd Army Agricultural College. 1 other rank to H.Q., Cavalry Division as Batman. 1 other rank from Hospital.	
			1 Rdg. Horse evacuated to M.V.S.	
—	4th		4 other ranks proceed to the U.K. for demobilization. 1 other rank from Hospital.	WC
—	5th	15.00	Divisional Commander (Maj. Gen. Sir. N.E. Peyton, K.C.B.K.C.V.O, D.S.O.) visited the Regt. and inspected stables and billets of "C" Squadron.	WC

WAR DIARY or **INTELLIGENCE SUMMARY**

Army Form C. 2118.

VOL. XLIX   From 1.4.19 to 30.4.19

15th "The King's" Hussars.

Place	Date	Hour	Summary of Events and Information	Remarks and references to Appendices
BEDBURG	5th		Lieut. G.F.A. Douglas proceeded on leave to the U.K.	W
			4 other ranks proceeded to the U.K. for demobilisation.	
	6th		Hussar Brigade (less 3rd Hussars, "O" and "Y" Batteries, R.H.A.) ordered to move to an area about KERPEN on 7th instant (Ref.I.L. 1/100,000)	
			Billeting parties of the Regt. proceeded to KERPEN.	W
			Lieuts. J.P. Tennant, M.C. and A.B. Smith proceeded on leave to the U.K.	
			4 other ranks to U.K. for demobilisation. 1 Rg. Lewis destroyed.	
	7th	09.00	The Regt. paraded at southern exit of BLERICHEN (Ref.I.L. 1/100,000) and marched in the following order:-	
			Headquarters: "B" Squadron : "C" Squadron : "A" Echelon : "B" Echelon.	
			Route :- THORR - HEPPENDORF - SINDORF. Dress :- Marching Order.	
			The Regt. arrived in KERPEN at 11.30 hours: Squadrons and H.Q. billeted in Soll. LÖRSFELD on KERPEN (Ref.I.L. 1/100,000 : M.III. 8.R.). Transport in Soll. LÖRSFELD on KERPEN - SINDORF Road, 1½ miles N. of KERPEN.	W
			Lieut. G.F.H. Clarke proceeded on leave to the U.K.	
			4 other ranks demobilised whilst on leave in the U.K.	

Army Form C. 2118.

WAR DIARY or INTELLIGENCE SUMMARY.

(Erase heading not required.)

VOL. XLIX From 1.4.19 To 30.4.19

15th "The Kings" Hussars

Place	Date	Hour	Summary of Events and Information	Remarks and references to Appendices
KERPEN	8th	12.45	A.D.V.S. Cavalry Division inspected horses proposed for casting in the Square. 1 other rank rejoined from Hospital. Lieut. T.C.J. Bradshaw proceeded on leave to the U.K.	WL
—	9th	12.00	IV Corps Commander visits Regimental Headquarters. 4 other ranks proceeded to the U.K. for demobilization. 1 other rank to Hospital. 9 Reg. horses evacuated to M.V.S.	WL
—	10th		Lt. Col. St. Combe, D.S.O. and Lt. S.P.L.A. Litgow rejoined from leave to U.K. Lt. R.C. Skellow rejoined from course at No. 6. Veterinary Hospital, ROUEN. 1 other rank from Hospital. 4 other ranks to the U.K. for demobilization. 1 other rank from 1st Bn. Gloucester Regt. on transfer. 2 Reg. horses evacuated to M.V.S. 2 Reg. horses to Animal Collecting Camp, COLOGNE.	WL
—	11th		Capt. C.H. Liddell proceeded on leave to the U.K.	WL
—	12th		16 other ranks proceeded to the U.K. for demobilization.	WL

Army Form C. 2118.

WAR DIARY
or
INTELLIGENCE SUMMARY.
(Erase heading not required.)

VOL. XLIX. From 1.4.19 To 30.4.'19.

15th "The King's" Hussars.

Place	Date	Hour	Summary of Events and Information	Remarks and references to Appendices
KERPEN	13th		Capt. R.H.O. Starkey proceeded on leave to the U.K. from H.Q. Hussar Brigade.	W.C.
	14th		Lt. R.H.E. Athy joined Regt. from the U.K. Other ranks rejoined from Hospital.	W.C.
		10.00	G.O.C. Cavalry Division visited Regimental H.Q. at KERPEN.	
		11.30	Farewell visit of Brig. Gen. G.A. Legard, C.M.G., D.S.O. to officers of the Regt. on relinquishing command of Hussar Brigade.	W.C.
	15th		1 other rank joined from Base.	W.C.
	16th		1 other rank rejoined from Hospital.	K.C. W.C.
	17th		2 other ranks admitted to Hospital. Lt. R.C. Stellin proceeded to the U.K. for demobilization ; 2/Lt. J. Staggars proceeded on leave and 1 O.R. evacuated to M.V.S.	W.C.
	18th		3 Rlg. horses and 1 Lt. O.R. evacuated to M.V.S. Capt. A. J. Brace D.S.O. M.C. proceeded to the U.K. on leave to the U.K. 6 other ranks proceeded to the U.K. for demobilization. 5 other ranks to the U.K. for re-engagement leave and struck off strength. 2 Rdg. horses evacuated to M.V.S.	W.C.

Army Form C. 2118.

WAR DIARY or INTELLIGENCE SUMMARY.

(Erase heading not required.)

VOL. XLIX

Sqn. From 1.4.19. To 30.4.19.

15th "The King's" Hussars

Place	Date	Hour	Summary of Events and Information	Remarks and references to Appendices
KERPEN	19th	14.30	Conference for Comdg. Officers was held at H.Q., Unseen Brigade	H.C.
			BERGERHAUSEN. Detachment of 3 officers 100 other ranks of 1/5th Argyle & Sutherland Highlanders reported their Battalion. 3 officers, 96 other ranks of 52nd Bn. Gordon Highlanders joined in relief of the above party. 1 Rgt. Horse Evacuated to M.V.S.	
	20th	10.45	Guard Parade for C.of E. Y.M.C.A Hall, KERPEN. The following attended and paraded in the Square at 10.15 hours :— Band as a Band. 2 Officers, 20 other ranks of 'A','B', & 'C' Squadrons. 1 Officer, 20 other ranks of Headquarters. Lt.Col. H. Combe D.S.O. commanded the parade. Lt.Col. F.E. Rhodes M.C. rejoined from leave to the U.K. 2/Lt. Sir H.R.K. Floyd Bt. proceeded on leave to the U.K. 1 Reg. Horse to Animal Collecting Camp COLOGNE.	H.C. H.C.

Army Form C. 2118.

WAR DIARY or INTELLIGENCE SUMMARY.

VOL. XLIX. From 1.4.'19. To 30.4.'19.

15th "The King's" Hussars

(Erase heading not required.)

Place	Date	Hour	Summary of Events and Information	Remarks and references to Appendices
KERPEN.	22/4	10.30 a.m.	Court of Enquiry held at "C" Sqn. Officers Mess. President: Capt. C.H. Shaw.	W.
			1 other rank to the U.K. to attend Educational Training Course.	W.
			1 other rank of Army Gymnastic Staff struck off attached strength.	W.
	23/4		1 other rank joined 3rd Res. Bn. Monmouth Regt. on transfer.	W.
			2nd Lt. Lewis joined from 17th Lancers.	
	24/4		2 Lt./Qr.Mr. Innes reported from M.V.S.	W.
	25/4	11.00 a.m.	G.O.C. Hussars Brigade inspected all horses of the Regt. in the Square.	W.
		14.15	Lecture by G.O.C. Hussar Brigade in Y.M.C.A. Hut, KERPEN. All Officers attended. Subject :- "Polo".	
	26/4	10.20	Gen. Sir H.R. Robertson G.C.B., K.C.V.O., D.S.O., A.D.C. (G.O.C. British Army of the Rhine) visited Officers of the Regt. at Regt. H.Q. KERPEN.	W.
			Lt. Q.P. Lennant M.C. reported from leave to the U.K.	W.
			1 other rank to Hospital. 3 Rly. horses to M.V.S.	
	27/4	09.30	Divine Service for C.of E. in Y.M.C.A. Hall, KERPEN. The following attended and paraded in the Square at 09.00 :- Band as a Band.	W.

WAR DIARY or INTELLIGENCE SUMMARY

Army Form C. 2118.

VOL. XLIX

From 1.4.19. To 30.4.19.

15th "The King's" Hussars

Place	Date	Hour	Summary of Events and Information	Remarks and references to Appendices
KERPEN.	27th (cont.)		2 Officers, 15 other ranks of "A", "B" & "C" Squadrons.	MC
			1 Officer, 15 other ranks of Headquarters.	
			Lt. R.F.E. Rhodes, MC. commanded the parade.	
			Maj. Gen. F.A. Nicolson, MC. and Capt. C.H. Shaw proceeded on leave to the UK.	
			Lts. T.C.V. Bradshaw and D.H.H. Clarke rejoined from leave to the UK.	
			3 other ranks joined Regt. from the UK. 1 other rank to Hospital.	
	28th		Capt. C.H. Liddle, Lts. A.B. Smith and L.J.L. Loudon, MC. rejoined from leave to the UK.	MC
			1 other rank joined from 3rd Echelon. 1 other rank admitted to Hospital.	
	29th	9.00	Comdg. Officer inspected 15th Hussars Squadron and Transport of Mobile Striking Force in the Square, KERPEN.	MC
		10.30	G.O.C. Hussar Brigade inspected Mobile Striking Force (Composite Regiment found by Hussar Brigade) in grass meadow 1 mile South of BLATZHEIM (Ref. I.L. 1/100,000).	MC
			1 Reg. horse received from Base.	
			Capt. R.H.O. Hanbury rejoined from leave to the UK.	MC
	30th			

Army Form C. 2118.

WAR DIARY or **INTELLIGENCE SUMMARY.**

VOL. XLIX

From 1.4.19
To 30.4.19
15th "The King's" Hussars

(Erase heading not required.)

Place	Date	Hour	Summary of Events and Information	Remarks and references to Appendices
KERPEN	30th (contd)		25 other ranks joined from U.K. as reinforcements. 2 Rdg. horses evacuated to M.V.S.	M

WAR DIARY or INTELLIGENCE SUMMARY

Army Form C. 2118.

VOL. XLIX

From 1.4.19
To 30.4.19. 15th The King's Hussars

Summary of Casualties during April, 1919.

Place	Date	Hour	Summary of Events and Information	Offrs	O.R.	Horses: Rdg./L.D.	Pack	Remarks
			INCREASE.					
			From Hospital.	-	4	-	-	
			" Base.	1	30	1	-	
			" Infantry (on transfer)	-	2	-	-	
			" 17th Lancers.	-	-	28	-	
			" M.V.S.	-	-	2	-	
			TOTALS	1	36	31	-	
			DECREASE.	Offrs	O.R.	Rdg./L.D.	Pack	
			To Hospital.	-	5	-	-	
			" U.K. for demobilization	1	15	-	-	
			" H.Q. Cavalry Division.	-	1	-	-	
			" U.K. for re-engagement leave	-	5	-	-	
			" U.K. (9th Lancers)	-	-	3	-	
			" 9th Lancers	-	-	1	-	
			" Animal Collecting Camp.	-	-	19	-	
			" H.Q. Hussar Brigade.	-	-	3	-	
			" M.V.S. (Struck off strength)	-	-	30	-	
			TOTALS	1	26	56	-	

	Officers	O.Rks.	Rdg.	Lt.Drht.	Pack.
Present Strength of Regiment	33	288	274	61	25
Attached	5	100	3	-	-
30.4.19 TOTALS	38	388	277	61	25

Herbert Combe Lt. Col.
15th Hussars 1.5.19

CONFIDENTIAL.

WAR DIARY

OF

15TH "THE KING'S" HUSSARS

MAY, 1919.

VOLUME No. XLIX.

WAR DIARY
or
INTELLIGENCE SUMMARY.

Army Form C. 2118.

VOL. XLV

From 1.5.19.
To 31.5.19.
15th - The King's - Hussars

Place	Date	Hour	Summary of Events and Information	Remarks and references to Appendices
KERPEN	1st.		Lieut. W.P. Alcock, M.O. proceeded on leave to the United Kingdom. 1 other rank rejoined from hospital.	H.
-.-	2nd.	10.30.	Cavalry Memorial Service held in Y.M.C.A. Hut, BERGHEIM. 6 all ranks per Squadron and H.Q. attended and were conveyed by lorry to the service.	H.O.
			3 other ranks proceeded to U.K. for demobilisation. 13 other ranks to U.K. for re-engagement leave. 1 other rank rejoined from hospital. 7 riding horses despatched to Base. 4 riding horses evacuated by V.S.	
-.-	3rd.	10.30	F.G.C.M. held at Regimental H.Q., KERPEN. 1 other rank to P. & R.T. Course, ALDERSHOT. 1 other rank to Course at School of Cookery, COLOGNE. 1 light draught horse evacuated to M.V.S.	H.
-.-	4th.	09.30	Divine Service for C.of E. in Y.M.C.A. Hall, KERPEN. The following attended and paraded on square outside Orderly Room at 09.15 hrs- Band as a Band. 1 Officer, 15 other ranks per Sqn. 1 Officer, 15 other ranks of H.Q.	H.

Army Form C. 2118.

WAR DIARY
or
INTELLIGENCE SUMMARY.
(Erase heading not required.)

VOL XLX

From 1.5.19
To 31.5.19
15th - The King's - Hussars

Instructions regarding War Diaries and Intelligence Summaries are contained in F. S. Regs., Part II. and the Staff Manual respectively. Title pages will be prepared in manuscript.

Place	Date	Hour	Summary of Events and Information	Remarks and references to Appendices
KERPEN	4th (cont.)		Captain C. H. Liddell commanded the parade. 1 other rank rejoined from hospital. 1 other rank from Base	H.C.
—	5th.		1 other rank rejoined from hospital. 3 Riding Horses evacuated to M.V.S.	H.C.
—	6th.		16 other ranks proceed to UK. to attend Regtl. Old Comrades Association Dinner on 10th inst. 2 other ranks proceeded to UK. on demobilization.	H.C.
—	7th.		Capt. A.F. Bruce DSO, MC. Lieut. G.F.T.S. Douglas & 2/Lt. J. Haggas rejoined from leave to the United Kingdom. 29 other ranks Northumberland Hussars joined Regiment and taken on strength.	H.C.
—	8th.		Lt. Col. H. Combe DSO., Capts. C.H. Liddell & R.H.O. Stanbury proceeded to UK. to attend R.O.C.A. Dinner on 10th inst.	H.C.
—	9th.	18.00	9 riding horses were despatched to Animal Collecting Camp, DUREN. Lecture by Rev. Canon MEYRICK in Y.M.C.A. Hall, KERPEN. Subject: "Life & Amusements of the Ancient Romans"	H.C.

Army Form C. 2118.

WAR DIARY or INTELLIGENCE SUMMARY.

(Erase heading not required.)

VOL XLX

From 1.5.19.
To 31.5.19.
15th The King's Hussars

Place	Date	Hour	Summary of Events and Information	Remarks and references to Appendices
KERPEN	10th		Regimental Old Comrades Association Dinner held at Cafe Mexico.	W.
			LONDON.	
	11th		Brig. Gen. P. Hambro, CB, CMG, visited the Regiment. 10 riding horses joined from 1st Field Sqn. 1 other rank to hospital.	W. W.
	12th		2 other ranks to hospital.	W.
	13th		1 other rank to Corps Animal Collecting Camp, DUREN, for duty. 2 riding horses evacuated to M.V.S.	W.
	14th		1 other rank joined from Northumberland Hussars and taken on strength. 1 other rank from hospital.	W.
	15th		Lieut. L.T. Negrum rejoined from leave to the U.K. 1 other rank to hospital. Riding horse attached 9th C.F.A. struck off strength. Riding horse to M.V.S.	W.
	16th		Tactical Exercise for Battallion Officers; rendezvous on road outside Brigade H.Q., BERGERHAUSEN, at 09.15 hours.	W.
	17th		Lieut. W.P. Alcock, M.C. proceeded to attend course at Cavalry School.	W.
			NETHERAVON.	
			3 other ranks proceeded to U.K. for demobilization; 1 other rank to hospital.	

Army Form C. 2118.

WAR DIARY
or
INTELLIGENCE SUMMARY.
(Erase heading not required.)

VOL XLX

From 1.5.19
To 31.5.19

15th The King's Hussars

Place	Date	Hour	Summary of Events and Information	Remarks and references to Appendices
KERPEN	18th	09.30	Divine Service for C. of E. in Y.M.C.A. Hall, KERPEN. The following attended and paraded on square outside Orderly Room at 09.15 hours:- 1 Officer, 13 other ranks per Sqn. & H.Q. Band as a Band.	H.
	19th		Lieut. Col. H. Cooke, D.S.O. Commanded the Parade. 1 other rank joined from U.K. and taken on strength. 1 other rank to Hospital.	H.C.
	20th		Comdg. Officer inspected one mounted man and one cyclist in new Divisional marching order.	H.C.
			Lieut. A.C. Straker joined from 3rd Echelon and taken on strength.	H.
	21st		Lieut. H. Ind. proceeded to U.K. for demobilization. Maj. Rev. J.D. Pitkin M.C. (C.F. attached) proceeded to U.K. for demobilization. 1 other rank to Cavalry School, NETHERAVON. 1 other rank from Hospital. 5 riding horses evacuated to M.V.S.	H.
	22nd	11.00	Conference for Comdg. Officers & Squadron Leaders was held at H.Q. Hussar Brigade.	H.C.

Army Form C. 2118.

WAR DIARY
or
INTELLIGENCE SUMMARY.
(Erase heading not required.)

VOL. XLX

From 1.5.19
To 31.5.19
15th The Kings Hussars

Place	Date	Hour	Summary of Events and Information	Remarks and references to Appendices
KERPEN	23rd	18.00	Lecture by Lt. Col. Tyshan on the fallacies of Bolshevism in R.A.S.C. Hall, HORREM. All available Officers and other ranks attended and proceeded by lorries to HORREM.	H
—	24th	10.30	Captain C.H. Liddell member of F.G.C.M. held at H.Q. 10th Hussar. Lieut. B.J.L. Banks joined from U.K. and taken on strength. 1 riding horse to M.V.S. 3 riding horses of Senior Chaplain to Div. H.Q. Divine services were held as under:—	H
—	25th	11.00	Parade service for C. of E. in Y.M.C.A. Hall. The following attended:— Band as a Band. 1 Officer, 13 other ranks per Sqdn. 15 other ranks of H.Q. and paraded on square outside Orderly Room at 10.45 hours. Lieut. R.F.G. London, M.C. commanded the parade.	H
		09.00	Service for Presbyterians and other Nonconformists in Y.M.C.A. Hall, KERPEN. 10 other ranks per Sqdn. attended. 1 other rank admitted to hospital.	H

Army Form C. 2118.

WAR DIARY or INTELLIGENCE SUMMARY.
(Erase heading not required.)

VOL. XIX

From 1.5.19
To 31.5.19

15th The King's Hussars

Place	Date	Hour	Summary of Events and Information	Remarks and references to Appendices
KERPEN	26th	11.00	Capt. C.H. Liddell (O.C. Hussar Bde. Mobile Striking Force) attended conference at 1st Northern Bde. H.Q., COLOGNE. Capt. C.H. Shaw returned from leave to the U.K.	H.
	27th		1 other rank joined from H.Q. Cavalry Divn. and taken on strength	H.
			1 other rank from hospital	H.
	28th		1 other rank from hospital	
	29th		1 other rank (Bandmaster) joined from U.K. and taken on strength	
			9 other ranks Northumberland Hussars joined and taken on strength	H.
			1 other rank to H.Q. Cavalry Divn. as servant to G.O.C.	
			22 Z. riding horses to the 24 Vety. Hospital, COLOGNE. In despatch to the 1st Bde.	
	30th	09.00	Lecture by Sergeant, Army Signals, on instruction in the use of Carrier Pigeons in Y.M.C.A. Hall, KERPEN: All officers attended. Lieut. A. Ireland proceeded to the United Kingdom for demobilization.	H.
			3 other ranks to hospital	
			7 riding horses to M.V.S.	

Army Form C. 2118.

WAR DIARY
or
INTELLIGENCE SUMMARY.

VOL XLV

From 1.5.19.
to 31.5.19.

15th The Kings - Chasers

(Erase heading not required.)

Instructions regarding War Diaries and Intelligence Summaries are contained in F. S. Regs., Part II. and the Staff Manual respectively. Title pages will be prepared in manuscript.

Place	Date	Hour	Summary of Events and Information	Remarks and references to Appendices
KERPEN.	31/5	17.00	Comdg. Officer attended Conference at Divisional H.Q. Lieut J.W. McBroukan admitted to hospital.	MC.

Army Form C. 2118.

WAR DIARY
or
INTELLIGENCE SUMMARY.

VOL. XLX

From 1.5.19
To 31.5.19. 15th The King's Mustard

(Erase heading not required.)

Place	Date	Hour	Summary of Events and Information	Remarks and references to Appendices
			Summary of Training during month of May, 1919.	
			Daily (except Sundays.)	
			Subaltern Officers :- Equitation : 07.00 hrs HC
			Foot Drill : 09.30 " HC
			N.C.O's. :- Foot Drill : 09.30 hrs

Instructions regarding War Diaries and Intelligence Summaries are contained in F. S. Regs., Part II. and the Staff Manual respectively. Title pages will be prepared in manuscript.

Army Form C. 2118.

WAR DIARY
or
INTELLIGENCE SUMMARY.
(Erase heading not required.)

Instructions regarding War Diaries and Intelligence Summaries are contained in F. S. Regs., Part II. and the Staff Manual respectively. Title pages will be prepared in manuscript.

Summary of Events and Information

Summary of Casualties during May, 1919.

Place	Date	Hour					INCREASE	Offrs.	O.R.	Horses Rdg.	Horses L.D.P.			DECREASE	Offrs.	O.R.	Horses Rdg.	Horses L.D.P.	Remarks and references to Appendices
							From United Kingdom	1	33	-	-			To U.K. for demob.	2	3	-	-	
							Hospital	-	3	-	-			Hospital	-	5	-	-	
							Northumberland Hussars	-	39	-	-			H.Q. Cav. Division	-	1	-	-	
							3rd Echelon	1	-	-	-			M.V.S.	-	-	23	1	
							H.Q. Cavalry Divn.	-	1	-	-			Base	-	-	9	-	
							1st Field Sqdn.	-	-	10	-			9ᵏ C.F.A.	-	-	1	-	
							H.Q. Hussar Bde.	-	2	-	-								
							TOTALS	2	76	12	-			TOTALS	2	9	33	1	-

	Offrs.	O.R.	Rdg.	L.D.P.	Pack	Total
Present Strength of Regiment	32	309	422	61	25	508
Attached	2	115	7	-	-	-
TOTALS	34	424	429	61	25	508

Herbert Forte L/Col.
Comdg. 15ᵗʰ Hussars
31/5/19.

15th "The King's" Hussars.

War Diary

for

June, 1919.

VOLUME L.

Army Form C. 2118.

WAR DIARY
or
INTELLIGENCE SUMMARY.
(Erase heading not required.)

VOL. L.   From 1.6.19
           to 30.6.19
           15th "The King's" Hussars

Place	Date	Hour	Summary of Events and Information	Remarks and references to Appendices
KERPEN	1st.	10.00	Divine Service for C.I.E. in Y.M.C.A. Hall. KERPEN: The following attended and paraded on the Square outside Orderly Room at 09.45:- Band as a Band.	
			1 Officer, 13 other ranks per Sqdn.	
			1 Officer, 13 other ranks of H.Q.	A.C.
			Captain C.H. Shaw commanded the parade.	
			1 other rank (Army Gymnastic Staff) joined for duty and taken on attached strength.	
	2nd.		Educational Classes commenced & held daily from 14.00 to 17.00 in room next to Regtl. Canteen.	A.C.
			3 other ranks joined from 53rd Bn. Middlesex Regt. and taken on attached strength. 1 other rank admitted to Hospital.	
-.-	3rd.	10.00	Parade in honour of H.M. The King: The following attended and paraded on the Square outside Orderly Room at 10.00:- Band as a Band.	A.C.
			3 Officers, 34 other ranks per Sqdn. & H.Q.	

Army Form C. 2118.

WAR DIARY or INTELLIGENCE SUMMARY.

VOL. L.

From 1.6.19
To 30.6.19.

15th "The King's" Hussars

(Erase heading not required.)

Instructions regarding War Diaries and Intelligence Summaries are contained in F. S. Regs., Part II. and the Staff Manual respectively. Title pages will be prepared in manuscript.

Place	Date	Hour	Summary of Events and Information	Remarks and references to Appendices
KERPEN	3rd (late)		Dress:- Church Parade order. 1 Officer, 36 other ranks of Gordon Highlanders. Lieut. Col. H. Combe, D.S.O. Commanded the parade. Remainder of day observed as a holiday.	AC
—	4th		1 other rank proceeded to Course at P. & R.T. School, RIEHL. 3 other ranks joined on posting from Northumberland Hussars.	AC
—	5th		1 other rank rejoined from Educational Course in U.K. 1 other rank admitted to hospital. 3 Riding Horses evacuated to M.V.S. 2 other ranks admitted to hospital: 1 other rank rejoined from hospital.	AC
—	6th		Comdg Officer inspected horses of "C" Sqn in watering order, in the Square, KERPEN.	AC
—	7th		3 other ranks joined from 10th Bn. Argyll & Sutherland Hrs, and taken on attached strength.	AC
—	8th	09.00	Divine service for Nonconformists in Y.M.C.A. Hall, KERPEN: 10 other ranks per Sqn attended.	AC

Army Form C. 2118.

WAR DIARY
or
INTELLIGENCE SUMMARY.
(Erase heading not required.)

From 1.6.19
To 30.6.19
15th "The King's" Hussars

VOL. L.

Instructions regarding War Diaries and Intelligence Summaries are contained in F.S. Regs., Part II. and the Staff Manual respectively. Title pages will be prepared in manuscript.

Place	Date	Hour	Summary of Events and Information	Remarks and references to Appendices
KERPEN	8th	(Cato)	Lieut. G.H.H. Clarke, one other rank and 2 Riding Horses absorbed in establishment of H.Q. Hussar Bde. and struck off strength.	M.C.
—	9th	09.30	Divnl. gas officer tested Small Box Respirators of personnel of Mobile Striking Force.	M.C.
			Lieuts. R. Snee and F.A. Lilsley rejoined from M.H. Base Veterinary Hospital.	
			2 other ranks to U.K. for demobilization (from M.H. Base Vety. Hospital)	
			2 other ranks of 1/141st Divnl. Employment Coy. joined and taken on attached strength.	
—	10th		2 other ranks rejoined from hospital.	M.C.
			2 Riding Horses evacuated to M.V.S.	
—	11th		Major Hon. F.A. Nicolson M.C. rejoined from leave to the U.K.	M.C.
			Lieut. P.P. Tennant proceeded on short leave to France.	
			1 Riding Horse received from M.V.S.	
—	12th	11.30	Lecture by Command Paymaster to all Units of Cavalry Division, in M.T. Coy. Recreation Hall, HORREM. The following attended :—	M.C.

WAR DIARY or INTELLIGENCE SUMMARY.

Army Form C. 2118.

VOL. L. From 1.6.19 To 30.6.19

15th "The King's" Hussars.

Place	Date	Hour	Summary of Events and Information	Remarks and references to Appendices
KERPEN	12th (Contd.)		Adjutant, 2nd i/c Sqdns, Transport Officer, Quartermaster, Sqdn QMSs, 2 Orderly Room Clerks.	HC
			1 other rank admitted to hospital	
—	13th		Maj. Hon. F.A. Nicolson, M.C. was President and Capt. H.T. Brace, D.S.O., M.C. a member of a F.G.C.M. which assembled at H.Q. 10th Hussars at 09.30.	HC
			Lieut. F.A. Lilley proceeded on leave to the United Kingdom	
			2 other ranks admitted to hospital. 1 other rank rejoined from hospital.	
—	14th	10.30	Divine Service for C.of.E. in Y.M.C.A. Hall, KERPEN. The following attended and paraded in the Square outside Orderly Room at 10.15:-	HC
			Band as a Band.	
			1 Officer, 13 other ranks per Sqdn.	
			1 Officer, 13 other ranks of H.Q.	
			Major Hon. F.A. Nicolson, M.C. commanded the parade.	
			1 Riding Horse evacuated to M.V.S.	
—	15th		1 other rank (Army Gymnastic Staff) proceeded to 10th Hussars and struck off attached strength.	HC

Army Form C. 2118.

WAR DIARY
or
INTELLIGENCE SUMMARY.
(Erase heading not required.)

VOL. L. From 1.6.19 To 30.6.19
15th "The King's" Hussars.

Place	Date	Hour	Summary of Events and Information	Remarks and references to Appendices
KERPEN	16th	10.30	F.G.C.M. held in room next to Regtl. Canteen.	WC
			60 other ranks joined from U.K. as reinforcements.	
—	17th	04.35	Orders received from Hussar Brigade for Mobile Striking Force to concentrate at noon.	WC
			Personnel of 15th Hussars paraded on the Square, KERPEN at 11.00 under Lieuts R. Snee and J.A.F. Dalgety. The party then marched to the concentration point at Artillery Barracks, COLOGNE.	WC
			Captain C.H. Liddell commanded Hussar Brigade Mobile Force.	
			5 Riding Horses evacuated to M.V.S.	
—	18th		G.O.C. Cavalry Division inspected training of Instructors in the Regiment as under:-	WC
		09.30	Equitation Class in the field half-way between KERPEN and SCHLOSS LORSFELD (on the KERPEN - SINDORF Road: Ref: I.L. 1:100,000: M.3.)	WC
		10.15	Foot Drill on the Square KERPEN.	
		10.30	Physical and Recreational Training on the Square, KERPEN.	

WAR DIARY or **INTELLIGENCE SUMMARY.**

Army Form C. 2118.

VOL. L.

From 1.6.19
To 30.6.19.
15th "The Kings" Hussars

Place	Date	Hour	Summary of Events and Information	Remarks and references to Appendices
KERPEN	18th	(Cont)	Lecture by G.O.C. Hussar Brigade. Subject "POLO". All available Officers attended.	AC
—	19th		1 other rank (F.Q.M.S.) proceeded to the U.K. on transfer to the Home Establishment.	AC
			2 other ranks rejoined from hospital.	AC
—	20th		4 other ranks (attached H.Q. Cav. Divn.) taken on strength.	AC
			1 other rank absorbed in establishment of H.Q. Cav. Divn. and struck off the strength.	
			1 Riding Horse despatched to 1st Signal Sqn. R.E.	
			5 Riding Horses and 1 Lt. Draft received from M.V.S.	
—	21st		Lieut. G. A. Windsor proceeded to PARIS for duty with Provost Marshal's Branch and struck off strength.	AC
			Lieut. J. Arnott proceeded on leave to the United Kingdom.	
			Lieut. O. C. F. Bradshaw rejoined from hospital.	
			2 Lt. Draft and 3 Riding Horses evacuated to M.V.S.	
—	22nd	10.00	Divine Service for C. of E. in Y.M.C.A. Hall, KERPEN.	AC
			The following attended and paraded on the square outside Orderly Room at 09.45 :-	

WAR DIARY or INTELLIGENCE SUMMARY

Army Form C. 2118.

VOL. L.

From 1.6.19
To 30.6.19

15th "The King's - Queens"

Place	Date	Hour	Summary of Events and Information	Remarks and references to Appendices
KERPEN	22nd (Contd)		Band as a Band.	
			1 Officer, 13 other ranks per Span.	
			1 Officer, 13 other ranks of H.Q.	
			Lieut. Col. H. Combe, D.S.O. commanded the parade.	HC
			Capt. H.L. Brace, D.S.O., M.C. and 2/Lieut. J.J. Meyrick proceeded on leave to the United Kingdom.	
			Lieut. R.B. Harvie proceeded to the U.K. for demobilization.	
			1 other rank rejoined from P+R.T. Course in the U.K.	
			1 other rank rejoined from hospital.	
	23rd	06.45	Riding School for recruits and untrained men commenced.	HC
			2/Lieut. H. McE. B. Bramwell proceeded on leave to the United Kingdom.	
	24th		2/Lieut. R.L. Agnew proceeded on leave to the United Kingdom.	HC
			Lieut. D.P. Tenfant, M.C. rejoined from leave in France.	
			1 other rank rejoined from Course at P+R.T. School, RIEHL.	
	25th		34 other ranks joined from U.K. as reinforcements.	HC
			60 other ranks of 150th Labour Coy. joined for duty and taken on attached strength.	

WAR DIARY
or
INTELLIGENCE SUMMARY.
(Erase heading not required.)

Army Form C. 2118.

VOL. L.

From 1.6.19.
To 30.6.19.
15th "The Kings" Hussars.

Place	Date	Hour	Summary of Events and Information	Remarks and references to Appendices
KERPEN	26th		2/Lieut. J.H.C. Wilson proceeded on leave to the United Kingdom.	MC
-	27th		50 other ranks of 30th Labour Coy. joined for duty and taken on attached strength. 1 other rank admitted to hospital. 1 other rank rejoined from hospital.	MC
-	28th		Captain R.H.O. Hanbury, M.C. proceeded on leave to the United Kingdom	MC
-	-	10.00	All horses of the Regiment (except those out at grass) were paraded in watering order in the Square, KERPEN for checking. 1 other rank admitted to hospital. 1 Riding Horse (attd. M.T. Coy. Cav. Div.) having died, is struck off strength.	MC
-	29th			
-	30th	11.00	A Board of Officers, as under, assembled at "B" Sqdn Forge to examine 1 other rank as to his fitness for Appointment of Shoeing Smith :- Major Hon. F.H. Nicolson, M.C. Captain C.H. Shaw. Captain W.A. Dickerson, R.A.V.C.	MC

Army Form C. 2118.

WAR DIARY
or
INTELLIGENCE SUMMARY.
(Erase heading not required.)

VOL. L. From 1.6.19.
To 30.6.19.
15th The Kings - Hussars.

Summary of Training for Month of June 1919.

Times of Training	Days on which Training is carried out	Nature of Training	Place of Training
06.45 to 08.00	Daily (except Sundays)	Riding School for Recruits.	Field half-way between KERPEN and SCHLOSS LORSFELD.
10.00 to 11.00	Daily (except Sats. & Sunday)	Foot Drill for Recruits.	The Square, KERPEN.

Herbert Combes Lieut. Colonel.
Comdg. 15th The Kings - Hussars.

WAR DIARY
or
INTELLIGENCE SUMMARY

Army Form C. 2118.

VOL. L. From 1.6.19. To 30.6.19. 15th The King's Hussars

(Erase heading not required.)

Summary of Events and Information

Summary of Casualties during June 1919.

INCREASE.	Offrs.	O.R.	Horses Rdg.	L.D.	Pack.		DECREASE.	Offrs.	O.R.	Horses Rdg.	L.D.	Pack.
From Hospital	-	9	-	-	-		To Hospital	-	10	-	-	-
Northumberland Hrs.	-	3	-	-	-		United Kingdom for demob.	1	2	-	-	-
United Kingdom (taken on)	-	94	-	-	-		Hussar Brigade (absorbed in establishment.)	1	1	2	-	-
H.Q. Cav. Div. (absorbed)	-	4	6	1	-		United Kingdom (Transfer to Home establishment)	-	1	-	-	-
M.V.S.	-	-	-	-	-		Provost Marshall's Branch. PARIS.	1	-	-	-	-
							H.Q. Cav. Div. (absorbed in establishment.)	-	1	1	-	-
							1st Signal Sqdn.	-	-	1	-	-
							M.T. Egy. Cav. Div.	-	-	1	-	-
							M.V.S.	-	-	14	2	-
TOTALS.	-	110	6	1	-		TOTALS.	3	15	18	2	-

	Officers.	Other Ranks.	Riding	Lt.Drft.	Pack.
Present Strength of Regiment :-	30	369	415	61	24
Attached	3	236	10	-	-
TOTALS	33	605	425	61	24

Remarks and references to Appendices:

T. Mincofser Brig: for Lieut: Col:
Leury 15" The King's Hussars

CONFIDENTIAL.
****

WAR DIARY

OF

15TH "THE KING'S" HUSSARS.

FOR

JULY, 1919.

VOLUME LI.

WAR DIARY *or* **INTELLIGENCE SUMMARY.**

Army Form C. 2118.

VOL LI. From 1.7.19. To 31.7.19. 15th "The Kings' Hussars.

Place	Date	Hour	Summary of Events and Information	Remarks and references to Appendices
KERPEN	1st		Personnel of Hussar Bde Mobile Striking Force rejoined Regiment.	
—	—		Lt. H. Jackson, D.C.M. proceeded on leave to the U.K.	AL
—	—		Capt. Rev. L.W. Wright, C.of.E. Chaplain and 1 other rank taken on attached strength. 1 other rank to the U.K. for demobilization.	
—	2nd		Lt. Col. H. Combe, D.S.O. proceeded on leave to the U.K.	HL
—	—		Lt. Q.P. Tennant, M.C. proceeded to the U.K. for demobilization.	HL
—	3rd		Capt. C.H. Shaw was Member of F.G.C.M. at H.Q. 1st Field Sqdn. at 10.30 hrs.	HL
—	4th		3 Rdg. horses evacuated to MVS. 1 other rank admitted to hospital.	HL
—	5th		Capt. C.T. Liddell proceeded on leave to the U.K.	HL
—	—		Lt. V.C.J. Bradshaw proceeded to the U.K. for demobilization.	
—	6th	16.00	Divine Service for C.of.E. in Y.M.C.A. Hut, KERPEN. The following paraded in the Square at 09.45 hrs :— 2 Offrs., 1 Sgt., 32 other ranks per Sqdn. 1 Officer, 1 Sgt., 20 other ranks of H.Q. Band as a Band. Major Hon. F.A. Nicolson, M.C. commanded the parade.	HL

Army Form C. 2118.

WAR DIARY
OR
INTELLIGENCE SUMMARY.

From 1.7.19
To 31.7.19.
VOL. LI
15th "The King's" Hussars

(Erase heading not required.)

Place	Date	Hour	Summary of Events and Information	Remarks and references to Appendices
KERPEN	7th.		5 other ranks of the Regt. proceeded to COLOGNE en route to PARIS to partake in "Victory March".	H.C.
—	8th.		Capt. R.H.C. Hanbury H.C. and 2/Lt. T.J. Arnott rejoined from leave to the U.K. 2/Lt. T.J. Myrick rejoined from leave to the U.K.	H.C.
—	9th.		Capt. J.H. Kellett, R.A.V.C. struck off attached strength of Regt. Detachment 1/5th Gordon Highlanders (1 officer, 100 other ranks) proceeds to rejoin their Battalion.	H.C.
—	10th.		Lieut. J.A.T. Dalgety proceeded on leave to the U.K. Lieut. R.H.E. Abdy proceeded on leave to the U.K. 1 other rank joined on transfer from Inniskilling Dragoons. 1 other rank admitted to hospital. 1 other rank rejoined from hospital.	H.C.
—	11th.		IV Corps Commander visited the Regt. and inspected training of recruits on the square, KERPEN. Lt. H.C. Witsey : 2/Lt. J.H.C. Wilson and R.L. Agnew rejoined from leave to the United Kingdom. 1 other rank admitted to hospital.	H.C.

Army Form C. 2118.

WAR DIARY
or
INTELLIGENCE SUMMARY.
(Erase heading not required.)

VOL. LI

From 1.7.19
To 31.7.19.
15th "The King's" Hussars

Instructions regarding War Diaries and Intelligence Summaries are contained in F. S. Regs., Part II. and the Staff Manual respectively. Title pages will be prepared in manuscript.

Place	Date	Hour	Summary of Events and Information	Remarks and references to Appendices
KERPEN	12th		2/Lt. L. T. Pegrum proceeded on leave to the U.K. 2/Lt. H. McC. B. Bramwell rejoined from leave to the U.K. 30 other ranks proceeded to attend Course at Army Gym and Commercial College, COLOGNE. 1 other rank to Course at Army School of Musketry, DREVE.	H.Q.
—	13th	09.00	Divine service for Nonconformists in Y.M.C.A. Hall, KERPEN. 6 other ranks per S.Q.M.S. attended.	
		10.00	Parade service for C.O.E. in Y.M.C.A. Hall, KERPEN. The following attended and paraded on the Square at 09.45 hrs:— Band as a Band. 1 Officer, 13 other ranks per Sqn. 1 Officer, 13 other ranks of H.Q.	H.Q.
—	15th		Capt. R.H.O. Danbury, M.C. commanded the parade. Capt. H.J. Brace, D.S.O., M.C. rejoined from leave to the U.K. 2 other ranks proceeded to the U.K. on re-posting to their former Regts. and are struck off the strength.	H.Q.
—	16th		D/Sjt. Jordison, D.C.M. rejoined from leave to the U.K.	H.Q.

Army Form C. 2118.

WAR DIARY
or
INTELLIGENCE SUMMARY.
(Erase heading not required.)

VOL. LI

From 1.7.19.
To 31.7.19.

15th The King's Hussars

Place	Date	Hour	Summary of Events and Information	Remarks and references to Appendices
KERPEN	16th (contd)		1 other rank joined from III Corps Animal Collecting Camp and taken on the strength.	HQ
—	17th		Lt. Col. H. Crouch, D.S.O. returned from leave to the U.K.	HQ
			Lt. H.S.V. Tufton joined from the U.K. and taken on strength	
			1 other rank returned from hospital.	
—	18th		2 other ranks to course at School of Cookery, COLOGNE.	HQ
			1 other rank admitted to hospital.	
—	19th	09.30	Horses as detailed were paraded on the square for malleining	HQ
			1 other rank to course at School of Cookery, COLOGNE.	
		14.00	Regimental Sports were held at SCHLOSS LORSFELD.	
—	20th	10.00	Parade service for C.of.E. in Y.M.C.A. Hall, KERPEN. The following attended and paraded on the square at 09.45 hrs.	HQ
			Band as a Band.	
			1 Officer, 13 other ranks per Sqdn.	
			1 Officer, 13 other ranks of H.Q.	
			Capt. H.T. Brace, D.S.O., M.C. commanded the parade.	

Army Form C. 2118.

WAR DIARY
or
INTELLIGENCE SUMMARY.
(Erase heading not required.)

From 1.7.19
To 31.7.19
15th "The Kings" Hussars

Place	Date	Hour	Summary of Events and Information	Remarks and references to Appendices
KERPEN	20th (cont)		Lt. L.J.G. Loncton, M.C. proceeded on leave to the U.K.	M.C.
			1 other rank admitted to hospital.	
			2 Rdg. Horses evacuated to M.V.S.	
-	21st	0.9.40	All horses of the Regt. were paraded on the square for malleining.	M.C.
			1 other rank (Army Gym. Staff) joined for duty.	
			1 L.t. Orks Horse rejoined from M.V.S.	
-	22nd		Lt. Col. H. Conte, D.S.O. proceeded on special leave to the U.K.	M.C.
			1 other rank joined from 19th Hussars and taken on strength	
			1 other rank (R.A.S.C. attached) proceeded to the U.K. for demobilization	
-	23rd	11.40	Lecture by Command Paymaster in M.T. by Recreation Hall, HORREM.	M.C.
			Subject:- "The Pay & Mess Book". The following attended :-	
			Adjutant, 2nd/Lt Sgans. Q.M., R.Q.M.S., S.Q.M.Ss. and 2 Orderly Room Clerks.	
			40 other ranks of 30th Labour Coy. joined and taken on attached strength.	
			Capt. C.H. Liddell rejoined from leave to the U.K.	
			1 other rank admitted to hospital. 1 other rank rejoined from hospital.	
			1 Rdg. horse evacuated to M.V.S.	

WAR DIARY or INTELLIGENCE SUMMARY

Army Form C. 2118.

VOL. LI

From 1.7.19
To 31.7.19

15th "The King's" Hussars

Place	Date	Hour	Summary of Events and Information	Remarks and references to Appendices
KERPEN	24th		1 other rank to H.Q. Cavalry Division as orderly to the G.O.C.	H.C.
"	25th		1 other rank to hospital	K.
"	"		1 Rfn. Lowe died and struck off strength.	
"	"		Lt. R. Snee proceeded on leave to the U.K.	H.C.
"	27th		2 Rfg. horses evacuated to M.V.S.	
"	"		Lt. L.A.F. Dalgety rejoined from leave to the U.K.	H.C.
"	"		1 other rank to course at P & R.T. School, RIEHL.	K.C.
"	28th	10.00	Commander-in-Chief, British Army of the Rhine, visited Regt.	
			H.Q. at SCHLOSS LORSFELD and Inspected training of the Regt.	H.C.
			as under :—	
			Recruits of 'A' Sqn at Riding School.	
			" " 'B' " Foot Drill.	
			" " 'C' " Physical Training.	
			N.C.O's at Sword Drill.	
			Lt. Col. H. Combe, D.S.O. rejoined from leave to the U.K.	
			Lt. B. L. Banks proceeded on leave to the U.K.	
			10 Rifn. horses rejoined from Advanced Remt. Section, COLOGNE.	

Army Form C. 2118.

WAR DIARY
or
INTELLIGENCE SUMMARY.
(Erase heading not required.)

From 1.7.19
To 31.7.19 "The Kings' Hussars"
15th

VOL. L1

Place	Date	Hour	Summary of Events and Information	Remarks and references to Appendices
KERPEN	29th	09.30	Educational Classes for N.C.O.'s commenced. 1 other rank joined from the U.K.	H.C.
—	30th	09.30	Classification of Horses of H.Q. and 'A' Sqn. by Veterinary Officer.	H.C.
—	—	09.30	Classification of Horses of 'B' and 'C' Sqns. by Veterinary Officer. Lieut. R.T. Pegrum rejoined from leave to the U.K. 1 other rank admitted to hospital. 1 Rdg. Horse received from Remt. Depot, COLOGNE.	H.C.
—	31st	10.00	The C.O. inspected all Officers' Chargers in watering order on the Square. Maj. Hon. F.A. Nicolson M.C. was President of a F.G.C.M. at H.Q., 1st Field Sqn. at 11.00 hrs. 1 other rank admitted to hospital. Lieut. F.A. Tilsley proceeded to the U.K. for demobilization. 5 Riding Horses received from M.V.S.	H.C.

Herbert Combe Lt Col.
Cmdg. 15th Hussars
1.8.19.

Army Form C. 2118.

WAR DIARY
or
INTELLIGENCE SUMMARY.

From 1.7.19
To 31.7.19

15th "The King's" Hussars

VOL. LI

(Erase heading not required.)

Summary of Training for Month of July 1919.

Times of Training	Days on which Training is carried out.	Nature of Training	Place of Training
06.45 to 08.00	Daily (except Sundays).	Riding School for Recruits.	SCHLOSS LÖRSFELD.
10.00 to 11.00	Daily (except Sats. & Sundays)	Foot Drill for Recruits.	The Square, KERPEN.

Herbert Combe Lt. Colonel.
Comdg. 15th "The King's" Hussars.

31.7.19.

Army Form C. 2118.

WAR DIARY
or
INTELLIGENCE SUMMARY.
(Erase heading not required.)

From 1.7.19 To 31.7.19 "15th "The Kings" Hussars."

VOL. LI

Instructions regarding War Diaries and Intelligence Summaries are contained in F.S. Regs., Part II. and the Staff Manual respectively. Title pages will be prepared in manuscript.

Place	Date	Hour	Summary of Events and Information	Remarks and references to Appendices
			Summary of Casualties during July 1919.	Activity Ente "15th The Kings" Hussars.

INCREASE.

	Offrs.	O.R.	Horses Rdg.	Horses L.D.	Horses Pack
From Hospital	-	4	-	-	-
Iniskilling Dragoons	-	1	-	-	-
III Corps Animal C.C.	-	1	-	-	-
United Kingdom	1	1	-	-	-
19th Hussars	-	1	5	1	-
M.V.S.	-	-	11	-	-
Adv. Remt. Sect. COLOGNE	-	-	-	-	-
	1	8	16	1	-

DECREASE.

	Offrs.	O.R.	Horses Rdg.	Horses L.D.	Horses Pack
To Demobilization	3	1	-	-	-
Hospital	-	10	-	-	-
M.K. on re-posting	-	2	-	-	-
M.V.S. (included 1 Rdg. died)	-	-	13	-	-
	3	13	13	-	-

	Officers	Other Ranks	Riding	L.Drht.	Pack
Present Strength of Regiment	29	365	419	60	25
Attached	1	152	13	-	-
TOTALS	30	517	432	60	25

CONFIDENTIAL.

WAR DIARY

OF

XVTH (THE KING'S) HUSSARS.

FOR

AUGUST, 1919.

VOLUME LII.

WAR DIARY or **INTELLIGENCE SUMMARY**

Army Form C. 2118.

VOL LII.

From 1.8.19. To 31.8.19.

XV*(The King's) Hussars*

Place	Date	Hour	Summary of Events and Information	Remarks and references to Appendices
KERPEN	1st.		1 other rank admitted to hospital.	HC
—	2nd		Lt. Sir A.K. Hoyd. Bt. proceeded on leave to the U.K. Lt. B.J.L. Banks rejoined from leave.	HC
—	3rd.			HC
—	4th.		1 other rank (M.T. R.A.S.C.) joined Regt. for attachment.	HC
—	5th.		Lt. A.B. Smith proceeded on leave to the U.K.	HC
—	6th.		11 other ranks joined from U.K. as reinforcements. 5 Rdg. horses received from IV Corps Heavy Artillery.	HC
—	7th.	09.30	Regt. ordered to find Composite Sqn. for review in COLOGNE. Composite Sqn. paraded in grazing field for practice. All horses of the Regt. were paraded on the square for re-classification by a Bde. Committee in the following order:- 'A' Sqn : 09.00 hours 'B' Sqn : 11.00 hours 'C' Sqn : 13.45 hours Sigs. & Transpt. : 15.30 hours. 1 other rank admitted to hospital.	HC

WAR DIARY or INTELLIGENCE SUMMARY

Army Form C. 2118.

VOL. LII

From 1.6.19.
To 31.8.19.

XVth (The King's) Hussars

Place	Date	Hour	Summary of Events and Information	Remarks and references to Appendices
KERPEN.	8th.		Capt. C.H. Liddell proceeded to No 3 Cavalry Depot, SCARBOROUGH, for duty.	WC
			Lt. R.R. Abty rejoined from leave.	
		10.00	Bde. Composite Regt. paraded for practice on Bde. Sports Ground.	
			6 other ranks proceeded to the U.K. for posting to 19th Hussars.	
			49 other ranks of 30th Labour Coy joined for attachment.	
-.-	9th.	08.30	Parade of Composite Sqdn. on the Square.	WC
			1 Reg. Horse evacuated to M.V.S.	
-.-	10th.		1 other rank rejoined from hospital.	WC
-.-	11th.	09.30	Parade of Composite Sqdn. for practice.	WC
			Lts. R. Knee and L.J.G. Souchon, M.C. rejoined from leave.	
			40 other ranks of 30th Labour Coy. proceeded to rejoin their unit.	
			1 other rank rejoined from Hospital.	
			1 Reg. Horse evacuated to M.V.S.	
-.-	12th.	09.30	Parade of Composite Sqdn. for practice.	WC
			Lt. A.C. Straker proceeded on leave to the U.K.	
			1 other rank to Course at School of Cookery, COLOGNE.	

Army Form C. 2118.

WAR DIARY
or
INTELLIGENCE SUMMARY.
(Erase heading not required.)

VOL. LII.

From 1.8.19.
To 31.8.19.

XVth. (The King's) Hussars

Instructions regarding War Diaries and Intelligence Summaries are contained in F. S. Regs., Part II. and the Staff Manual respectively. Title pages will be prepared in manuscript.

Place	Date	Hour	Summary of Events and Information	Remarks and references to Appendices
KERPEN	12th	(contd)	1 other rank to Course of Instruction in Sanitation at 9th San. Section.	A
—	—		2 Ridg. horses evacuated to M.V.S.	
—	13th		Capt. R.H.O. Stanbury, M.C. proceeded on leave to the U.K.	A
—	—		3 other ranks admitted to hospital.	
—	—		1 other rank of 30th Labour Coy. proceeded to rejoin his unit.	
—	—		1 Rdg. horse destroyed.	
—	14th		1 other rank rejoined from hospital.	A
—	15th	06.00	Composite Sqdn. under the command of Maj. Hon. H.A. Nicolson, M.C. paraded on the Square and marched to Artillery Barracks, COLOGNE, to take part in a review on 18th inst.	A
—	—	10.30	Capt. C.H. Shaw and Lt. R.H.L. Abby were members of a F.G.C.M. held at H.Q. "O" Battery, R.H.A.	
—	—	22.00	Information received that the Regt. would proceed to Ireland at an early date.	
—	—		2 other ranks admitted to hospital; 1 other rank rejoined from hospital.	

WAR DIARY or INTELLIGENCE SUMMARY

Army Form C. 2118.

Instructions regarding War Diaries and Intelligence Summaries are contained in F. S. Regs., Part II. and the Staff Manual respectively. Title pages will be prepared in manuscript.

VOL. LII.

From 1. 8. 19
To 31. 8. 19

XVth. (The King's) Hussars

(Erase heading not required.)

Place	Date	Hour	Summary of Events and Information	Remarks and references to Appendices
KERPEN	16th		1 other rank rejoined from hospital.	AC
—	17th			AC
—	18th	09.30	F.G.C.M. held in room next to Regtl. Canteen.	
			2 other ranks transferred to M.M.P.	AC
			15 'S' horses proceeded to Corps Animal Collecting Camp, for sale.	
			5 Rdg. horses rejoined from M.V.S.	
—	19th		Lt. Sir H.R.K. Floyd, Bt. rejoined from leave: Capporits again rejoined Regt.	AC
			Lt. L. J. Loncken, M.C. and 1 other rank admitted to hospital.	
			1 other rank proceeded to U.K. for demobilization.	
			1 other rank joined from H.Q. Hussar Bde.	
—	20th	10.30	Maj. Hon. J. A. Nicolson, M.C. was President of F.G.C.M. held in room next to Regtl. Canteen.	AC
			3 other ranks of 7th Bn. Middlesex Regt. transferred to 15th Hussars and taken on strength. 1 other rank rejoined from hospital.	
			Lt. A.B. Smith rejoined from leave.	
—	21st		1 other rank rejoined from hospital.	

Army Form C. 2118.

WAR DIARY
or
INTELLIGENCE SUMMARY.

(Erase heading not required.)

VOL LII.

From 1.8.19
To 31.8.19.

XV= (The King's) Hussars

Instructions regarding War Diaries and Intelligence Summaries are contained in F. S. Regs., Part II. and the Staff Manual respectively. Title pages will be prepared in manuscript.

Place	Date	Hour	Summary of Events and Information	Remarks and references to Appendices
KERPEN	22nd		1 other rank proceeded to the U.K. for demobilization.	AC
			1 Rdg. horse died. 1 Rdg. and 1 Lt. Drft. horse evacuated to M.V.S.	
-"-	23rd		Lt. B.L. Banks proceeded on leave to the U.K.	
			Capt. J.T.L. Grant, M.C. R.A.M.C. proceeded to 10th Hussars and struck off attached strength.	AC
			Capt. E.A.P. Martland, R.A.M.C. joined from 10th Hussars and taken on attached strength.	
			1 Rdg. horse evacuated to Remount Depot, COLOGNE.	AC
-"-	24th		Lt. S.P.L.A. Litgow proceeded on leave to the U.K.	
-"-	25th		Lt. J.V.S. Douglas proceeded on leave to the U.K.	AC
			1 other rank to Provost School, COLOGNE.	
			1 other rank rejoined from hospital.	AC
			1 Rdg. horse rejoined from M.V.S.	
-"-	26th		Lt. J. Haggas proceeded on leave to the U.K.	AC
			2 Rdg. horses rejoined from HQ Hussar Bde.	
			4 Rdg. horses evacuated to M.V.S.	

Army Form C. 2118.

WAR DIARY
or
INTELLIGENCE SUMMARY.

(Erase heading not required.)

VOL. LII. From 1.8.19
To 31.8.19

XVth. (The King's) Hussars.

Place	Date	Hour	Summary of Events and Information	Remarks and references to Appendices
KERPEN	27th		Maj. Hon. J.A. Nelson M.C., Lt. R.L. Iver and 2 other ranks proceeded to KILKENNY as advance party.	MC
—	28th		2/Lt. J.J. Arnett proceeded on leave to the U.K. Capt. A.F. Brace D.S.O., M.C. proceeded to the U.K. for duty at Cavalry School NETHERAVON. 2/Lt. H.McC.B. Bramwell proceeded on leave to the U.K.	
—	—	11.00	Court of Enquiry as under was held in room next to Regtl. Canteen. President :- Capt. C.H. Shaw. Member :- Lt. L.T. Pegrum. Lt. Sir H.R.K. Hoyle Bt. 2 other ranks of 14th at Divnl. Employment Coy. rejoined their Unit and struck off attached strength. 1 other rank rejoined from hospital.	MC
—	29th	09.00	Court of Enquiry, as under, was held in room next to Regtl. Canteen. President :- Capt. C.H. Shaw. Members :- Lt. J.A.J. Dalgety. 2/Lt. R.L. Agnew.	MC
		10.30	F.G.C.M. was held in room next to Regtl. Canteen. Lt. L.T. Pegrum and 7 other ranks proceeded with equipment (wagons etc) to entrain at DUREN en route to the U.K.	

Army Form C. 2118.

WAR DIARY or INTELLIGENCE SUMMARY

(Erase heading not required.)

VOL. LII.

From 1. 8. 19.
To 31. 8. 19.

XVth (The King's) Hussars

Place	Date	Hour	Summary of Events and Information	Remarks and references to Appendices
KERPEN	29th (Contd)		4 other ranks proceeded to the U.K. for demobilization. 1 other rank taken on strength from H.Q. II Corps. 7 Rdg. horses evacuated to M.V.S.	AC
—	30th		All horses of the Regt. were paraded in Watering Order on the Square for veterinary inspection, as under:— A Squadron :- 09.00 hrs. B Squadron :- 09.30 hrs. C Squadron :- 10.00 hrs. Sigs. + Transport :- 10.30 hrs. S.Q.M.S.'s attended lecture by Comd. Paymaster on Pay and Mess Books at M.T. Theatre, HORREM at 10.30 hours. Lt. F.J.G. Loudon, M.C. rejoined from hospital. 1 other rank rejoined from hospl. 5 N.C.O.s proceeded to KILKENNY as advance party. 1 other rank proceeded to join 3rd Hussars on re-posting. 1 other rank admitted to hospital. 1 other rank 30th Labour Coy. proceeded to join that unit and struck off attached strength.	AC

WAR DIARY or **INTELLIGENCE SUMMARY**

Army Form C. 2118.

From 1.8.19
To 31.8.19.
XVth (The King's) Hussars

VOL. LII.

Place	Date	Hour	Summary of Events and Information	Remarks and references to Appendices
KERPEN	30th		6 Rdy. horses were evacuated to 39th M.V.S.	A.C.
— .—	31st		1 other rank (servant) to Cavalry School, NETHERAVON	A.C.
			1 other rank proceeded to join advance party at KILKENNY.	
			1 other rank admitted to Hospital	
			Herbert Corbet Lt. Col.	
			Cmdg. 15th Hussars	31/8/19

WAR DIARY or INTELLIGENCE SUMMARY

Army Form C. 2118.

From 1.8.19
To 31.8.19

VOL LII.

XVth. (The King's) Hussars.

Remarks and references to Appendices

Place	Date	Hour	Summary of Events and Information	

Summary of Training for Month of August 1919.

Times of Training.	Days on which Training is carried out.	Nature of Training.	Place of Training.
06.45 to 08.00	Daily (except Sundays).	Riding School for Recruits.	SCHLOSS LORSFELD.
10.00 to 11.00	Daily (except Sats. & Sundays)	Foot Drill & Physical Training for Recruits.	The Square, KERPEN.

Training temporarily ceased from 16.8.19: Regt. received orders to proceed to IRELAND.

Herbert Combe. Lt. Colonel.
Comdg. XVth. (The King's) Hussars.

1.9.19.

Army Form C. 2118.

WAR DIARY *or* **INTELLIGENCE SUMMARY.**

VOL LII. From 1.8.19 To 31.8.19.

XVth (The King's) Hussars

Lt Colonel Herbert Gordon (Comdg.) 31.8.19.

Summary of Casualties during August 1919=

Increase	Offrs.	O.R.	Horses Rdg.	L.D.	P.	Decrease	Offrs.	O.R.	Horses Rdg.	L.D.	P.
From Hospital	1	7	.	.	.	To Hospital	1	9	.	.	.
United Kingdom	.	11	.	.	.	United Kingdom for duty	2	.	.	.	.
Hussar Bde.	.	1	2	.	.	U.K. for demobilization	.	6	.	.	.
7th Bn Nissex Regt (transfers)	.	3	.	.	.	U.K. for re-posting	.	6	.	.	.
H.Q. II Corps	.	1	.	.	.	3rd Hussars	.	1	.	.	.
IV Corps H. Artillery	.	.	5	.	.	M.M.P.	.	2	.	.	.
39th M.V.S.	.	.	6	.	.	Corps Animal Collecting Camp	.	.	15	.	.
.	.	.	.	.	.	39th M.V.S. (included 1 Rdg. Antwerpen) (1 Rdg. sick off)	.	.	24	1	.
.	.	.	.	.	.	Remt. Depot. COLOGNE.	.	1	.	.	.
	1	23	13	.	.		3	24	40	1	.

	Officers.	Other Ranks.	Riding	L. Draft.	Pack.
Present Strength of Regiment	28	399	379	59	25
Attached	1	176	14	.	.
TOTALS	29	575	393	59	25

BEF
CAV DIV
Hussar Bde

9 M.G. Sdn

1919 APR
To
1919 AUG

FROM 1 CAV DIV 9 BDE
BOX 1116

CONFIDENTIAL.

WAR DIARY

of

9th Machine Gun Squadron.

for

APRIL, 1919.

Volume. XXXIX.

Reserve HUSSARS M.G. SQ.

Confidential

Army Form C. 2118.

WAR DIARY
or
INTELLIGENCE SUMMARY.
(Erase heading not required.)

9th Machine Gun Squadron

Instructions regarding War Diaries and Intelligence Summaries are contained in F.S. Regs., Part II. and the Staff Manual respectively. Title pages will be prepared in manuscript.

Place	Date 1919 April	Hour	Summary of Events and Information	Remarks and references to Appendices
KASTER	1		In billets	Germany
"	2		In billets. 1 Rider destroyed. 2 Riders evacuated.	1 K.
"	3		In billets. N.C.O. inspected horses for casting. 24 O.R. to England for Demobilisation. 1 Charger taken on strength from Reven No. 13.	
"	4		In billets. 1 Officer & 34 O.R. 1/4 Gordon Highlanders attached to the Sqdn.	
"	5		In billets. C.O.C. Cavalry Divn. visited the Sqdn. at 14.30. Football match with 'D' Bty. R.H.A. Revel. 'D' Bty 5, 9th R.G.S. 1. Instructions received to move to new area on the 7th.	
"	6		In billets. Billeting party proceeded to new area. 20 Riders struck off the strength. A.D.V.S. inspected horses for casting. 30 O.Rs taken on strength from 5th M.G. Sqdn.	
"	7		The Brigade marched to an Area between Beuven & Cologne. Germany the Sqdn being billeted at Bleatzheim. 1 Rider accidentally killed.	1 L.
BLATZHEIM	8		In billets. Inspection of Class Z horses by A.D.V.S.	
"	9		In billets. 12 Riders & 2 Pack struck off. 45 O.Rs struck off. 8 O.Rs to W.R. for demobilisation.	
"	10		In billets.	
"	11		In billets.	
"	12		In billets. 1 O.R. to W.R. for demobilisation.	
"	13		In billets. Divine Service at 09.00 for Presbyterians, Wesleyans & Non Conformists.	

Confidential.   Army Form C. 2118.

WAR DIARY
or
INTELLIGENCE SUMMARY.
(Erase heading not required.)

9th Machine Gun Squadron   II

Place	Date 1919 April	Hour	Summary of Events and Information	Remarks and references to Appendices
Blatzheim	14		In billets. Brig. General D'A. Legard paid a farewell visit to the Sqdn. Yesterday. He presented medals to the remaining members of the Sqn. Football team. 2 Riders taken on strength.	Germany 1L.
"	15		In billets. 6 Riders & 1 Pack taken on strength.	
"	16		In billets.	
"	17		In billets. Cinema show in the Recreation Room at 19.30	
"	18		Good Friday. In billets. Service for Non-conformists, Wesleyans & Presbyterians at 10.30. 3 Riders & 1 mule struck off.	
"	19		In billets. 50 O.Rs. struck off. 1 Rider struck off.	
"	20		Easter Sunday. In billets. C. of E. service & Holy Communion at 18.30. 10 O.R., R.A.O.C. attached the Sqdn.	Nim
"	21		In billets.	
"	22		In billets.	
"	23		In billets. Personnel of 1/14 Londons reported their 'attalion.	
"	24		In billets. Health inspection by the Medical Officer at 14.00. Cinema show in Recreation Room at 18.30. 10 Off. & 40 O.Rs. of 52nd Gordon Highlanders attached to the Sqn. adv.on. 1 Rider taken on strength. 1 Rider destroyed. 10 R. taken on strength from 5th M.G. Sqdn. Lieut. B. Eade M.C. & 43 ORs struck off.	
"	25		In billets.	
"	26		In billets. General Sir Wm. Robertson, C. in C. visited the Squadron at 11.00.	

Confidential

WAR DIARY
or
INTELLIGENCE SUMMARY.
(Erase heading not required.)

9th Machine Gun Squadron

Army Form C. 2118.

III

Place	Date	Hour	Summary of Events and Information	Remarks and references to Appendices
Blakfurmany	1919 April 27		In billets.	Germany
"	28		In billets.	1L.
"	29		In billets. G.O.C. 9th near Brigade inspected the mobile force formed from the Brigade, west of Blankheim at 10.30 The Squadron turned out 2 complete sub-sections, 9 G.S. limbs.	
"	30		In billets. G.O.C. 9th near Brigade, made a tour round the sqdn at 11.30, inspecting billets, stores, shops etc.	

Strength of the Squadron.

	Officers	O.Rs.	Horses Rid.	L.D.	Pack
	10	123	177	71	40
Attached	1	42			

W Moncrieff
Major.
Commanding 9th Machine Gun Squadron.

Army Form C. 2118.

WAR DIARY
or
INTELLIGENCE SUMMARY.
(Erase heading not required.)

9th Machine Gun Squadron.

May, 1919

Volume 40.

Confidential

Army Form C. 2118.

WAR DIARY
or
INTELLIGENCE SUMMARY
(Erase heading not required.)

9th Machine Gun Squadron

Instructions regarding War Diaries and Intelligence Summaries are contained in F. S. Regs., Part II. and the Staff Manual respectively. Title pages will be prepared in manuscript.

Place	Date May	Hour	Summary of Events and Information	Remarks and references to Appendices
Belgium	1		In billets. Horse Inspection by A.D.V.S.	Germany
	2		In billets.	1 L.
	3		In billets. Cinema show at 18.30 in Recreation Room.	
	4		In billets. 8 O.R. struck off. 1 Rider struck off.	
	5		In billets. Started grazing proportion of horses daily. 3 Off. & 22 O.R. allowed a lecture at Herpen by the Matermal Smith. Kit inspection & boots inspection complete. & spurs.	
	6		In billets. 1 Rider struck off.	
	7		In billets. 45 Offs. & O.Rs. attended a performance by the Kirkos Theatrical Party at Herpen. 1 O.R. admitted hospital.	
	8		In billets. 4 O.R. struck off.	
	9		In billets. 25 men attended lecture at Herpen. 2 L.D. & 2 R.H. struck off.	
	10		In billets. Cinema show in evening. 10 Riders taken on strength.	
	11		In billets. 1 Hack struck off.	
	12		In billets. 1 O.R. rejoined from hospital. 1 O.R. struck off.	
	13		In billets. 1 O.R. admitted hospital.	
	14		In billets. 3 O.R. struck off.	
	15		In billets. 4 Riders & 2 L.D. struck off.	
	16		In billets. 1 L.D. struck off. Capt. H. P. Ancot struck off (transferred to Horse Depot Camp).	
	17		In billets. Cinema show in evening.	
	18		In billets. 6 of B. Service at 11.30.	
	19		In billets. 1 O.R. admitted hospital. 1 L.D. struck off.	

Army Form C. 2118.

WAR DIARY
or
INTELLIGENCE SUMMARY.
(Erase heading not required.)

9th Machine Gun Squadron

Place	Date	Hour	Summary of Events and Information	Remarks and references to Appendices
Blakhim	20		In billets. 2/Lt Weir proceeded to Dunecourt 4/6 Bn for duty as gas officer. 1 O.R. & 2 Horses attached. 1 Pack & 1 L.D. struck off.	1 L.
	21		In billets.	
	22		In billets. Health inspection by M.O.	
	23		In billets. 85 all ranks attended a very interesting lecture on Bolshevism at Howem	
	24		In billets. Cinema show in evening. 1 O.R. returned from hospital.	
	25		In billets.	
	26		In billets.	
	27		In billets. Mobile horse standing to at 2 hours notice. Evening 3 hours notice. 4 L.D. & 2 Riding struck off.	
	28		In billets. 1 O.R. admitted hospital.	
	29		In billets.	
	30		In billets. All officers attended a lecture on the war by Major Aycox given by a Sergeant from Army H.Q. also concert in evening by the "Snipes" Party. Eighty L.D. wagon.	
	31		In billets.	

Strength of the Squadron

	Officers	O.Rs.	Horses Rg	L.D.	Pack
	9	109	168	63	36
Attached	1	40			

J W Morrieff Major,
Commanding 9th Machine Gun Squadron

Confidential.

WAR DIARY
or
INTELLIGENCE SUMMARY. Hussar M.G. Squadron
(Erase heading not required.)

Army Form C. 2118.

June, 1919.

Volume number, 41.

Place	Date	Hour	Summary of Events and Information	Remarks and references to Appendices

Confidential

Army Form C. 2118.

WAR DIARY
INTELLIGENCE SUMMARY.
(Erase heading not required.)

Hussar Machine Gun Squadron

Place	Date	Hour	Summary of Events and Information	Remarks and references to Appendices
Bensberg	June 1919 1		In billets. Church of England Service in morning. Cinema performance in evening.	Germany
	2		In billets.	1L
	3		In billets.	
	4		In billets. The mobile section paraded in marching order & was inspected by the C.O. at 09.30.	
	5		In billets. Ride taken on the strength.	
	6		In billets.	
	7		In billets.	
	8		In billets. Cinema show in the evening.	
	9		In billets. Personnel of Mobile Force proceeded to KERPEN for gas test. S.S.M. Little awarded the M.S.M.	
	10		In billets.	
	11		In billets. O.C. Proceeded on leave to U.K.	
	12		In billets. Health Inspection by the M.O. at 14.00 hours.	
	13		In billets.	
	14		In billets.	
	15		In billets.	
	16		In billets.	
	17		In billets. Orders received at 04.00 hours for Mobile Force to concentrate at Brigade rendezvous at 12.00 to-day. Moved off at 11.00. Lieut. W.M. Forbes 2/Lieut. W.B. Shook M.M. 54 O.R. and 47 horses detached with Mobile Force.	

Confidential.

Army Form C. 2118.

WAR DIARY
INTELLIGENCE SUMMARY.
(Erase heading not required.) Hussar Machine Gun Squadron

II.

Instructions regarding War Diaries and Intelligence Summaries are contained in F. S. Regs., Part II. and the Staff Manual respectively. Title pages will be prepared in manuscript.

Place	Date	Hour	Summary of Events and Information	Remarks and references to Appendices
Blatzheim	June 1919 18		In billets. 1 O.R. struck off strength. Lieut. G. E. Booth taken on the strength from 9th M. G. Squadron. 1 Raw & 1 L.D. taken on strength.	Germany 1 L.
	19		In billets. Health Inspection by M.O. at 14.00 hours.	
	20		In billets. Cinema show in evening.	
	21		In billets. G.O.C. Cavalry Division visited the Squadron at 11.30 & made a tour round the village, inspecting stables, mess Rooms etc.	
	22		In billets.	
	23		In billets.	
	24		In billets.	
	25		In billets. 1 O.R. struck off the strength.	
	26		In billets. Health Inspection by M.O. at 14.00 hours. O.C. 11th M.G. Sqdn. Designated	
	27		In billets. 50 O.Rs. of 30th Labour Coy. attached to the Sqdn. changed from 9th M.G. Sqdn. to Hussar M.G. Squadron.	
	28		In billets. 9 O.Rs. of 52nd Londons arrived from Hussar Brigade H.Q. 10 O.Rs. of 30th Labour Coy. posted to Hussar Brigade H.Q. Official message received at 20.15 hours that "Peace is signed".	
	29		In billets.	
	30		In billets.	

Strength of the Squadron.

	Officers	O.Rs.	Horses Rid.	L.D.	Pack.
	9	105	172	68	35
Attached	1	86			

M. Morvey, Major
Commanding Hussar M. G. Squadron.

Confidential.

Army Form C. 2118.

WAR DIARY
or
INTELLIGENCE SUMMARY.

(Erase heading not required.)

Hussar M.G. Squadron.

July 1919

Volume No. 42

Instructions regarding War Diaries and Intelligence Summaries are contained in F. S. Regs., Part II. and the Staff Manual respectively. Title pages will be prepared in manuscript.

Place	Date	Hour	Summary of Events and Information	Remarks and references to Appendices

Confidential

Army Form C. 2118.

WAR DIARY
or
INTELLIGENCE SUMMARY.
(Erase heading not required.)

Instructions regarding War Diaries and Intelligence Summaries are contained in F. S. Regs., Part II. and the Staff Manual respectively. Title pages will be prepared in manuscript.

Hussar Machine Gun Squadron

Place	Date July	Hour	Summary of Events and Information	Remarks and references to Appendices
BLATZHEIM	1		In billets. 1 Rider struck off.	Germany
	2		In billets. Health inspection at 14:00.	1L
	3		In billets. Cinema shows in evening.	
	4		In billets.	
	5		In billets.	
	6		In billets. 1 Officer & 24 O.Rs attended a Thanksgiving Service at KERPEN at 10.00.	
	7		In billets. 60 Indian Dyees arrived. 10 being sent to Brigade H.2.	
	8		In billets. 1 O.R. to England for Demob.	
	9		In billets. Personnel of 52nd Gordon Highlrs rejoined their Btn.	
	10		In billets. 20 O.Rs went by lorry to Cologne Races.	
	11		In billets. 1st Corps Commander paid a visit to the Sqdn. A.D.V.S. inspected horses at 11.30. Health Inspection at 14.00. Cinema Shows at 18.00.	
	12		In billets. 25 O.Rs. went to Cologne Races by lorry.	
	13		In billets. C. of E. Service at 11.30. 1 O.R. to M.G. School, DROVE for course of Instruction.	
	14		In billets.	
	15		In billets.	
	16		In billets. Squadron mounted & Dismounted Sports Meeting in afternoon & evening.	
	17		In billets.	

Confidential.

Army Form C. 2118.

WAR DIARY
or
INTELLIGENCE SUMMARY
(Erase heading not required.)

Hussar Machine Gun Squadron

Instructions regarding War Diaries and Intelligence Summaries are contained in F. S. Regs., Part II. and the Staff Manual respectively. Title pages will be prepared in manuscript.

Place	Date July	Hour	Summary of Events and Information	Remarks and references to Appendices
BLATZHEIM	18		In billets. Health Inspection at 14.00. Cinema Show in evening.	Germany
	19		In billets. Performance by Waspo "Concert" Party at 20.00.	
	20		In billets. Lieut. G. E. Booth rejoined from hospital.	
	21		In billets.	
	22		In billets. 4 Indian syces proceeded to Divisional H. Qrs. 2 Riders struck off.	14.
	23		In billets.	
	24		In billets.	
	25		In billets. Health Inspection 14.00. Cinema films 18.00. 1 O.R. rejoined.	
	26		In billets. Performance by "Prongs" Concert Party at 19.30.	
	27		In billets. 1 O.R. taken on strength. 1 Rider struck off. R. B. Horses	
			in 15 to form Church. 6 Riders & 9 L.D. struck off	
	28		In billets	
	29		In billets. Part of men taking part in a ceremony by Division Horses &	
			spurs proceeded to Cologne to be attached to Lancer M. G. Sqdn.	
	30		1 O.R. taken on. 4 Riders & 9 L.D. taken on and 1 L.D. struck off.	
	31		In billets. Remainder of Chen's party proceeded to Lancer M.G.	

Strength of the Squadron.

	Officers	O.Rs.	Mlg.	L.D.	Horses	Pack.
	9	105	65	66		35
Attached		141				
11 Indian syces		46				

[signature] Major
COMMANDING HUSSAR M. G. SQUADRON.

Confidential

Army Form C. 2118.

WAR DIARY
or
INTELLIGENCE SUMMARY.

(Erase heading not required.) Hussar M.G. Sqdn

IF.

August, 1919.

Volume No. 43

Instructions regarding War Diaries and Intelligence Summaries are contained in F. S. Regs., Part II. and the Staff Manual respectively. Title pages will be prepared in manuscript.

Place	Date	Hour	Summary of Events and Information	Remarks and references to Appendices

Confidential.

Army Form C. 2118.

WAR DIARY
or
INTELLIGENCE SUMMARY.
(Erase heading not required.)

Instructions regarding War Diaries and Intelligence Summaries are contained in F. S. Regs., Part II. and the Staff Manual respectively. Title pages will be prepared in manuscript.

Army Form C. 2118.

Place	Date	Hour	Summary of Events and Information	Remarks and references to Appendices
Blabberinany	Aug 1		In billets. 100 men of the Squadron spent the day in Cologne at the Cavalry Division Shows	Husser Machine Gun Squadron spent the day in Cologne at Germany
	2		In billets. 100 men to Cologne for Cav. Div. Shows.	I.L.
	3		In billets.	
	4		In billets. 80 men to Cav. Div Shows at Cologne	
	5		In billets. 100 " " " "	
	6		In billets. Lieut J.E. Booth admitted hospital	
	7		In billets.	
	8		In billets. 2 ORanks to D.A.R.M. Gas Drum for Police duty	
	9		In billets. All horses inspected by Claim fication committee	
		09.45 to 13.30		
	10		In billets.	
	11		In billets. 2 Rates returned from Div. H.Qrs.	
	12		In billets.	
	13		In billets.	
	14		In billets. Cinema Performance in evening.	
	15		In billets. Health Inspection by M.O.	
	16		In billets.	
	17		In billets.	
	18		In billets. 60 O.R. went by lorry to Army Horse Show at Cologne.	
	19		In billets. 80 ORs. to Horse Show at Cologne. Lieut J.E. Booth rejoined from Hospital. 2 Rates taken on strength.	
	20		In billets.	

Confidential

Army Form C. 2118.

WAR DIARY
or
INTELLIGENCE SUMMARY.
(Erase heading not required.) Hussar Machine Gun Squadron

Instructions regarding War Diaries and Intelligence Summaries are contained in F. S. Regs., Part II. and the Staff Manual respectively. Title pages will be prepared in manuscript.

Place	Date	Hour	Summary of Events and Information	Remarks and references to Appendices
Malplaquet	Aug.21		In billets. Cinema Performance in evening	Germany
	22		In billets. 14 O.R. to W.K. for Demob. Leave by Major Spencer Johnson on rear hunting. 30 O.Rs taken on a length.	16
	23		In billets.	
	24		In billets.	
	25		In billets. Squadron parade – dismounted machine gun inspected by C.O. at 14.45.	
	26		In billets. 15 L.D. and 3 Pack struck off.	
	27		In billets. 9 Riders	
	28		In billets. 1 O.R. to W.K. for demobilization.	
	29		In billets. "Equipment and reward of the Squadron entrained at DUREN at 11.30. Lieut a Bailey in charge.	
	30		In billets. 98 of the Labour Coy personnel attached proceeded to Morcam for duty with Animal Collecting Camp. 63 O.Rs. of R.F.A. attached from C.R.H.A. to help move horses to W.K.	

Strength of the Squadron.

	Officers	O.Rs	Indians	Horses	R	P
	8	118	63	Horses	143	43
Attached.			45		53	

J.M. Morency Major
COMMANDING HUSSAR M. G. SQUADRON

BEF
Cav. Div
Lancer Bde H.Q

1919 APR to 1919 SEPT

CONFIDENTIAL.

WAR DIARY

"LANCER" BRIGADE HEADQUARTERS.

for the month of

APRIL 1919.

VOLUME LVII.

Army Form C. 2118.

WAR DIARY
or
INTELLIGENCE SUMMARY
(Erase heading not required.)

Instructions regarding War Diaries and Intelligence Summaries are contained in F.S. Regs., Part II. and the Staff Manual respectively. Title pages will be prepared in manuscript.

Place	Date	Hour	Summary of Events and Information	Remarks and references to Appendices
COLOGNE.	APRIL 1919 1st.	p.m.	About 200 men from the Brigade proceeded by Boat from COLOGNE for demobilization. Fine, sunny weather.	
"	2nd.	p.m.	The Brigadier proceeded to Divisional H.Q. to see the Divisional Commander. At 12.00 hours 2nd. Cavalry Brigade became the "LANCER BRIGADE".	
"	3rd.	p.m.	Following infantry companies were attached to Regiments to assist in grooming :- 9th. Lancers. Offrs. 4 O.Rs. 134 12th. Lancers. " 2 " 114 17th. Lancers. " 2 " 100 These Companies all come from LIGHT DIVISION and will be of great assistance. The situation as regards grooms on April 1st. is shown in Appendix I.	
"	4th.	p.m.	The Divisional Commander visited the 3 Regiments, M.G. Squadron and Batteries. 9th. Lancers warned that they might have to move to ETZWEILER.	
"	5th.	p.m.	Brig-General N. HAIG, future Commander of the Brigade paid a visit to COLOGNE.	
"	6th.	p.m.	30 "Z" Horses were sent to Animal Collecting Camp at DEUTZ. Leave for other ranks in this Brigade re-opened at the rate of 3 per diem.	
"	7th.	p.m.	All Horse Accounts of Units inspected by Major MICHOLLS, 17th. Lancers. This inspection has been ordered weekly.	
"	8th.	p.m.	Brigadier visited X Corps. Notification of following appointments received :- Brig-General N. HAIG / C.B., C.M.G. / to Command LANCER Brigade. Captain C.A. HEYDEMAN, M.C. 2nd. Dragoon Guards to be Brigade Major. Lieut. (T/Capt.) H. GORING, 3rd. Hussars to be Staff Captain.	
"	9th.	p.m.	The Divisional Commander inspected the 1st. M.V.S. and 3rd. C.F.A.	

Army Form C. 2118.

WAR DIARY
or
INTELLIGENCE SUMMARY.
(Erase heading not required.)

Instructions regarding War Diaries and Intelligence Summaries are contained in F. S. Regs., Part II. and the Staff Manual respectively. Title pages will be prepared in manuscript.

Place	Date	Hour	Summary of Events and Information	Remarks and references to Appendices
COLOGNE.	APRIL 10th.		Horse Accounts inspected by Major MICHOLLS, 17th. Lancers.	
"	11th.		General GODLEY Commanding IV Corps, under which Corps, Cavalry Division now is, visited Regiments, Batteries, and Machine Gun Squadron in COLOGNE.	
"	12th.		Notification of formation of 5th. Brigade R.H.A. received, viz "E", "G" and "O" Batteries under Command of Lieut-Colonel WEST. "H" Battery to waste to Cadre.	
"	13th.		52 Horses selected from "H" Battery for transfer to other Units of the Brigade, to complete establishment.	
"	15th.		Lieut-Colonel MELVILL. D.S.O., 17th. Lancers proceeded on leave.	
"	17th.		Information received that 9th. Lancers would move next week to EXHIBITION GROUND West of the HOHENZOLLERN BRIDGE.	
"	19th.		Orders received from the Division that in the event of a Mobile Force being required, Each Brigade would find an Composite Regiment about 220 strong plus 1 Section M.G. Squadron and 1 Section R.H.A.	
"	20th.		"H" Battery R.H.A. having reverted to Cadre, left the Brigade and moved to ICHENDORF with a view to subsequent transfer to ENGLAND.	
"	21st.		70 Horses received by 17th. Lancers from Remount Department. 29 of these for "HUSSAR" Brigade, remainder distributed to Units of this Brigade.	
"	22nd.		Advanced party of 9th. Lancers now in "WHITE CITY" but elements of "REMOUNTS" and Animal Collecting Camp still in occupation. Division asked to move them.	
"	23rd.		Captain H. GORING, Special Reserve, 3rd. Hussars joined Brigade as Staff Captain. "WHITE CITY" now clear of Remount Personnel and work progressing satisfactorily.	
"	26th.		9th. Lancers arrived in "WHITE CITY". Capt. F.W. WILSON-FITZGERALD. D.S.O., M.C., rejoined the Royal Dragoons. Captain D.V. CREAGH. M.C., took over duties of Brigade Major.	

Army Form C. 2118.

WAR DIARY
or
INTELLIGENCE SUMMARY.

(Erase heading not required.)

Instructions regarding War Diaries and Intelligence Summaries are contained in F. S. Regs., Part II. and the Staff Manual respectively. Title pages will be prepared in manuscript.

Place	Date	Hour	Summary of Events and Information	Remarks and references to Appendices
COLOGNE.	APRIL 30th.		Brig-General NEIL HAIG, C.B., C.M.G., took over Command of "LANCER" Brigade.	
			(signature) Captain, for G.O.C., Lancer Brigade.	

APPENDIX I

GROOMING STATE 2nd. CAVALRY BRIGADE - APRIL 1st. 1919.

Unit.	Animals.	Grooms.	Non-grooms.	Horses to grooms.	Horses to men.	Total ration strength O.R's.
9th. Lancers.	349	107	51	3.3	2.2	158
12th. Lancers.	597	99	87	6.5	3.2	186
17th. Lancers.	596	69	68	8.6	4.3	137
2nd. M.G.Sqdn.	261	112*	38	2.3	1.9	150

Bands are included in grooming strength of 9th. Lancers, but are shewn as not grooming in 12th. Lancers and 17th. Lancers. - Strength as follows :- 9th. Lancers 30, 12th. Lancers 25, 17th. Lancers 35.

* Includes 30 men still due for demobilization.

APPENDIX "A" attached to Lancer Brigade War Diary for the month of APRIL, 1919.

Strength of Units of the Brigade.

	31.3.19.		30.4.19.	
	Offrs.	O.Rs.	Offrs.	O.Rs.
Brigade H.Q.	2	38	6	37
2nd. Signal Troop.	1	29	1	22
9th. Lancers.	19	267	28	162
12th. Lancers.	24	180	17	154
17th. Lancers.	29	218	21	143
"G" Battery R.H.A.			5	158
2nd. M.G. Squadron.	9	117	6	124
3rd. C.F.A	5	83	3	78
1st. M.V.S.	3	29	2	24

CONFIDENTIAL

WAR DIARY

"LANCER" BRIGADE HEADQUARTERS.

for the month of

MAY 1919

VOLUME LVIII.

Army Form C. 2118.

WAR DIARY
INTELLIGENCE SUMMARY
(Erase heading not required.)

Instructions regarding War Diaries and Intelligence Summaries are contained in F. S. Regs., Part II. and the Staff Manual respectively. Title pages will be prepared in manuscript.

Place	Date	Hour	Summary of Events and Information	Remarks and references to Appendices
COLOGNE.	1919 MAY.			
	1st.		1 Squadron 12th. Lancers and 1 Squadron 17th. Lancers stood too from reveille in case mounted troops were required to operate against "May Day" demonstrations. They were not required and stood down at 19.45 hours.	
	2nd.		Notification received that the Commander in Chief would inspect the interior economy of 12th. Lancers and "G" Battery R.H.A. One Squadron 9th. Lancers placed at the disposal of 6th. Corps for Ceremonial purpose till May 8th.	
	3rd.		Commander in Chief inspected 12th. Lancers and "G" Battery R.H.A.	
	4th.		"G" Battery R.H.A. and 1 Squadron 9th. Lancers placed at disposal of NORTHERN Division till May 8th. for Ceremonial purposes.	
	7th.		Conference on Commanding Officers' at brigade Headquarters, agenda attached.	APP. I.
	8th.		brigade Major on leave 21 days. H.R.H. DUKE OF CONNAUGHT reviewed NORTHERN Division including 1 Squadron 9th. Lancers in morning and in the afternoon visited 17th. Lancer Barracks	
	9th. 10th. 11th.		Nothing to record.	
	12th.		G.O.C. and Staff Captain visited 9th. Lancers barracks and stables.	
	13th.		G.O.C. visited 3rd. Cavalry Field Ambulance.	
	14th.		G.O.C. visited barracks and stables of 17th. Lancers. Staff Captain attended conference at "Q".	
	15th.		G.O.C. and Staff Captain visited barracks and stables of 12th. Lancers.	

Army Form C. 2118.

WAR DIARY
or
INTELLIGENCE SUMMARY.
(Erase heading not required.)

Instructions regarding War Diaries and Intelligence Summaries are contained in F. S. Regs., Part II. and the Staff Manual respectively. Title pages will be prepared in manuscript.

Place	Date	Hour	Summary of Events and Information	Remarks and references to Appendices
COLOGNE.	1919. May			
"	16th.		Divisional Commander and Brigadier visited 9th. and 12th. Lancers. Board of Officers reconnoitred some land selected by Brigadier-General with a view to turning out 300 horses.	
"	17th.		G.O.C. and Staff Captain visited 2nd. Machine Gun Squadron.	
"	18th.		Nothing to record.	
"	19th.		G.O.C. and Staff Captain visited stables and barracks of 2nd. Machine Gun Squadron.	
"	20th.		Conference of Adjutants and Quartermasters at Brigade Office. Notification from VIth Corps that 2 hours notice for Mobile Squadron no longer required, but would remain available. Leave allotment reduced to one vacancy per day per brigade as a temporary measure owing to uncertainty whether Germans will sign Peace Terms.	
"	21st.		Divisional Commander and Brigadier visited 3rd. Cavalry Field Ambulance, 17th. Lancers and 2nd. Machine Gun Squadron barracks and stables.	
"	22nd.		Staff Captain attended conference at VI Corps on operations to be undertaken should the Army advance.	
"	23rd.		Orders issued to Units amending composition of Mobile Force, in accordance with VI Corps orders to Cavalry Division.	
"	24th. 25th.		Nothing to record.	

Army Form C. 2118.

WAR DIARY
INTELLIGENCE SUMMARY
(Erase heading not required.)

Instructions regarding War Diaries and Intelligence Summaries are contained in F. S. Regs., Part II. and the Staff Manual respectively. Title pages will be prepared in manuscript.

Place	Date	Hour	Summary of Events and Information	Remarks and references to Appendices
COLOGNE.	1919 May			
	26th.		Orders received that Lt-Col FANE. 12th Lancers would Command the Composite Regiment in the event of the Army advancing, and not a C.O. found by Dragoon Brigade as originally arranged. Also Col. FANE to Command the Brigade during the absence of Brig-General. HAIG, 10 days sick leave. Lancer Squadron to come under orders of G.O.C. Northern Division on J-3 day instead of J-2 day.	
	27th.		Divisional Commander held Conference of O.Cs. and Squadron Leaders, "G" Battery Commander and O.C. 2nd M.G. Sqdn at 17th Lancers Barracks. Various internal economy questions discussed-training of recruits, musketry, equitation. VIth Corps ordered Troops to be confined to Barracks owing to strikes and disturbances in Cologne, but restrictions removed again in evening.	
	28th.		Nothing to record.	
	29th.		G.O.C. VIth Corps visited barracks of 12th Lancers, "G" Battery. R.H.A., 9th Lancers, 17th Lancers.	
	30th.		O.in.C inspected 17th and 9th Lancers at Stables.	
	31st.		Brigade Major returned from leave.	
			The Weather during the month was remarkably fine, not a single wet day being experienced throughout the month.	

B. [signature]
Captain for,
G.O.C. "Lancer" Brigade.

APPENDIX "A" attached to Lancer Brigade War Diary for the month of MAY, 1919.

Strength of Units of the brigade.

	30.4.1919.		31.5.1919.	
	Offrs.	O.R's.	Offrs.	O.R's.
Brigade H.Q.	6	37	5	41
2nd.Signal Troop.	1	22	1	31
9th. Lancers.	28	162	31	269
12th. Lancers.	17	154	23	283
17th. Lancers.	21	143	28	281
"G" Battery.	5	158	6	187
2nd. M.G.Sqdn.	6	124	9	161
3rd. C. F. A.	3	78	5	170
1st. M. V. S.	2	24	1	27

APPENDIX I.

9th. Lancers.   3rd. C.F.A.
12th. Lancers.   1st. M.V.S.
17th. Lancers.   Camp Cmdt.
"G" Battery.   Supply Offr.
2nd. M.G.S.

POINTS DECIDED AT CONFERENCE HELD AT BRIGADE H.QRS. 7/5/1919.

1. MOBILE COLUMN. DUTY C.O. and REGIMENT.

In future Regiments will find Regimental H.Q. and Duty C.O. for periods of 21 days in turn. The Roster is as follows, beginning on Monday 12th. inst. from 12.00 hours inclusive.

     1st. Period   -   17th. Lancers.
     2nd. ..   -   9th. Lancers.
     3rd. ..   -   12th. Lancers.

Each of the above Regiments will provide in turn a duty Mobile Squadron for a period of 7 days. This Squadron will be ready to turn out at 2 hours notice.

The Roster is as follows, beginning on Monday 12th. inst. from 12.00 hours inclusive.

     1st. Period. -   17th. Lancers.
     2nd. ..   -   9th. Lancers.
     3rd. ..   -   12th. Lancers.

The 12th. Lancers will be responsible for these duties till 12.00 hours 12th. inst. exclusive.

1 Section "G" Battery and 1 Sub-section, 2nd. M.G.Sqdn. will also be at 2 hours notice. Details to be arranged by O's. C. these Units.

The Duty C.O. will not normally be absent from the vicinity of his billeting Area while on duty, though there is no objection to the Duty C.O's. will exchanging duties should he desire week end leave. C.O's. will invariably arrange in advance through Brigade H.Q. before taking short leave in the Country.

2. COMMANDING OFFICERS.

The G.O.C., and 1 C.O., or, in the absence of the G.O.C., 2 C.O's. will always be with the Brigade, and a similar system will be observed in Regiments.

3. INFANTRY REINFORCEMENTS.

Attention was drawn to the fact that, Infantry personnel transferred to Cavalry should be carefully selected as they could not be subsequently re-transferred.

4. BRIGADE ARMOUR-ers SHOP.

Decided not to have one.

5. SUPPLY OF BEDDING.

B.S.O. now trying to arrange, and will report in due course.

6. EDUCATION.

The proposed policy was shewn to Commanding Officers. It was decided to work on these lines and the Education Officer has been ordered to deal with Units as to Army Certificates Classes, and, Instruction of Band Boys.

7. LEAVE.

Extensions are not to be asked for from W.O. except under very urgent circumstances, Officers will ask for the leave they want before proceeding to U.K.

9	STEEL HELMETS.	To be worn by all guards and sentries and on all Marching Order Parades.
9	INSPECTION OF HORSES ATTACHED TO R.A.F.	This duty will be performed by the Duty C.O., who will forward a certififcate to this Office by 12.00 hours each Saturday to say this has been done. He will be accompanied by the O.C., 1st. M.V.S., The Duty Regiment will detail an N.C.O. to visit these horses daily and give instructions in grooming etc.

8/5/1919.

(sd.) H. GORING., Captain,
Staff Captain, Lancer Brigade.

CONFIDENTIAL.

WAR DIARY.

of

LANCER BRIGADE HEADQUARTERS.

for the month of

~~June~~ MAY, 1919.

VOLUME. LIX.

Army Form C. 2118.

WAR DIARY

~~INTELLIGENCE SUMMARY.~~

(Erase heading not required.)

Instructions regarding War Diaries and Intelligence Summaries are contained in F. S. Regs., Part II. and the Staff Manual respectively. Title pages will be prepared in manuscript.

Place	Date 1919	Hour	Summary of Events and Information	Remarks and references to Appendices
COLOGNE.	JUNE			
	1st.		No change.	
	2nd.		do.	
	3rd.		do.	
	4th.		do.	
	5th.		do.	
	6th.		G.O.C., returned from sick leave.	
	7th.		G.O.C., inspected horses of 12th. R. Lancers.	
	8th.		G.O.C., " " " 9th. Lancers.	
	9th.		No change.	
	10th.		do.	
	11th.		do.	
	12th.		do.	
	13th.		do.	
	14th.		do.	
	15th.		Information received that J - 3 Day would, in all probability be the 17th. instant.	
	16th.	4 A.M.	Warning order received that J. Day, i.e. the day selected for the advance in the event of the enemy not signing the Peace terms, would be June 20th.	
		11.00	Lancer Squadron moved to OLBERG, where, on arrival, it came under the orders of the LONDON DIVISION.	
		16.00	Detachments of Dragoon and Hussar Brigades arrived in Brigade Area and came under the orders of Lieut-Colonel FANE, C.M.G., D.S.O., Commanding Composite Regiment.	
	17th.		Composite Regiment came under orders of NORTHERN DIVISION.	
	18th.		No change.	

Army Form C. 2118.

WAR DIARY
INTELLIGENCE SUMMARY

(Erase heading not required.)

Instructions regarding War Diaries and Intelligence Summaries are contained in F. S. Regs., Part II. and the Staff Manual respectively. Title pages will be prepared in manuscript.

Place	Date 1919. JUNE.	Hour	Summary of Events and Information	Remarks and references to Appendices
COLOGNE.	19th.		Mobile Regiment under Command of Lieut-Colonel FANE, moved from Brigade Area to WERMELSKIRCHEN. Information received that J. Day was postponed.	
	20th.		Party of French Officers inspected Brigade H.Qrs. and 1st. M.V.S.	
	21st.		G.O.C., visited 2nd. M.G. Squadron.	
	22nd.		No change.	
	23rd.		do.	
	24th.		do.	
	25th.		do.	
	26th.		G.O.C., visited 12th. R. Lancers.	
	27th.		G.O.C., visited 2nd. M.G. Squadron.	
	28th.		Information received that Pease had been signed and that the Mobile Regiment, less Lancer Squadron would return on June the 30th., billetting in COLOGNE night 30/1st. Lancer Squadron would return on 1st. G.O.C., proceeded on 14 days leave, Lieut-Colonel MELVILLE took Command of the Brigade.	B.O.O.No.3.
	29th.		No change.	
	30th.		Composite Regiment, less Lancer Squadron staged the night in COLOGNE Area.	

30/6/1919.

D. J. [signature] Captain.

for G.O.C. Lancer Brigade.

SECRET.
****

Copy No....... 14

June 28th. 1919.

LANCER BRIGADE ORDER NO. 3.
----

1. In the event of Peace being signed without any further advance taking place, orders may be expected for the Mobile Force to re-join the Division.

2. Moves to effect this are given over-leaf.

3. The date of "A" day will be notified later.

4. Acknowledge.

                                                    D.V. Cr_____
                                                       Captain.

                             Brigade Major, Lancer Brigade.

Distbn. :-

1	9th. Lancers.	8	1st. M.V.S.
2	12th. Lancers.	9	Camp Cmdt.
3	17th. Lancers.	10	2nd. Signal Tp.
4	"G" Battery.	11	Supply Officer.
5	2nd. M.G. Sqdn.	12	Cav. Div. G.
6	3rd. C.F.A.	13	File.
7	Capt. BOLES.	14	War Diary.

Date	Unit.	From	To	Remarks.
"A" Day.	Mobile Force (less Lancer Sqdn.)	Present billets	COLOGNE.	Under orders which are being issued by Northern Division. Units will be accomodated as in previous stage through COLOGNE.
"E" Day.	Lancer Sqdn.	Present Area.	COLOGNE.	Under orders which are being issued by London Divn.
"B" Day.	Dragoon Sqdn. Hussar Sqdn. M.G. Detachments.	COLOGNE	Rejoin Units.	Under orders to be issued by O.C. Mobile Force. If weather hot to march c early, but in any case to be clear of HOHENZOLLERN BRIDGE by 10.30 hrs.

APPENDIX "A" attached to Lancer Brigade War Diary for the month of JUNE 1919.

Strength of Units of the Brigade.

	31.5.1919.		30.6.1919.	
	Offrs.	O.Rs.	Offrs.	O.Rs.
Brigade H.Q.	5	41	5	39
Lancer Signal Tp.	1	31	1	16
9th. Lancers.	21	269	34	276
12th. Lancers.	23	283	29	224
17th. Lancers.	28	281	33	264
"G" Battery.	6	187	5	208
Lancer M.G.S.	9	161	8	153
Lancer F.A.	3	76	2	59
1st. M.V.S.	1	27	1	29

****

APPENDIX "B"

The following are the numbers of reinforcements received by this Brigade for the month of JUNE 1919.
****

Cavalry Reinforcements   261

Labour Corps.   456

****

WAR DIARY.

for the

MONTH of JULY, 1919.

VOLUME LI.

LANCER BRIGADE HEADQUARTERS.

Army Form C. 2118.

WAR DIARY

INTELLIGENCE SUMMARY

(Erase heading not required.)

Instructions regarding War Diaries and Intelligence Summaries are contained in F. S. Regs., Part II. and the Staff Manual respectively. Title pages will be prepared in manuscript.

Place	Date	Hour	Summary of Events and Information	Remarks and references to Appendices
	1st.		Lancer Squadron. Mobile Regiment rejoined the Brigade. Lt-Col.O.FANE.DSO., assumed Command of Lancer Brigade.	
	2nd.		Information received that attached Infantry would rejoin their Units on 5th inst. G.O.C.,IVth Corps inspected the Brigade in Barracks.	
	3rd.		No change.	
	4th.		No change.	
	5th.		Attached Infantry rejoined their Units.	
	6th.		Parade Services were held by all Units to Commemorate Peace; The Divisional Commander attended the Service held at 12th Royal Lancers and 9th Lancers.	
	7th.		Syces arrived and were distributed as follows; 50 to the 9th Lancers., 30 to the 12th Lancers., 75 to the 17th Lancers, and 30 to the Lancer M.G.Sqdn.	
	8th.		No change.	
	9th.		Detachments from the Lancer Brigade taking part in the Victory March proceeded to PARIS. Detail as follows:- C.in.C's escort., 1 Sgt 13 O.Rs. 17th Lancers. Dismounted detachment, 2 Officers 15 O.Rs - 5 from each Regiment.	
	10th.		No change.	

Army Form C. 2118.

WAR DIARY
or
INTELLIGENCE SUMMARY.
(Erase heading not required.)

Instructions regarding War Diaries and Intelligence Summaries are contained in F. S. Regs., Part II. and the Staff Manual respectively. Title pages will be prepared in manuscript.

Place	Date	Hour	Summary of Events and Information	Remarks and references to Appendices
	11th.		No change.	
	12th.		G.O.C., Lancer Brigade., visited Brigade Horse Farm.	
	13th.		Brigadier General.NEIL.HAIG. C.B.,C.M.G. resumed Command of the Brigade on return from leave,U.K.	
	14th.		No change.	
	15th.		Nonchange.	
	16th.		No change.	
	17th.		No change.	
	18th.		Divisional Commander inspected recruits and Instructors of 12th Royal Lancers and 9th Lancers. Brigade Party for Victory March, returned from PARIS.	
	19th-20th.		No change.	
	21st.		One Troop 12th Lancers placed at the disposal of VIth Corps in view of threatened Civil disturbances in the neighbourhood of the Zoological Gardens. The Troop was turned out but not required to act.	
	22nd-29th.		No change.	
	30th.		One Squadron 17th Lancers detailed for escort duty to General FAYOLLE.	

[signature]
Captain for,
G.O.C.,Lancer Brigade.

CONFIDENTIAL.

WAR DIARY of LANCER BRIGADE HEADQUARTERS.

for the month of AUGUST, 1919.

****

VOLUME. IX

Army Form C. 2118.

WAR DIARY
or
INTELLIGENCE SUMMARY
(Erase heading not required.)

Instructions regarding War Diaries and Intelligence Summaries are contained in F.S. Regs., Part II, and the Staff Manual respectively. Title pages will be prepared in manuscript.

Place	Date	Hour	Summary of Events and Information	Remarks and references to Appendices
COLOGNE.	Aug: 1919. 1st. 4th.		No training was carried out during this period owing to the Divisional Horse Show week being observed as a holiday.	A/A
	6th.		12th Lancers provided 2 Troops as escort for General GOURAND.	A/A
	7th.		Rehearsal Parade took place for Ceremonial Parade to be held on the 12th inst.	A/A
	11th.		Practice Parade took place of the Composite Lancer Regiment under Lieut Colonel.C.FANE., and "G" Battery RHA. for the Review to be held on 18th. (postponed from 12th).	A/A
	12th		The D.R.(Major, General BIRCHBECK. K.C.B.,C.M.G.) inspected the horses of one squadron each of the 9th, 12th and 17th Lancers.	A/A
	13th		Practice Parade took place of the Composite Regiment under Lieut Colonel C.FANE CMG.DSO.12th Lancers, and "G" Battery RHA. for Review to be held on 18th inst.	A/A
	15th.		Dragoon and Hussar Composite Regiments(less 3rd Hussar Squadron) and "E" Battery RHA. concentrated in Cologne for Review 18th.	A/A
	16th.		Dress Rehearsal took place of Troops of Cavalry Division on EXERZIER PLATZ, East of LONGRICH for Review on 18th inst.	A/A
	18th.		Review of Troops of the Rhine Army by the Army Council took place on EXERZIER PLATZ., East of LONGERICH at 10-45 Hours.	A/A
	20th.		"S" horses despatched to Rhine Army Animal Collecting Camp for sale on 21st: 12th Lancers 126, Lancer M.G.Sqdn. 70 horses.	A/A
	29th.		Equipment of 12th Lancer and 17th Lancers and Lancer M.G.Sqdn despatched from NIPPES Goods Station 12th Lancers at 12.23 hrs. 17th and Lancer M.G.Sqdn at 14.07 hrs.	A/A
	30th.		Equipment of 9th Lancers, "G" Battery RHA., Lancer F.A., Lancer Bde H.Q.Lancer Signal Troop and 1st.M.V.S., despatched from NIPPES Goods Station at 12.23.	A/A

H. Goring Captain for
G.O.C. Lancer Brigade.

Army Form C. 2118.

WAR DIARY of Headquarters, LANCER BRIGADE.

INTELLIGENCE SUMMARY.

SEPTEMBER, 1919.
(Volume LXI).

(Erase heading not required).

Instructions regarding War Diaries and Intelligence Summaries are contained in F. S. Regs., Part II. and the Staff Manual respectively. Title pages will be prepared in manuscript.

Place	Date	Hour	Summary of Events and Information	Remarks and references to Appendices
COLOGNE.	1st	22.30	Horses of 12th Lancers (324) were despatched from DEUTZ Goods Station.	A.G.
	2nd	12.25	Personnel of 12th Lancers were despatched from BUIR.	A.G.
		22.30	Balance of 12th Lancers horses (47) despatched from DEUTZ Goods Station.	
	3rd		Lieut. (T/Captn) H. GORING (S.R.) 3rd Hussars, Staff Captain Lancer Brigade, appointed Brigade Major Lancer Brigade, as from 7.8.19. vice Captn. D.V. CREAGH MC, 7th Hussars.	A.G.
	4th		G.O.C. inspected Inniskilling Dragoons at SINDORF.	A.G.
	8th	22.30	Horses of 9th Lancers (334) despatched from COLOGNE-DEUTZ Goods Station.	A.G.
	9th	22.30	Horses of G/R.H.A. (176), 9th Lancers, balance (91), Lancer Field Amb. (44) and Lancer Signal Troop (16) despatched from COLOGNE-DEUTZ (Goods).	A.G.
	10th	22.30	Horses of Bde H.Q. (21), 1st Mob.Vet.Sec. (24), Lancer M.G.Sqdn. (207), 17th Lancers (65) despatched from COLOGNE-DEUTZ (Goods).	A.G.
	13th	09.30	Personnel of 9th Lancers (4 Offrs., 41 O.R.), G/R.H.A. (1 & 73), Lancer Field Amb. (1 & 73), Lancer Sig.Troop (1 & 9), 1st Mob.Vet.Sec. (7 O.R.), Lancer Bde. H.Q. (7 O.R.), Lancer M.G. Sqdn. (13 O.R.), 17th Lancers (4 & 66), despatched from DEUTZ Station (Goods).	A.G.

H. Goring
Captain.
Brigade Major.
Lancer Brigade.

BEF
Cav. Div.
Lancer Bde

9 Lancers

1919 APR to 1919 AUG

FROM 1 CAV DIV 2 BDE
BOX 1113

WAR DIARY or **INTELLIGENCE SUMMARY.** 9ᵗʰ Lancers

Army Form C. 2118.

Place	Date	Hour	Summary of Events and Information	Remarks and references to Appendices
Düren	April 1ˢᵗ		Regimental Routine. 1 O.R. Transferred from 2ⁿᵈ Dragoon Guards to 17ᵗʰ Lancers and 1 O.R. Posted to 9ᵗʰ Lancers.	1 O.R. joined Reg. 1 O.R. to 17 H.P.
	2ⁿᵈ		Regimental Routine. Major-General Sir W.E. Peyton, K.C.B., K.C.V.O., D.S.O. assumed the command of 2ⁿᵈ Cavalry Division on 30.3.19 vice Major General R.L. Mullens C.B. to England. 1ˢᵗ Cavalry Division becomes the "Cavalry Division of the Army of the Rhine". The 2ⁿᵈ Cavalry Brigade becomes in future the Lancer Brigade. 5 Sd. R. Drive and 10.3 light draught horses evacuated.	
	3ʳᵈ		"C" Squadron proceeded on Route to Do. local- to Major General R.L. Mullens on his departure from the 2ⁿᵈ Cavalry Division. 3 Officers 1 Sgt. & 35 O.R's proceeded to Cologne to collect horses from Deutz and Artillery Barracks.	2 O.R. from H.P.
	4ᵗʰ 5ᵗʰ		Regimental Routine. 2/Lieut H.S. Robinson DCM Promoted Lieutenant. The Divisional Commander inspected the barracks, stables and horses. Lieut. Corps inspected the horses attached to R.A.F. No. 12 Squadron. Regimental Routine. 2 Officers and 100 O.R's K.R.R.C attached to the Regt. 2 O.R's Demobilised.	1 O.R. Sqt. to H.P. 10 O.R. to H.P. 10 O.R. & H.P. 10 O.R. from H.P.
	6ᵗʰ		Regimental Routine. 2 O.R's Demobilised. 2/Lieut Gilroy joined and Posted to "A" Sqdn.. 2 Reserve horses from "A" Battery, 1 Riding from Div. H.Q., 69 Riding, 1 S.D from 17ᵗʰ Lancing & 35 Riding from 12ᵗʰ Lancers and taken on the strength of the Regt.	1 O.R. from H.P. a.d.c.

WAR DIARY
or
INTELLIGENCE SUMMARY.
(Erase heading not required.)

Army Form C. 2118.

Instructions regarding War Diaries and Intelligence Summaries are contained in F. S. Regs., Part II. and the Staff Manual respectively. Title pages will be prepared in manuscript.

Place	Date	Hour	Summary of Events and Information	Remarks and references to Appendices
Dinan	7th		Regimental Routine. 1 N.C.O. & 10.R. Proceed on leave.	10.R from H.P.
"	8th		Regimental Routine.	
"	9th		Regimental Routine. 1 N.C.O. & 10.R. Demobilised. 3 O.R's from France to the Regt. from Escort/co.	10.R from H.P. 10.R's class 2 Reserve
"	10th		2/Lt E.J TYNDALL demobilised. 2 horses evacuated. 7/Lieut THOMAS 5th Lancers posted to the Regt.	
"	10th		Regimental Routine. 2 O.R's demobilised. Medical Inspection of Regt.	10 R to H.P. 10.R from H.P.
"	11th		Regimental Routine. 1 N.C.O & 3 O.R's Demobilised. 2/Lieut POWELL inspected the horses attached to ho. 12 Sqdn. R.A.F. LIEUT(T/Capt.) DUFF is taken on the strength from 8.11.19. 6 Riding horses evacuated. 39 horses from "2" and "N" Batteries R.H.A taken on the strength. LIEUT JOICEY rejoined the Regt.	12.R Demobilised
"	12th		Regimental Routine. 3 N.C.O's & 10.R. Demobilised. 3 Riding and 28 L. Draught horses to the Regt. Retreat attendance to 18.35 hours. 1 Ride horse evacuated.	11.R & 4 H.P.
"	13th		Regimental Routine. 2 O.R's Proceed on leave. Voluntary service for all denominations at 11.0 hours.	11.R & 4 H.P.
"	14th		Regimental Routine. 1 O.R Proceed on leave. CAPT. C.W. NORMAN rejoined the Regt.	10.R & class 2 Army Reserve. 10.R & H.P.
"	15th		Regimental Routine. 9 N.C.O's K.R.R. rejoined their Regt. 11 O.R's from 20th Bn. K.R.R. joined the Regt.	
"	16th		Hq. A & B Squadrons moved from their present Block to Block C in barracks.	A.D.C.

Army Form C. 2118.

WAR DIARY
or
INTELLIGENCE SUMMARY.
(Erase heading not required.)

Instructions regarding War Diaries and Intelligence Summaries are contained in F. S. Regs., Part II. and the Staff Manual respectively. Title pages will be prepared in manuscript.

Place	Date	Hour	Summary of Events and Information	Remarks and references to Appendices
Bonn	17th	cont	A Field General Court Martial assembled at Orderly Room for the trial of No 1/5324 Pte ALLEN. LIEUT.E.C.RADCLIFFE a member, with 2/Lieuts PIRD and ERSKINE under instruction. I.O.R Demobilised. All draught horses shown as "2" reclassified "X", 4 Riding & 1 L Draught evacuated.	
	18th		The Medical Officer inspected the Regt. An order issued (?) Board in order assembled at 8. His stin. CAPT NORMAN, LIEUTS McFARLANE, RADCLIFFE. Retreat altered to 18.40 hrs.	
	19th		Regimental Routine. 16.15 13 Bde R.H.A. Point to Point Meeting	20 R from H.P
	20th		Regimental Routine	1 O.R to H.P. 3.O.R to Colm 2 waves.
	21st		Regimental Routine. No 1/5324 Pte ALLEN tried by F.G.C.M. on 17.11.19 for desertion. His was 16/3 service was found "not Guilty" of desertion but "Guilty" of absence without leave and was sentenced to 90 Days F.P No 2 with additional dispulin	2.O.R to H.P. 10.R from H.P.
			As 2 Days for under R.W. 1.O.R Proceeded on leave. LIEUT CAMPBELL & 2/Lt MOWMAN and 12.O.R Proceeded to COLOGNE on billeting Party.	
	22nd		Regimental Routine T/Lieut H.J. ROBINSON DCM Demobilised	1.O.R to H.P.
	23rd		Medical Officer inspected the Regt.	
	24th		Regimental Routine. 21 O.R's K.R.R. rejoined Their Regt. and were replaced by another 21. 4 Horses evacuated. 1 Charger (Mint CAMPBELL) joined the Regt.	1 O.R from H.P. 4O.R from H.P.
	25th		Regimental Routine. Regiment warned to move to COLOGNE. 15 horses and 114 O.R's rejoining to bring the Regt. 3 Horses evacuated	3. R.K.S. a.D.C.

A5834 Wt. W.4973 M687. 750,000 8/16 D. D. & L.Ltd. Forms/C.2118/13.

Army Form C. 2118.

WAR DIARY
or
INTELLIGENCE SUMMARY.
(Erase heading not required.)

Instructions regarding War Diaries and Intelligence Summaries are contained in F.S. Regs., Part II. and the Staff Manual respectively. Title pages will be prepared in manuscript.

Place	Date	Hour	Summary of Events and Information	Remarks and references to Appendices
Burao	26th	cont	Regiment marched from "DIREN" to "WHITE CITY" COLOGNE. 17 Horses taken on the strength of the Regt. 5 Horses transferred to 3rd Hussars.	10.R H.P.
"	27th		Regimental Routine.	
"	28th		Regimental Routine. 1st days Race meeting at KALK.	10.R16 H.P
"	29th		Regimental Routine. 2nd days meeting at KALK. LIEUT BROWN (ESSEX YEO) Demobilised. Medical Officer Demobilised.	Set Litton rejoined the Regt. 1.OR dem Holsted.
"	30th		C.O. Inspected the complete Squadron under CAPT CHISHOLM, LIEUTS KELLY, MCFARLANE, DALY and MACDONNEL.	1 OR from MP 10A to H.P 60.R Demobilised

A.D. Campbell
Lieut
A/Adj. 9th Lancers

Army Form C. 2118.

WAR DIARY
or
INTELLIGENCE SUMMARY.
(Erase heading not required.)

V.F. 9th Lancers

Instructions regarding War Diaries and Intelligence Summaries are contained in F.S. Regs., Part II. and the Staff Manual respectively. Title pages will be prepared in manuscript.

Place	Date	Hour	Summary of Events and Information	Remarks and references to Appendices
COLOGNE.	May 1st		The C.O. inspected the Composite Squadron at 15.30 hours	2 O/R pm O.R. 20 " to 21 "
"	2nd		Regimental Routine. The M.O. inspects the Regiment. 4 horses (cast) despatches to 4K Corps Animal Collecting Camp.	9 O/R to U.K. " from hospl
"	3rd 4th		Regimental Routine. A Riding horse taken on the strength. The Regiment was ordered to find one squadron from the Cavalry Squadron 1 Officer to U.K. to hospl at the inspection of the Northern Division by H.R.H. The Duke of Connaught next 1 to to troops week. In view of this each Squadron paraded 30 horses for the selection of a Cockpull Bay and Black troop.	
"	5th		The Squadron selected for the inspection with the Northern Division paraded at 06.30 hours under Major G.H. PHIPPS-HORNBY, Capt. E.W. NORMAN 2nd in command and foot leaders Lieut. L.P.C KELLY, Lieut. R.K. MACFARLANE and Lieut. C.C. LOMAX. R.A.M.C. joined the Regiment for duty as M.O.	1 O/R to hosp Capt. E.W. SPARKES
"	6th		The Squadron paraded on the Racecourse KALK for rehearsal	
"	7th		The Squadron paraded again on the Racecourse for rehearsal Bathing parade at the KAHER WILHELM BAD in the afternoon.	
"	8th		The Squadron paraded with the NORTHERN DIVISION on the EXERZIER PLATZ East of LINDERICH for the inspection by H.R.H The DUKE of CONNAUGHT at 11.00 hours.	
"	9th		Regimental Routine. The medical Officer inspected the Squadron Regiment during the morning. Bathing parade in the afternoon.	3 O/R to to hosp
"	10th 11th		Regimental Routine. 11 horses were evacuated or transferred. Lieut. E.R. JOICEY and Col. HASSETT proceed to England to attend a course of instruction at the Cavalry School NETHERAVON	1 conveyor application kit gone

A5534 Wt. W4973 M687 750,000 8/16 D. D. & L. Ltd. Forms/C.2118/13.

WAR DIARY or INTELLIGENCE SUMMARY

Army Form C. 2118.

(Erase heading not required.)

Instructions regarding War Diaries and Intelligence Summaries are contained in F. S. Regs., Part II. and the Staff Manual respectively. Title pages will be prepared in manuscript.

Place	Date	Hour	Summary of Events and Information	Remarks and references to Appendices
COLOGNE	May 12th		Regimental Routine. 2 Horse evacuated to M.V.S.	1 Off/for 3 sergts
"	13th		The A.D.V.S. inspected horses which it was intended to cast. In number of a Court of Enquiry at H.Q. 2nd H.G.S.	1 Off/for 3 sergts
"	14th		Horse cast by A.D.V.S. yesterday proceeded to HOHRATH. Bathing Parade during the afternoon. 4 O.R., 1 recruit joined.	2 Off/for 3 sergts
"	15th		Regimental Routine.	1 Off/for 3 sergts
"	16th		G.O.C. Cavalry Division & James Bell inspected the lines, rooms & recreation Rooms of the Regiment. A Board consisting of Capt. E.W. NORMAN, Lieut C.W. WYNN and the Veterinary Officer assembled to cast 2 O.R. as showing unfit.	1 Off/ 3 sergts
"	17th		Regimental Routine.	1 Off/3 sergts
"	18th		Parade service for Roman Catholics at the "White City". 2 chargers sent to Brig-General. D. F. BEALE-BROWNE, D.S.O. at Brussels. 3 horses evacuated to No 1 A.V.S.	1 Off/3 sergts
"	19th		The Mobile Squadron under Capt C.W. NORMAN came on duty at 12:00 hours. 5 Off/ an OR
" to	20th		The Veterinary Officer inspected all horses of the Regiment with defective eyesight. Lieut. L.F.C. KELLY, M.C. sat as Member of a Court of Enquiry, reassembling at H.Q. 2nd M.G.S.	
"	21st		Regimental Routine. Bathing Parade. Major A.C.S. BOYLE M.C. joined Regiment	
"	22nd		Owing to the Autumnal weather the German Civil Service would sign the Peace Terms these were temporarily postponed from today.	1 Off/ 3 sergts
"	23rd		A Field General Court Martial assembled at Orderly Room at 10:00 hours for the trial of Rfm. W.G. LAW 2 D.B R Rfle K.R.R.C. attached 9th Lancers. Lieut. C.C. LOMAX attached 9th Lancers — Bathing parade.	2 Off/ 3 sergts

A 584. Wt. W4973 M687 750,000 8/16 D.D. & L. Ltd. Forms/C.2118/13.

Army Form C. 2118.

WAR DIARY
or
INTELLIGENCE SUMMARY.
(Erase heading not required.)

Instructions regarding War Diaries and Intelligence Summaries are contained in F. S. Regs., Part II. and the Staff Manual respectively. Title pages will be prepared in manuscript.

Place	Date	Hour	Summary of Events and Information	Remarks and references to Appendices
COLOGNE	Friday 24th		A Class of Instruction in Lewis, Sword & Rifle for all Lieutenants commenced under the R.S.M.	100 F troops
"	25th		Col. E.S. Power down to the Dining Hall at noon hour	
"	26th		Regimental Routine	1000 for troops
"	27th		Regimental Routine	1" " "
"	28th		Lieut. J.E.G. POWELL to return to the strength having proceeded to England (resigned) 2 to th troops from Divisional Baths parade at 1400 hours in due purl E. W. WYNN.	
"	29th		G.O.C. 57 Corps inspected the Indoor rifle range & stables this morning	
"	30th		The Commander-in-Chief inspected the Regiment took home reveille from 1 Belch steps etc. The C.O. inspects the Lieutenants in the Square and proved the point of the lower drill. Battalion parade in the afternoon.	
"	31st		Regimental Routine. 60 O.R. for the Northern Command Labour Centre (Arms from England) for proving purposes.	

H. Malthin Sheehan
Capt.

V.F.

Confidential

War Diary

of

9TH (Q.R.) Lancers.

from 1st June 1919 to 30th June 1919.

(Volume .)

Army Form C. 2118.

WAR DIARY
or
INTELLIGENCE SUMMARY.
(Erase heading not required.)

Instructions regarding War Diaries and Intelligence Summaries are contained in F. S. Regs., Part II. and the Staff Manual respectively. Title pages will be prepared in manuscript.

Place	Date	Hour	Summary of Events and Information	Remarks and references to Appendices
COLOGNE	June 1st		Regimental Routine. 1 horse evacuated to No 1 M.V.S.	1 Rly to M.V.S. 1 OR to RRE to Hosp
"	2nd		Regimental Routine. Regiment detailed to find Regt H.Q. for local Mobile Force. 2 O.R. demobilised. 1 O.R. rejoined. I.N.C.O. & O.R. 5 O.R. K.R.R. proceeded to rejoin their Batt.	1 OR. journal 6 " K.R.R. to unit 1 OR Labour Corp Hosp
"	3rd		Observed as a holiday (Wednesday) the birthday of H.M. the King. Regt parade at 10.00 hours. 1 O.R rejoined. 1 O.R. re-enlisted for 3 years.	1 OR rejoined 3 OR to B on Bumps for Druside
"	4th		Regimental Routine. Bathing parade at 14.00 hours under Lieut L.H.H. HARRIS. The C.O. inspected 13 OR. K.R.R wishing to transfer to Cavalry. 2nd Lieut J R McDONNELL detained in England by Medical Board.	1 OR rejd from Hos.
"	5th		Regimental Routine. All K.R.Rs attached to A.Q and C Squadron paraded at 09.00 hours for drill under Lieut BROWN. K.R.R. Medical Inspection by the Medical officer during the morning. 1 N.C.O and 12 O.R. 51st Bn. Northumberland Fusiliers and 1 N.C.O. and 12 O.R. 52nd Northumberland Fusiliers attached for a 3 weeks course of Instruction in Equitation and Horse Management. 1 O.R. proceeded on leave. The band played in the grounds of the White City at 18.30 hours. 1 O.R. K.R.R. joined 1 O.R. K.R.R proceeded to rejoin his unit. CAPT. G.H. BENSON demobilised.	1 OR KRR joined " " to unit
"	6th		Regimental Routine. Bathing parade at 14.00 hours under LIEUT R.K McFARLANE. 1 N.C.O and 1 O.R. proceeded on leave. 1 horse died. 1 horse evacuated to No 1 M.V.S. 1 O.R. L.C. proceeded to rejoin his unit. 1st Day of SOUTHERN DIVISION race meeting at KALK.	1 Rly Died " to M.V.S. 1 OR Labour Corp to unit 1 OR RRE to Hos.
"	7th		3 Classes of 51st & 52nd Northumberland Fusiliers for Riding School commenced under S.S.M. SPENCER D.C.M., S.S.M. GUNNERSON M.S.M. and S.Q.M.S. HEPWORTH. Oil issue FRSON NSTI SSTILC Forms/C.2118/13. Water on tubs 0800-12.00 hours. The C.O. inspected 1 O.R. K.R.R wishing to transfer to Cavalry. 1.O.R. proceeded on leave.	3 OR Gordon Hylrs 1 Riffle Bolt 1 journal 1 OR RRE to Hos

Army Form C. 2118.

WAR DIARY
or
INTELLIGENCE SUMMARY.
(Erase heading not required.)

Instructions regarding War Diaries and Intelligence Summaries are contained in F.S. Regs., Part II. and the Staff Manual respectively. Title pages will be prepared in manuscript.

Place	Date	Hour	Summary of Events and Information	Remarks and references to Appendices
COLDENE.	June 7th (cont)		3.O.R. Gordon Highlanders and 1.O.R. T.B. joined. – 2nd Day of SOUTHERN DIVISION rare meeting at KALK.	
"	8th		Col. E. Parade service held in Dining Hall at 11.00 hours. 1.O.R. proceeded on leave. 1. N.C.O. K.R.R. joined. 1. N.C.O. K.R.R. proceeded to join his unit.	1 N.C.O. K.R.R. joined from [...] to unit. [...] [...] Regts in U.T.
"	9th		Local Mobile Duty Squadron came on duty at 12.00 hours under command CAPT. C.W. NORMAN. 1.O.R. proceeded on leave. CAPT. C.W. NORMAN is detailed as 2nd in command of the Mobile Squadron vice CAPT. C.T. CHISHOLM. 1st 1.O.R. from Q.V.R. joined for Sanitary Duties	3 O.R. proceeded on leave. 1 O.R. and 1 are to join [...] [...] [...] Q.V.R. joined for [...] [...]
"	10th		Regimental Routine. All K.R.R's attached to "A" & "B" Squadrons paraded at 09.00 hours under LIEUT. BROWN K.R.R. for drill. A Court of Enquiry consisting of MAJOR G.H. PHIPPS-HORNBY M.C. as president and CAPT. C.W. NORMAN & LIEUT. C.W. WYNN assembled to enquire into the loss of 4 bicycles at 10.15 hours. 1.O.R. proceeded on leave. Officers Class B Football under S/M. S. Taylor commenced parades Tuesday, Thursday and Saturday at 18.00 hours.	2 O.R.s K.R.R. [...] [...] [...]
"	11th		A Court of Enquiry consisting of B. MAJOR G.H. PHIPPS-HORNBY as president, CAPT. C.W. NORMAN and LIEUT. C.W. WYNN assembled at Regt. H.Q. to enquire into the loss of 4 bicycles. Riding parade at 14.00 hours under LIEUT. B.H. ALLFREY. LIEUT. I.P. G. KELLY M.C. & O.R.s K.R.R. proceeded on leave. – 2.O.R. K.R.R. joined. – 2.O.R. K.R.R. proceeded to join their unit.	2 O.R.s K.R.R. joined
"	12th		The Command Pay master gave a lecture on the new system of Pay and Mess Books at H.Q.R.F.M. CAPT. A. MATHER-JACKSON. LIEUTS. T.F. COLVIN M.C., L.H.H. HARRIS, H.W. DURNFORD, A.D. CAMPBELL and S.Q.M.S.'s attended. All K.R.R.s attached to H.Q. and C. Squadron paraded at 09.15 hours for drill under LIEUT BROWN K.R.R. 2.O.R. proceeded on leave. The Band played in the grounds of the White City at 18.30 hours. 1.O.R. to Divisional H.Q.	1 Officer and [...] [...] to U.K. for [...] [...]

A 8341 Wt. W4973 M687 750,000 8/16 D.D. & L. Ltd. Forms/C.2118/13.

Army Form C. 2118.

WAR DIARY
or
INTELLIGENCE SUMMARY.
(Erase heading not required.)

Instructions regarding War Diaries and Intelligence Summaries are contained in F. S. Regs., Part II. and the Staff Manual respectively. Title pages will be prepared in manuscript.

Place	Date	Hour	Summary of Events and Information	Remarks and references to Appendices
COLOGNE.	June 13th.		Regimental Routine. Bathing parade at 14.00 hours under 2nd Lieut. J.D. GILROY. 1 O.R. proceeded on leave. 1 O.R. demobilized. LIEUT DAGG. K.R.R. joined for attachment.	1 Off. K.R.R. joined 1 O.R. to tr. transp. to Denmark 1 O.R. to Hosp.
"	14th.		G.O.C. Rhine Brigade inspected officers ride at 09.00 hours in the 17th Lancers Riding School at 9.30 he inspected 11 W.O. and N.C.O.'s whose names had been forwarded as efficient instructors. 1 O.R. proceeded on leave. 1 O.R. and 1 O.R. K.R.R. joined. Officers ride under Lieut. R.K. McFARLANE ceased.	1 O.R.S. joined from U.K. 1 O.R. K.R.R. joined
"	15th		R.C. church parade at 07.40 hours. C. of E. Church Service at 11.30 hours. 1 N.C.O. + 1 O.R. proceeded to No 11 V.S. to take over duties v/c Camp duties at Brigade grazing camp. 2 O.R. proceeded 2 Rty. Minst. on leave. 1 Nurse (charge Capt. BENSON) Mounted to H.Q. 9th Bde. 1 Horse (charge of LLOYD-REES Off. transferred to Army Redition Camp.	
"	16th.		Mobile Squadron came off duty. All Ranks of Mobile Squadron paraded at 10.30 found with box respirators which were tested in Tear Gas. 2 O.R. proceeded to H.Q. 2 M.G.S. to attend Brigade Course of Cooking. Officers Ride under R.S.M. A/S.Q's White and Deadman and Cpl. Deadman also attended to instruction. 2 K.R.R. officers attended cordwine riding under 2 S.M. GUMMERSON. H.S.M. N.C.O's football class and musketry class under R.S.M. and S.M. WESTGATE. 20 horses sent to Brigade grazing camp. 103 recruits joined from England.	1 S.R. K.R.R. and 1 M.S.M. returned from Hosp. 9 O.R.s K.R.R. joined 4 O.R.
"	17th		Regimental Routine. All K.R. R's attached to "A" + "B" Squadrons paraded under LIEUT. DAGG K.R.R. to Div. The C.O. inspected infantry volunteers for transfer to Cavalry. The Mobile TOH. Co. paraded at 10.15 hours under Major BOVILL M.C. 1 NURNFORD, L RADCLIFFE commanding troops proceeded to 2 London Bde. at ENGLEKIRCHEN	2 N.R. K.R.R. and 2 O.R. K.R.R. joined 103 O.R.s joined from U.K. 1 O.R. London Bde. at ENGLEKIRCHEN

A 53.4 Wt.W4973 M687 750,000 8/16 D.D. & L. Ltd. Forms/C.2118/13.

Army Form C. 2118.

WAR DIARY
or
INTELLIGENCE SUMMARY.
(Erase heading not required.)

Instructions regarding War Diaries and Intelligence Summaries are contained in F. S. Regs., Part II. and the Staff Manual respectively. Title pages will be prepared in manuscript.

Place	Date	Hour	Summary of Events and Information	Remarks and references to Appendices
COLOGNE	June 17th/18		to duty.	1 O.R. to Hosp. 1 " from Hosp.
"	18.		The C.O. inspected all recruits who joined during the last month and the new draft of 09.45 hours. Bathing parade at 14.00 hours. 2nd LIEUT W. RICHARDSON, Dragoon Guards, of the Hostile force arrived 14.30 hours, and were billeted in the White City. Subject B.H.P.H formerly admitted into Hospital.	2 OR & RRS joined for attacht 2 " to Hosp 1 " rejoined for details 1 OR to Hosp
"	19th		Regimental Routine. All K.R.R.'s attached to A.Q and "C" Squadron paraded at 09.15 hours, 2 OR labour boy under LIEUT DAGG, K.R.R. for drill. Fah. S. Sergt Moxon inspected horses at the Brigade Grazing Camp. The Band played in the grounds of the White City at 18.30 hours. 60 O.R. from the Labour Corps joined for attachment. 1 horse Evacuated to No 11 V.H.S. 1 horse destroyed. 1 horse joined from advanced Remount Section.	Aug 6/11.61 3 OR labour boy 60 OR labour boy joined 1 horse joined 1 " Evacuated 1 " destroyed
"	20th		Regimental Routine. Bathing parade under 2 LIEUT B.F.S. MOUNTAIN. The Dragoons of the Hostile force ordered to go out to the outpost under Northern Division.	1 OR to Hosp 5 OR proceed from hosp 3 " to. Hosp 4 A.A.
"	21st		Regimental Routine. Three trench Colonels (Veterinary, Cavalry & artillery) walked round during Sunday stables. CAPT. C. W. NORMAN, LIEUT B.L. PRIOR PALMER conducted Kit inspn.	Officers 3 OR from H 1 struck off
"	22nd		C. of E. Parade Service in Dining Hall at 11.15 hours under 4 COLONEL R.H.R. BROCKLEBANK. R.S.O. Voluntary Evening Service in Church Army Hall at 18.00. Holy Communion Hotel de Nord Church at 07.30, 08.00, 08.45 hours.	Taught to write OR from Hosp.
"	23rd		Regimental Routine. Regimental H.Q came off duty with Hostile Force (Local), 2.O.R. proceeded to attend Brigade Course of Cooks at 2nd M.G.S. H.Q.	

A5834 Wt. W4973/M687. 750,000. 8/16. D.D.&L. Ltd. Form/C.2118/13.

Army Form C. 2118.

WAR DIARY
or
INTELLIGENCE SUMMARY.

(Erase heading not required.)

Instructions regarding War Diaries and Intelligence Summaries are contained in F. S. Regs., Part II. and the Staff Manual respectively. Title pages will be prepared in manuscript.

Place	Date	Hour	Summary of Events and Information	Remarks and references to Appendices
COLOGNE.	June 24th		The C.O inspected Class "A" Officers foot drill class and passed them off - at KRR's attached A + B Squadrons paraded at 09.15 hours under LIEUT SA & G. KRR to drill. The C.O. inspected 4.O.R. Infantry attached for final approval for transfer to Cavalry. Capt. H. Mather Jackson proceeded on leave. 1 O.R. died.	1 OR from Hosp.
"	25th		Officers Class B. foot drill parade on Mondays, Wednesdays and Fridays at from 10.15 to 11.15 hours and on Tuesdays and Thursdays from 14.00 hours to 15.00 hours. Recruits Foot drill parade 1.50 hours daily. A Court of Enquiry assembled to enquire into the case of No 58285 Rfn Brisk attached who sustained fatal injuries from exploding shell. President CAPT. C.W NORMAN. LIEUT LH.H. HARRIS, LIEUT A.D. CAMPBELL as members. FGR.	1 OR MRRC died 1 OR MRRC to Hosp. 2 SR to Hosp. 1 SR KRRC to WP
"	26th		The funeral of No 106 Rfn. BRISK took place at SÜDFRIEDHOF CEMETERY at 10.00hrs. 8.20 O.R. of Lancers under LIEUT. C.C. LOMAX and 30. O.R. KRR under LIEUT SA&G attended. For H. S. Sgt Goodridge inspected the Lottes turned out in the Grazing Camp.	1 SR from Hosp 1 OR to Land Forces to rest Officer & personal from Hosp
"	27th		Regimental Routine. Bathing parade under 2ND LIEUT. J.H.A.TENNANT at 14.00 hours. 2.2. O.R. Labour Corps joined for attachment.	2.2. OR Labour Corps joined 2 OR to Hosp 1 " KRRC from HP
"	28th		Regimental Routine. Peace Signed - Salute of 101 guns fired by R.F.A. at 18.00 hours	

43834 Wt.W4973/M684 750,000 8/16 D. D. & L. Ltd. Form/C.2118/13.

Army Form C. 2118.

WAR DIARY
or
INTELLIGENCE SUMMARY.
(Erase heading not required.)

Instructions regarding War Diaries and Intelligence Summaries are contained in F. S. Regs., Part II. and the Staff Manual respectively. Title pages will be prepared in manuscript.

Place	Date	Hour	Summary of Events and Information	Remarks and references to Appendices
COLOGNE	June 29th		C of E parade service in Dining room at 11.30 hours under Bt Major G.A. PHIPPS-HORNBY.	1 OR RAFF G sent to Hosp. 2 " joined 1 OR RE to Hosp 1 " joined 1 OR from Hosp 2 OR RRRC to Hosp 2 " joined 1 OR to Hosp.
	30th		Regimental Routine. L/Cpl Somerville N.C. Dragoon Squadron of Mobile Force arrived at 11.30 hours to one night on their way to rejoin their units. Divisional Fly officer inspected the Cookhouse at 12:00 hours. Local mobile Squadron carries on duty.	

J.F. Gloin Lieut.
a/adjt. 9th Lancers.

CONFIDENTIAL.

War Diary
of the

9th (QR) LANCERS.

(Volume 19)

From 1-7-19 To 31-7-19

WAR DIARY
or
INTELLIGENCE SUMMARY.
(Erase heading not required.)

Army Form C. 2118.

Place	Date	Hour	Summary of Events and Information	Remarks and references to Appendices
COLOGNE	July 1st		Regimental Routine. The K.R.R's attached to the Regiment paraded for drill and training under their own officers.	1. O.R.A.P.R. 2. A Programme
"	2nd		The following classes commenced. Recruits under officers under the R.S.M., N.C.O. Instructors to the R.S.M. Recruits & Signal and a Refresher Course under the NC.O.'s men musketry and a Refresher Course for NCOs. The NCO's & men of the 51st & 52nd Northumberlands Fusiliers attached to the Regiment joined their units. Bathing parade under Lieut. C.W. WYNN	2. Programme
"	3rd		Parade all K.R.R's under their own officers - Cpl. S.S. SMITH inspects the horses of the Regiment in the Brigade Group Camp.	
"	4th		Regimental Routine. 2 horses proceeded to WAHN Artillery Practice Camp 3Bdy RF for the use of officers there. Bathing parade under Lieut. 4/W. DURNFORD.	1. O.R. Rangs
"	5th		A Court of Enquiry assembled at Orderly Room to enquire into the injury by gun shot wound of Rfn FORRESTER, K.R.R.C attached to the 2nd am. Regiment- Cpl MARINER, Sgt GANT and Cpl DEEDMAN attended as witnesses.	1. Evidence for 3 - Enqd
"			He is selected for attachment to London Infantry Bde. for Officers making return to civil life.	
"	6th		C.O.'S Parade. Parties Devine at 11.30 hours under Lt.Col. R.H.R. BROCKLEBANK 20 O.R's per Sqdn and 10 OR from Head Qrtrs attended. A Party of 9 O.R. went to COLOGNE Race course for a rehearsal of duty to be performed at the Races on 18th + 124 instant. T/Major G.F. REYNOLDS reported to Regiment from Cavalry Division Headquarters and to take to Headquarters the 2nd in Command. 2 Officers and all O.R. K.R.R. reported their unit.	

Army Form C. 2118.

WAR DIARY
or
INTELLIGENCE SUMMARY.
(Erase heading not required.)

Instructions regarding War Diaries and Intelligence Summaries are contained in F.S. Regs., Part II. and the Staff Manual respectively. Title pages will be prepared in manuscript.

Place	Date	Hour	Summary of Events and Information	Remarks and references to Appendices
COLOGNE.	July 7th		All men of recently joined drafts were medically examined - Lieut A.D. CAMPBELL attached Shock taking at the Regimental Canteen.	1 O.R. & 4 H.Orps
"	8th		Today was observed as a holiday to commemorate the return of Mr Allen. 1 O.R. & H.K. Work was carried out as on a Sunday. Regimental Sports were held in the afternoon and a Special tea was provided. Lt. G.W. BREITMEYER & 1 O.R. detained from Regimental Routine Balking parade under Lieut L.P.G. KELLY, M.C.	1 O.R. for Regtl. Wkshop Off.
"	9th 10th 11th		Regimental Routine. Balking parade under Lieut. E.C. RADCLIFFE. The Veterinary officer malleins all horses of the Regiment except polo ponies and horses racing on Saturday	1 O.R. for shops
"	12th		3. O.R. from Capts. attached proceeded to the Army Science College Bonn for a course of instruction. The Veterinary officer malleins all polo ponies in the Army of the Rhine. COLOGNE Races on the Army of the Rhine were held to-day. Rhineland Jockey Club open to the Army.	1 O.R. for Course 100 for shops
"	13th		C. of E. Parade Service under Lt. Col. R.H.R. BRECKLEBANK, D.S.O. All R.C.'s met the R.C. Cavalry Chaplain at 07.45 hours for Parade mass. The Veterinary Officer malleins horses racing Yesterday, and inspects polo ponies malleined Yesterday.	
"	14th		Regimental Routine. Lieut. C.M. PETO having reported from England is reported to B Sqdn 30 pt &shp Second day of COLOGNE Races.	
"	15th		CAPT A.G. BOVILL. M.C. who posted to command "A" Squadron. Capt C.W. MORGAN 1 O.R. &Shop posto from "A" Squadron to command "B" Squadron.	
"	16th 17th		Regimental Routine. Balking parade under Lieut R.K. MACFARLANE. CAPT C. J. CHISHOLM M.C. as member of a F.G.C.M. assembled at H.Q. Qtrs. 1st K. Lancers. 2/Lt M.H. AIRD attended under instruction. 27.O.R. proceeded to QUADRATH to attend the examination for 3rd Class Certificate of Education. A Court of Enquiry assembled at Cavalry Barracks	1 O.R. for shops 1 O.R. for shops

Army Form C. 2118.

WAR DIARY
or
INTELLIGENCE SUMMARY.
(Erase heading not required.)

Instructions regarding War Diaries and Intelligence Summaries are contained in F.S. Regs., Part II. and the Staff Manual respectively. Title pages will be prepared in manuscript.

Place	Date	Hour	Summary of Events and Information	Remarks and references to Appendices
COLOGNE	July 17. contd.		To investigate the circumstances of an injury by gunshot wound to Pte. FORRESTER, K.R.R.C attached to the Regiment. Capt C.W. SPARKES A/c Sqt GANT and Capt WARINER attended as witnesses Riding hearts and Major J.H. KEMPLE having joined the Regiment from the 1st Reserve Regt CURRAGH, is posted to Head Quarters. Armourer S. Sgt CROOKS proceeded to CALAIS and was struck off the strength.	1 Rdg Offr 1 OR/Mt. Shop
"	18th 19th		Regimental Routine. Bathing parade under Instr. C.C. LOMAX. The Commanding Officer classified the horses of A. Squadron and picked the Entries for the Cav. Div Horse Show. Capt C.T. CHISHOLM and 10. OR. proceeded to the Brigade Armourer Capt to classify the horses of the Regiment, with the Belgium Veterinary Officer. Today, having been forced by Parliament, as a day off, National Holiday, was observed as a holiday. Capt A.E.G. GRANT M.C. having been ordered to report to the War Office whilst on leave in England, is struck off the strength.	
"	20th 21st		C.R.E. Parade Service under Capt. C.W. NORMAN Regimental Routine. 14 Riding horses were taken over from the Advanced Remount Depot COLOGNE. 2. OR. attended the Brigade Course for Cooks at the 2ND M.G. Sqdn H.Q.	1 Rdg Offr 1 OR/Mt. Shop
"	22ND		Regimental Routine. - Personnel of the 20th Bn. K.R.R.C. attached to the Regiment joins their unit.	1 Offr formerly attached 1 OR/Mt. Shop Rdg Offr
"	23RD		Old N.O.- in- Command of Squadrons and S.Q.M.S's. attended a lecture on the Annual System of Pay & Mess Books at HORREM- Bathing parade under 2/Lt FLAMS' fostering	1 OR/Mt. Shop
"	24th 25th		Regimental Routine. Lieut A.D. CAMPBELL and 5. OR. trumpets took 10 of the horse turned into the Brigade forging Camp. The Commanding Officer inspected and passed the Officers at football class. Bathing parade under 2/Lt. J.W. RICHARDSON. The C.O. inspected all horses leaf to the R.A.F. from the Brigade Lt. H.W. DURNFORD Sgt & number of a F.G.C.M. at H.Q. 17th (Lancs.) 2/Lt J.H.A TENNANT attached under instruction	10R AWL 1 Re/Mt. Shop

(16340) Wt W5309/P713 750,000 3/18 c. 2688 Forms/C2118/16. D., D. & L..., London, E.C.

Army Form C. 2118.

WAR DIARY
or
INTELLIGENCE SUMMARY.
(Erase heading not required.)

Instructions regarding War Diaries and Intelligence Summaries are contained in F. S. Regs., Part II. and the Staff Manual respectively. Title pages will be prepared in manuscript.

Place	Date	Hour	Summary of Events and Information	Remarks and references to Appendices
COLOGNE	July 26th		Regimental Routine. Lieut. C. W. BENNETT having been taken on the establishment of No. 3. Traffic Control Squadron is struck off the strength of the Regiment.	
"	27th		C. of E. Parade Service under the Commanding Officer.	200 NCOs stand Sickly + 10 Ofr. Exam.
"	28th		Capt. BUXTON (Veterinary Officer) and Capt. BODY. A.V.C. (No 1. M.V.S) classified the horses of the Regiment according to Veterinary categories.	100 ,, ,, ,, ,,
"	29th		The Lancer Brigade Board Consisting of Lt. Col. RUDD. R.A.V.C Major H.G. YOUNG D.S.O R.H.A and Major J H PHIPPS-HORNBY reclassified all horses of the Regiment. A lecture at which all Officers and O.R. attended, on Horse Saving Certificates was given in the Dining Hall.	22 by Exam.
"	30th		G.O.C. Lancer Bde inspected the Officers and Recruits Rodeo at 09.30 hours. Bathing Parade under Capt. J H DALY.	170 troop
"	31st		Regimental Routine. The R.E. Educational Officer commenced a Course for the N.C.Os. of the Regiment who have joined in for the test 2nd Class Certificate of Education. Examination.	200 from troop

H Mukk Jackson
Capt.
Adj. o/k Lancers

War Diary
of the
9th (QR) Lancers

From 1-8-19
To 31-8-19

9th LANCERS' WAR DIARY
or
INTELLIGENCE SUMMARY

Army Form C. 2118.

Place	Date	Hour	Summary of Events and Information	Remarks and references to Appendices
COLOGNE	Aug 1919			
	2nd		Cavalry Division Horse Show on COLOGNE Race-course. In consequence Routine was as for a Sunday. Monthly Stocktaking	108 OR.
	3rd		Church.	
	4th	A.M.	Regimental Routine. Cavalry Division Races. R.O.R. of 30th Labour Coy; attached to the Regiment left for duty with Cavalry Brigading Park. Cavalry Division Horse Show - In the two days show the Regiment won 6 first Prizes, 3 Seconds and 1 third. The first Prizes consisted of Best Troop Horse, Corporals & Privates; Best Troop Horse Sergeants; L.G.S. Wagon; Heavy-Weight Chargers (Major G.H. THIPPS-HORNBY); Officers 100 yards (Lt. A.D. CAMPBELL) and 120 yds. Hurdles (Other Ranks).	
	5th		Cavalry Division Races. 5 O.R. proceeds to the U.K. for Re-Engagement	108 OR strays
			Furlough.	
	6th		Regimental Routine. Balloting peread under 2/Lt D.C.F. ERSKINE.	1 Officer 1 horse
	7th		A composite Squadron from the Regiment attended a rehearsal with the 6th Corps of a Ceremonial Parade to be held at a later date. The 1" " Squadron was under the command of Capt A.C. BOVILL M.C., 2nd in command Lieut H.W. DURNFORD - Troop Leaders, Lieut L.H. HARRIS, Lieut R.K. MACFARLANE, Lieut D.L. PRIOR-PALMER, Lieut C.C. LOMAX. The strength of the Squadron was 68 O.R.	2" " strays
	8th		Regimental Routine. Balloting parade under Lt. R.A. LAMPREY. 2 O.R. Labour Corps attached.	1 Officer 1 horse strays

WAR DIARY or INTELLIGENCE SUMMARY

Army Form C. 2118.

Place	Date	Hour	Summary of Events and Information	Remarks and references to Appendices
COLOGNE	Aug 9th		Regimental Routine.	3 OR. R/Sgps
	10th		C. of E. Parade Service under Capt. C. J. CHISHOLM.	
	11th		The Composite Squadron rehearsed for Ceremonial Parade with the 6th Cav. Bde. attended another rehearsal on the EXERZIER PLATZ, north of MERHEIM.	2 OR. from UK. 2 to UK.
	12th		Maj-General Sir W. H. BIRKBECK K.C.B, C.M.G. Director of Remounts inspected the horses of B. & C. Squadrons.	
	13th		The Composite Squadron carried out another Practise Parade. A Board of the following Officers, Capt. C. J. CHISHOLM, Lieut. C. H. M. PETO & Lieut. B. H. ALLFREY assembled at Q.M. stores to verify the clothing account etc.	B. H. ALLFREY Bathing
	14th		Parade under Lt. R. K. McFARLANE. Commencement of a 14 Weeks Course of Physical Training for N.C.O's under the R.S.M. 4 Chargers chosen by Squadron Leaders for the use of Staff Officers at the VI Corps Ceremonial Parade paraded under the Riding Master for further training. All wheels of the Regiment were handed over to the Transport Sergeant to be prepared for shipment to England.	
	15th		Romman C. October attended Mass at 17th Lancers Barracks. Lt. L. H. HARRIS Set as member of a Board of Enquiry at Brigade H.Q.	Lt. L. H. HARRIS Bathing
	16th		Funeral under Lt. B. L. PRIOR-PALMER. Parade of Composite Squadron —	3 OR from Leave

WAR DIARY
or
INTELLIGENCE SUMMARY.
(Erase heading not required.)

Army Form C. 2118.

Instructions regarding War Diaries and Intelligence Summaries are contained in F.S. Regs., Part II. and the Staff Manual respectively. Title pages will be prepared in manuscript.

Place	Date	Hour	Summary of Events and Information	Remarks and references to Appendices
COLOGNE	Aug 17th		C. of E. Parade Service under Major G.H. PHIPPS-HORNBY.	2 O.R. from H.Qrs; 1 " " H.Qrs
	18th		The Composite Squadron paraded with the VI Corps for the Ceremonial Parade in honour of a visit of the Army Council. Army of the Rhine Horse Show at KALK.	10 O.R. o 4 Hrs.
	19th		Regimental Routine. Army Horse Show. In the Regiment won 1st Prize, Prize, 3 Seconds a 3 Thirds. 2-day Shows the Consisted of Best Pack Pony; Hotchkiss Park; Best Turn Out NCO or man; Best Troop Horse (Henry Wright Challenge (Major PHIPPS-HORNBY); Showing Competition (Cpl. S.S. SMITH).	3 O.R. o trap; 1 " 5 P.H.
	20th	2130	Regimental Routine. Bathing Parade under Lt. G.W. BREITMEYER.	10 O.R. o trap; 1 " " " ; 3 " " "
	21st		Regimental Routine.	
	22nd	2130	Regimental Routine.	
	23rd		All Riding School hrs. crews to-day running to Artillery turning to be packed for shipment to the U.K. COLOGNE Roman.	10 O.R. o trap; 1 " " H.Qrs; 1 " 5 P.H.; 1 " o trap; 1 " two trap
	24th		C of E Parade Service under Capt. C.J. CHISHOLM. Roman Catholic Service at 17 Lancers trenches.	
	25th		Regimental Routine.	3 " o trap; 1 " o trap.
	26th		Regimental Routine.	6 " o trap; 2 " 5 P.H.
	27th		Bathing Parade. Inoculation of Reform Corps by H.O. 2 O.R. proceeds to the U.K. on Re-Engagement Furlough.	

JHM

Army Form C. 2118.

WAR DIARY
or
INTELLIGENCE SUMMARY.
(Erase heading not required.)

Instructions regarding War Diaries and Intelligence Summaries are contained in F. S. Regs., Part II. and the Staff Manual respectively. Title pages will be prepared in manuscript.

Place	Date	Hour	Summary of Events and Information	Remarks and references to Appendices
COLOGNE	Aug. 28th 29th		Regimental Routine. The majority of the Regimental Transport Equipment was taken up to NIPPE'S Station, preparatory to loading it tomorrow - Balking Parade under 2/Lt J.H.A. TENNANT. 2 i/c in Command of Squadron and S.Q.M.S's attended a lecture on "the last Regiment of Troops before leaving the Army of the Rhine" at H.Q. 17th LANCERS.	taken up to NIPPES Stations 20/for tops
"	30th		Lieut B.H ALLFREY and a party of 12. O.R. proceeded to NIPPES Stations to load the Regimental Equipment. 2/Lieut. M.H AIRD and 7 O.R. proceeded with the Equipment to England (AINTREE). COLOGNE Races organized	
"	31st		Parade Service under Capt C.W NORMAN. CREFELD Races organized by the 1st Belgian Cavalry Brigade.	

31/8/19.

H. Walker Jackson - Capt.
Adj. 9th Lancers.

BEF
CAV. DIV.

LANCER Bde

12 LANCERS

1919 APR. to 1919 AUG

FROM 2 CAV DIV. 5 BDE
Box 1140

Own From Dragoon Bde 21.3."5.

Army Form C. 2118.

WAR DIARY
or
INTELLIGENCE SUMMARY.
Summary of Events and Information Later 5th Cav. Bde

(Erase heading not required.)

Instructions regarding War Diaries and Intelligence Summaries are contained in F. S. Regs., Part II. and the Staff Manual respectively. Title pages will be prepared in manuscript.

Place	Date	Hour	12th (PRINCE OF WALES' ROYAL) LANCERS.	Remarks and references to Appendices
	April 1st. 1919.		The Regiment was accomodated in the Artillery Barracks, RIEHL on the outskirts of COLOGNE. Accomodation good for men and horses but barracks very dirty. All ranks clearing up.	
	April 2-d. 1919.		Continued clearing up barracks. The following wire was received from Major-General W.H.GREENLY.C.M.G.,D.S.O. "Delighted to inform you that H.R.H.The Prince of Wales has consented to become Colonel in Chief of the Regiment. Please congratulate all ranks from me on this, the latest of the honours they have won".	07
	April 3rd 1919.		The G.O.C., Lancer Brigade inspected 35 horses selected for transfer to the 9th Lancers. 2 Officers and 114 other ranks of the 6th Battn. London Regt were posted to the regiment for duty to assist with the horses. 1 Officer and 15 other ranks of the 9th Lancers arrived from DUREN to conduct 35 horses by road tomorrow 4th inst.	07
	April 4th 1919.		35 horses were dispatched to the 9th Lancers. G.O.C., Cavalry Division of the Rhine inspected the regiment and Barracks. 12 other ranks of the 6th Battn London Regt joined the company for duty.	07

(19475) Wt W.4358/P.60 60,000 12/17 D. D. & L. Sch. Sta. Form/C.2118/13.

Army Form C. 2118.

WAR DIARY
or
INTELLIGENCE SUMMARY.
(Erase heading not required.)

Instructions regarding War Diaries and Intelligence Summaries are contained in F. S. Regs., Part II. and the Staff Manual respectively. Title pages will be prepared in manuscript.

Place	Date	Hour	Summary of Events and Information	Remarks and references to Appendices
12th (PRINCE OF WALES' ROYAL) LANCERS.				
	April 5th 1919.		General cleaning up of Barracks. Combined team of the regiment and the 6th London Regt played a football match with "H" and "G" Battery R.H.A. The later winning by 2 goals to 1. 9 other ranks, 6th London Regt and 1 other ranks of the regiment proceeded on leave.	JT
	April 6th 1919.		Church parade. Major H.M.MICHOLLS, 17th Lancers inspected the horse account of the regiment and found it satisfactory and up to date. 7 horses transferred to A.C.Camp, DEUTZ. 2 other ranks went on leave to the UNITED KINGDOM.	JT
	April 7th 1919.		Riding drill for young Officers and the band. Lance drill for all Officers in the afternoon under the Adjutant. 1 Officer and 20 other ranks proceeded to KASSEL to assist 9th Machine Gun Squadron to move to new area. 1 other rank went on leave to ENGLAND.	JT
	April 8th 1919.		Riding drill for all young Officers and band under the Adjutant. Lance drill for young Officers.	JT
	April 9th 1919.		Riding drill for young Officers and band. Lance drill for all Officers under the Adjutant. Officers' Mess meeting. One lorry arrived for attachment to the regiment from the R.A.S.C., M.T.Company. 2 other ranks went on leave to ENGLAND.	JT

Army Form C. 2118.

WAR DIARY
or
INTELLIGENCE SUMMARY.
(Erase heading not required.)

Instructions regarding War Diaries and Intelligence Summaries are contained in F. S. Regs., Part II. and the Staff Manual respectively. Title pages will be prepared in manuscript.

Place	Date	Hour	Summary of Events and Information	Remarks and references to Appendices
12th (PRINCE OF WALES' ROYAL)LANCERS.	April 10th 1919.		Riding drill as usual. Major G.M.NICOLLS, 17th Lancers inspected the horse account of the regiment and found it correct. 2 other ranks went on leave to ENGLAND. Football.	A
	April 11th 1919.		Riding drill as usual. The G.O.C., 4th Corps visited the regiment and walked around barracks. 1 other rank went on leave to ENGLAND.	A
	April 12th 1919.		Riding drill as usual. General cleaning up of barracks. Football match played between "A" and "B" Squadrons. No score.	A
	April 13th 1919.		Church parade. 1 other rank went on leave to the United Kingdom.	A
	April 14th 1919.		Riding drill under the Adjutant. Lance drill for all Officers. The Regiment came under orders to stand to and turn out at short notice at 06.00 hours for 7 days. Captain J.R.C.RAWNSLEY.M.C and one Officer per Squadron and 15 other ranks including one Hotchkiss Rifle Section per squadron and to be in readiness to turn out.	A
	April 15th 1919.		Riding drill under the Adjutant. Lance drill for young Officers. 1 other rank went on leave to ENGLAND.	A

Army Form C. 2118.

WAR DIARY
or
INTELLIGENCE SUMMARY.
(Erase heading not required.)

Instructions regarding War Diaries and Intelligence Summaries are contained in F. S. Regs., Part II. and the Staff Manual respectively. Title pages will be prepared in manuscript.

Place	Date	Hour	Summary of Events and Information	Remarks and references to Appendices
			12th (PRINCE OF WALES' ROYAL) LANCERS.	
	April 15th 1919.		Riding drill under the Adjutant. Large drill for all Officers at 14.00 hours. Major General Sir. W. E. PEYTON.K.C.B.,K.C.V.O.,D.S.O commanding the Cavalry Division of the Rhine visited the barracks and lunched with the Officers of the regiment. 1 other rank went on leave to ENGLAND.	07
	April 17th 1919.		Riding drill under the Adjutant. 1 other rank to ENGLAND on leave. Football in the afternoon.	07
	April 18th 1919.		Good Friday to be observed as a Sunday. No Church parades but suitable entertainments were held in allmainemas in the town. Squadron football competition of 6 a side. Won by "C" Squadron. Capt. D.C.H.RICHARDSON. M.C and Lieut R.S.T.MOORE joined the regiment from ENGLAND. Lieut R.S.T.MOORE was wounded in August 1914 and was taken a prisoner. 1 other rank went on leave to the United Kingdom. 1 other rank went to a dispersal station for demobilization.	07
	April 19th 1919.		The band paraded at No.1.Concentration Camp at 09.00 hours to play Cavalry and Artillery Demobilization party to the Boat. 1 other rank went on leave to ENGLAND.	07

WAR DIARY
or
INTELLIGENCE SUMMARY.

(Erase heading not required.)

Army Form C. 2118.

Place	Date	Hour	Summary of Events and Information	Remarks and references to Appendices
12th (PRINCE OF WALES' ROYAL LANCERS.	April 20th 1919.		Easter Sunday. Church Service at 10.45 hours followed by the Holy Communion. 1 other rank went to ENGLAND on leave.	7
	April 21st. 1919.		Exercise, the remainder of the day observed as a holiday. The 10th Brigade R.F.A held a steeplechase meeting at WEILLERSWIST, S.W. of COLOGNE. Lieut R. STRAKER. M.C winning the first race on "Rolleston" over a very difficult course. A very enjoyable afternoon was spent. 2 other ranks went on leave to ENGLAND	7
	April 22nd 1919.		Riding drill under the Adjutant. Lance drill for young Officers at 14.00 hours. All Officers' Chargers were inspected by the Commanding Officer. 1 other rank went on leave to ENGLAND.	7
	April 23rd 1919.		Riding drill under the Adjutant. Lance drill for all Officers in the afternoon. 4 riding horses posted to the regiment from the 17th Lancers. 1 L.D. Horse from the Lancer Brigade and 1 drum horse from the 10th Corps were posted to the regiment. 3 other ranks went on leave to ENGLAND,	7
	April 24th 1919.		Riding drill under the Adjutant. Lance drill for all Officers in the afternoon. 2 horses detached to the R.A.F. 2 other ranks went to ENGLAND on leave.	7

Army Form C. 2118.

WAR DIARY
or
INTELLIGENCE SUMMARY.
(Erase heading not required.)

Place	Date	Hour	Summary of Events and Information	Remarks and references to Appendices
12th (PRINCE OF WALES' ROYAL) LANCERS.				
	April 25th 1919.		Riding drill under the Adjutant and Lance drill in the afternoon for all Officers. The A.D.M.S., Cavalry Division of the Rhine inspected the Barracks and was very satisfied with the sanitary arrangements of the regiment. The A.D.V.S., Cavalry Division of the Rhine inspected the horses of the regiment. 2 other ranks went to ENGLAND on leave.	57.
	April 26th 1919.		Exercise. Football in the afternoon. 5 other ranks went to ENGLAND on leave.	57.
	April 27th 1919.		Church parade. The band played selections on the square at 12.00. 5 other ranks went to ENGLAND on leave.	57.
	April 28th 1919.		A composite Squadron formed in case of any disturbances in the town paraded 89 strong in marching order for inspection by the G.O.C., Lancer Brigade who complimented all ranks on their splendid turnout. The London Division held a steeplechase meeting at KALK. A very enjoyable afternoon. Rather cold.	57.
	April 29th 1919.		Riding drill under Captain J.R.C.RAWNSLEY.M.C Exercise. 2nd Day of the London Division Race meeting. 5 other ranks went to ENGLAND on leave.	57.

Army Form C. 2118.

WAR DIARY
or
INTELLIGENCE SUMMARY.
(Erase heading not required.)

12th (PRINCE OF WALES' ROYAL) LANCERS.

Summary of Events and Information

Place	Date	Hour		Remarks and references to Appendices
	April 30th 1919.		Riding drill under Captain J.R.O.RAWNSLEY.M.C. Exercise.	17

Rawnsley
Lieut Colonel.,
Commanding, 12th Royal Lancers.

Army Form C. 2118.

WAR DIARY
or
INTELLIGENCE SUMMARY.
(Erase heading not required.)

Instructions regarding War Diaries and Intelligence Summaries are contained in F. S. Regs., Part II. and the Staff Manual respectively. Title pages will be prepared in manuscript.

Place	Date	Hour	Summary of Events and Information	Remarks and references to Appendices
12th (PRINCE OF WALES' ROYAL) LANCERS	May. 1st 1919.		Composite Squadron standing too in case of any disturbances in the Town during Labour demonstrations. Orders received 19.45 hours, all quiet, Composite Squadron "Stand Down".	of
	May 2nd 1919.		Riding drill under the Adjutant for young Officers and band at 08.30 hours.	
			1 Officers and 24 other ranks attended Cavalry Memorial service at BERGHIEM. 2 other ranks went to ENGLAND on leave.	
			Captain J.A.PURDEY rejoined the regiment from War Office.	of
			All horses selected for jumping competition and riders paraded in the riding school under the Adjutant for instruction.	
			4 horses despatched to A.C.C. DUREN as unsuitable.	
	May 3rd 1919.		Riding drill under the Adjutant. 2 other ranks despatched to Cavalry Division Headquarters for Police duty.	
			Lieut R.G.HOFFNUNG GOLDSMID, Lieut F.T.BAINES, 2 servants and 4 Horses proceeded to Headquarters 4th Corps for duty.	
			The Commander in Chief, Rhine Army visited the regiment and inspected men's rooms, dining halls, reading rooms, cookhouses and stables.	
			4 other ranks joined the regiment from the CURRAGH., for duty with the band. 1 Officer and 50 other ranks from the 52nd Btn. Rifle Brigade attached to the regiment to assist in looking after the horses.	
			One other rank proceeded to ENGLAND on leave.	of

Army Form C. 2118.

WAR DIARY
or
INTELLIGENCE SUMMARY.
(Erase heading not required.)

Instructions regarding War Diaries and Intelligence Summaries are contained in F. S. Regs., Part II. and the Staff Manual respectively. Title pages will be prepared in manuscript.

Place	Date	Hour	12th (PRINCE OF WALES' ROYAL) LANCERS Summary of Events and Information	Remarks and references to Appendices
	May 4th 1919.		Church parade at 10.30 hours. The Band of the Regiment played selections on the square from 12.00 hours to 13.00 hours.	OT
	May 5th 1919.		Riding drill under the Adjutant. Lance drill for young officers at 14.00 hours. 1 other rank posted to regiment for duty as saddler 2 other ranks proceeded to ENGLAND on leave.	OT
	May 6th 1919.		Riding drill under the Adjutant at 08.30 hours. Tent pegging for all officers at 10.30 hours. Major W.R. STYLES assumed command of "A" Squadron. Captain J.A. PURDEY takes over duties as Pay Officer and Band President. 1 other rank to ENGLAND on leave. 1 other rank to Dispersal station.	OT
	May 7th 1919.		Riding drill under the Adjutant at 08.30 hours. Lance drill for young Officers at 14.00 hours. The Commanding Officer inspected this parade.	OT
	May 8th 1919.		Riding drill under the Adjutant at 08.30 hours. Tent pegging for all officers at 10.30 hours. 3 horses to A.C.C., DUREN.	OT
	May 9th 1919.		Riding drill under the Adjutant at 08.30 hours. 3 mules transferred to 17th Lancers. 2 other ranks to ENGLAND on leave. Polo for all officers at 14.30 hours	OT

Army Form C. 2118.

WAR DIARY
or
INTELLIGENCE SUMMARY.
(Erase heading not required.)

Instructions regarding War Diaries and Intelligence Summaries are contained in F. S. Regs., Part II. and the Staff Manual respectively. Title pages will be prepared in manuscript.

Place	Date	Hour	Summary of Events and Information	Remarks and references to Appendices
12th (PRINCE OF WALES' ROYAL) LANCERS	May 10th 1919.		Exercise under Squadron arrangements. General clean up of barracks. Lieut J.R.C.RAWNSLEY M.C. 1 servant and Sgt L.M.LAWRENCE.D.C.M proceeded to ENGLAND to attend the 1st Equitation course at NETHERAVON on the 19th May 1919.	JH
	May 11th 1919.		Church parade at 10.30 hours. The Regimental Band played selections on the square from 12.00 to 13.00 hours.	JH
	May 12th 1919.		Riding drill under the Adjutant at 08.30 hours. Lance drill at 14.00 hours. Lieut H.H.L.HIGGINS, Northumberland Hussars posted to the Regiment for duty. one other rank to ENGLAND on leave. Polo at 14.50 hours.	JH
	May 13th 1919.		Riding drill under the Adjutant at 08.30 hours. Tentpegging for all Officers at 10.30 hours. Lance drill at 14.00 hours. 17th Lancers took over the Duties of Headquarters Regiment for Mobile Regiment from 12.00 hours today. 2 other ranks posted to the regiment from the CURRAGH. One other rank to England on leave. One other rank to dispersal station.	JH
	May 14th 1919.		Officers paraded mounted with all arms for instruction under the Adjutant at 09.00 hours. Polo at 14.30 hours. One other rank to ENGLAND on leave.	JH

Army Form C. 2118.

WAR DIARY
or
INTELLIGENCE SUMMARY.
(Erase heading not required.)

Instructions regarding War Diaries and Intelligence Summaries are contained in F. S. Regs., Part II. and the Staff Manual respectively. Title pages will be prepared in manuscript.

Place	Date	Hour	Summary of Events and Information	Remarks and references to Appendices
12th (PRINCE OF WALES' ROYAL) LANCERS				
	May 15th 1919.		Riding drill under the Adjutant at 08130 hours. Lance drill at 14.00 hours. Practice for horses entered for the show at WIESBADEN at 14.30 hours. one other rank to ENGLAND on leave.	
	May 16th 1919.		All officers paraded mounted with all arms for instruction under the Adjutant at 08.30 hours. The Divisional Commander inspected the horses during stable hour. Polo at 15.00 hours. Horses entered for the WIESBADEN show practiced at 14.30 hours.	
	May 17th 1919.		1st Class ride under the Adjutant at 08.00 hours. Band ride under Captain F.F.F.SPICER.D.S.O at 08.00. Major W.R.STYLES assumed Command of the Mobile Force with Lieut A.F.DAVIDGE.M.G xxxi as 2nd in Command for week ending 26th inst. N.C.Os entered for the jumping competition to be held at WIESBADEN proceeded by train to Cavalry Barracks, WIESBADEN.	
	May 18th 1919.		Church parade at 10.30 hours. The Regimental Band played on the square from 12.00 to 13.00 hours. One other rank to ENGLAND on leave.	
	May 19th 1919.		Rides as detailed at 08.00 hours. Lance drill for young Officers at 14.30 hours.	

Army Form C. 2118.

WAR DIARY
or
INTELLIGENCE SUMMARY.
(Erase heading not required.)

Instructions regarding War Diaries and Intelligence Summaries are contained in F. S. Regs., Part II. and the Staff Manual respectively. Title pages will be prepared in manuscript.

Place	Date	Hour	Summary of Events and Information	Remarks and references to Appendices
12th (PRINCE OF WALES' ROYAL) LANCERS.	May 20th 1919.		1st class ride paraded at 08.00 hours under Lieut A.F.DAVIDGE.M.C. Band ride paraded under Captain F.F.F. SPICER.D.S.O at 08.00 hours. 2 other ranks rejoined from 1st Reserve Regiment, CURRAGH and posted to "A" and "C" Squadrons respectively.	of
	May 21st 1919.		Rides as detailed under Capt.F.F.SPICER.D.S.O. Remaining horses entered for the WIESBADEN horse show proceeded to WIESBADEN. Results of N.C.Os jumping competition, WIESBADEN open to all allied troops. 1st. L.Cpl. HEALY, 12th Royal Lancers on "BULLET". L.Cpl. HEALY is to be congratulated on his fine performance. All 4 horses jumped well.	of
	May 22nd 1919.		1st class ride paraded under the Adjutant at 08.00. Band ride under Capt.F.F.SPICER.D.S.O.	of
	May 23rd 1919.		1st class ride under the Adjutant at 08.00 hours. Band ride under Capt.F.F.SPICER.D.S.O. 2nd Lieut B.J.J.ELLERBECK attended a T.G.C.M held at 9th Lancers for instruction.	of
	May 24th 1919.		Rides as detailed under the Adjutant at 08.00 hours. Results of cross country race at the WIESBADEN show open to Officers of the Allied Armies. 2nd prize. Lieut R.S.T.MOORE on "GEORGE".	of
	May 25th 1919.		Church parade at 10.30 hours. The regimental band played selections from 12.00 to 13.00 hours on the square.	of

Army Form C. 2118.

WAR DIARY
or
INTELLIGENCE SUMMARY.
(Erase heading not required.)

Instructions regarding War Diaries and Intelligence Summaries are contained in F. S. Regs., Part II. and the Staff Manual respectively. Title pages will be prepared in manuscript.

Place	Date	Hour	Summary of Events and Information	Remarks and references to Appendices
12th (PRINCE OF WALES' ROYAL) LANCERS.				
	May 26th 1919.		Rides under the Adjutant as detailed. All subaltern Officers paraded with all arms for instruction under the Adjutant. The Mobile Squadron received orders to stand to at short notice owing to the uncertainty of the GERMAN'S signing the Peace Terms.	6↑
	May 27th 1919.		Rides as detailed paraded under the Adjutant at 08.00 All subalterns parade mounted with all arms under the Adjutant for instruction at 09.30 hours. Commanding Officer and Squadron leaders attended a conference at the 17th Lancers Headquarters given by the Divisional Commander.	6↑
	May 28th 1919.		Young Officers and Band parade with all arms for instructions at 08.00 hours. All subaltern officers parade for instruction in troop training at 09.30 to 10.30 hours. All subaltern officers paraded for lance drill at 14.30 hours. Capt.J.V.ADAIR.M.C proceeded to NIVELLE to assume command of the Cadre of the NORTHUMBERLAND hussars. Major A.B.REYNOLDS ordered to report to 12th Royal Lancers for duty. one other rank to ENGLAND on leave.	6↑

Army Form C. 2118.

WAR DIARY
INTELLIGENCE SUMMARY.
(Erase heading not required.)

Instructions regarding War Diaries and Intelligence Summaries are contained in F. S. Regs., Part II. and the Staff Manual respectively. Title pages will be prepared in manuscript.

Place	Date	Hour	Summary of Events and Information	Remarks and references to Appendices
12th (PRINCE OF WALES ROYAL) LANCERS	May 29th 1919.		1st class ride paraded with all arms under the Adjutant at 08.00 hours. All subalterns paraded at 09.30 hours for troop training. All subalterns paraded for Lance drill at 12.30 hours. The G.O.C., 6th Corps visited the regiment and inspected mens living rooms, dining halls, recreation rooms, cook houses and stables.	ot
	May 30th 1919.		1st Class ride paraded with all arms under the Adjutant at 08.00 hours. All subaltern officers paraded with all arms for instruction in troop training. Friendly game of Polo between 9th Lancers and 12th Lancers was played on the aerodrome at 14.30 hours. 9th Lancers won by 4 goals. Band played selections in the Y.M.C.A from 18.30 to 20.00 hours.	ot
	May 31st 1919.		All subalterns paraded at 08.00 hours for riding instruction.	ot

Coulthard
Lieut Colonel.,
Commanding, 12th Royal Lancers.

CONFIDENTIAL.

WAR &c DIARY.

12th (PRINCE OF WALES'S ROYAL) LANCERS.

June, 1919.

> 12TH
> (P. of WALES'S ROYAL)
> LANCERS.
>
> No. 8.769

Army Form C. 2118.

WAR DIARY
or
INTELLIGENCE SUMMARY.
(Erase heading not required.)

Instructions regarding War Diaries and Intelligence Summaries are contained in F. S. Regs., Part II. and the Staff Manual respectively. Title pages will be prepared in manuscript.

Place	Date	Hour	Summary of Events and Information	Remarks and references to Appendices
COLOGNE	June 1st, 19.		12th (Prince of Wales's Royal) Lancers. Parade Service was held in the Regimental Canteen at 10.30 hours. Band played Selections on the Square from 12.00 to 13.00 hours. 36 O.R's from 30th Labour Coy joined for duty.	
"	2nd, 19.		Band paraded for Riding School at 08.00 hours under the Adjutant. Subalterns paraded for Riding School at 09.15 hours with all arms.	
"	3rd, 19.		The Regiment parade at 10.00 hours on the Square to celebrate the King's Birthday. The Band was on parade and played selections. The remainder of the day was observed as a holiday.	
"	4th, 19.		The Band and Subalterns paraded for Riding Drill at 08.00 hours. 2 O.R's proceeded to Concentration Camp., HORREM for dispersal to ENGLAND as time serving soldiers. L/3509.Sgt.JACOBS.C.H. proceeded to NEWMARKET to undergo a course of instruction in Education. Captain.J.V.ADAIR.M.C rejoined from Northumberland Hussars.	
"	5th, 19.		The Band and Subalterns paraded for Riding Drill at 08.00 hours. The Veterinary Officer inspected the horses of "A" Squadron at 11.00 hours.	
"	6th, 19.		The Band and Subalterns paraded for Riding Drill at 08.00 hours. A Lecture was given to all Subalterns by Major.W.R.STYLES.	

Army Form C. 2118.

WAR DIARY
or
INTELLIGENCE SUMMARY.
(Erase heading not required.)

Instructions regarding War Diaries and Intelligence Summaries are contained in F. S. Regs., Part II. and the Staff Manual respectively. Title pages will be prepared in manuscript.

Place	Date	Hour	Summary of Events and Information	Remarks and references to Appendices
COLOGNE	June 7th, 19.		12th (Prince of Wales's Royal) Lancers. The Band paraded for Riding Drill at 06.00 hours. All Subalterns attended the Forge at 09.00 hours for an examination by Major W.R.STYLES on their knowledge of shoeing horses. The following Birthday honours were bestowed on the undermentioned:- Major.(T/Lt.Col).C.H.G.BLACK to be brevet Lt.Col. Capt.(A/Maj).H.V.S.CHARRINGTON,M.C to be brevet Major. Maj.(T/Lt.Col).A.B.REYNOLDS awarded the D.S.O. Capt.(A/Maj.).W.R.STYLES awarded the M.C. L/16958.Cook.Sgt.REID.F.H. awarded the M.S.M. L/3064.L/Sgt.KING.W.H. ———do——— 2 O.R's proceeded on leave to ENGLAND. The Southern Division held a Race Meeting at KALK., COLOGNE and the Goodwood Maiden Plate was won by Captain.J.V.ADAIR,M.C.	
"	8th,19.		Church Service was held at 09.00 hours in the Regtl Canteen. 1 O.R proceeded on leave to ENGLAND.	
"	9th,19.		Being Whitsun Monday the day was observed as a holiday. 1 O.R proceeded on leave to ENGLAND. 1 O.R joined from Reserve Regiment CURRAGH.	
"	10th,19.		All Subalterns paraded with their Chargers for Riding Drill at 09.00 hours. All Subalterns paraded at 14.15 hours for Lance Drill. The Veterinary Officer inspected the horses of Regtl Hqrs and "C" Squadron at 11.00 hours.	

Army Form C. 2118.

WAR DIARY
or
INTELLIGENCE SUMMARY.
(Erase heading not required.)

Instructions regarding War Diaries and Intelligence Summaries are contained in F. S. Regs., Part II. and the Staff Manual respectively. Title pages will be prepared in manuscript.

Place	Date	Hour	Summary of Events and Information	Remarks and references to Appendices
COLOGNE	June 11th,19.		(Prince of Wales's Royal/Lancers) Band Ride paraded under the Adjutant at 08.00 hours. Staff Ride for all Subalterns paraded under Major. W.R.SMYLES.M.C at 09.15 hours. 7 O.R's joined from Reserve Regiment., CURRAGH. 2 O.R's proceeded on leave to ENGLAND.	
"	12th,19.		Band and Subalterns paraded for Riding School at 08.00 hours.	
"	13th,19.		Band and Subalterns paraded for Riding School at 08.00 hours. 3 O.R's proceeded on leave to ENGLAND.	
"	14th,19.		The G.O.C., Lancer Brigade inspected Officers and N.C.O's (Instructors) of the Regiment at Lance Drill dismounted at 11.15 hours, and at mounted Drill at 12.00 hours. 1 O.R proceeded on leave to ENGLAND.	
"	15th,19.		Church Service was held at 10.15 hours in the Regimental Canteen. 1 O.R proceeded on leave to ENGLAND.	
"	16th,19.		Subalterns and Band paraded for Riding School at 08.00 hours. Officers and N.C.O's (Instructors) paraded at 09.15 hours. Lieut.R.P.SPENCER and 46 O.R's joined from Reserve Regiment., CURRAGH.	
"	17th,19.		Subalterns and Band paraded for Riding School at 08.00 hours. Officers and N.C.O's (Instructors) paraded at 09.15 hrs. (Contd).	

Army Form C. 2118.

WAR DIARY
or
INTELLIGENCE SUMMARY

(Erase heading not required.)

Instructions regarding War Diaries and Intelligence Summaries are contained in F. S. Regs., Part II. and the Staff Manual respectively. Title pages will be prepared in manuscript.

Place	Date	Hour	Summary of Events and Information	Remarks and references to Appendices
COLOGNE	June 17th, 19		(Contd). 30 Horses proceeded to Horse Farm for grazing. The Mobile Squadron proceeded to Rendezvous. 1 O.R. proceeded on leave to ENGLAND.	
"	18th, 19.		Exercise under Squadron Leaders. 100 O.R's joined from 30th Labour Company for duty.	
"	19th, 19.		Headquarters of Mobile Column under command of Lieut. Colonel. C. FANE C.M.G., D.S.O proceeded to Rendezvous. Band paraded for Riding School at 08.00 hours. Captain. D.C.H. RICHARDSON, M.C took over command of all details left in Barracks. 2 O.R's proceeded on leave to ENGLAND.	
"	20th, 19.		Band paraded for Riding School at 08.00 hours. Captain. J. McKAY, M.C. (RAMC) attached to the Regiment proceeded to the ENGLAND for duty.	
"	21st, 19.		Exercise under Squadron Leaders. 1 O.R proceeded on leave to ENGLAND.	
"	22nd, 19.		Church Service was held in the Regimental Canteen at 10.15 hours. 2nd London Brigade Group Sports were held at ENGELS-KIRCHEN, following events were won by L/4606. Pte. BALDOCK., 12th Royal Lancers. 440 yards. 220 Yards. The tug-of-war was won by Team from Composite Lancer Squadron consisting of 9th, 12th, and 17th Lancers. Brig. Gen. F.A. GUDGEON. C.B commended the Lancer Squadron for their fine exhibition.	

Army Form C. 2118.

WAR DIARY
or
INTELLIGENCE SUMMARY.
(Erase heading not required.)

Instructions regarding War Diaries and Intelligence Summaries are contained in F. S. Regs., Part II. and the Staff Manual respectively. Title pages will be prepared in manuscript.

12th (Prince of Wales's Royal)Lancers

Place	Date	Hour	Summary of Events and Information	Remarks and references to Appendices
COLOGNE	June 23rd,19.		Band paraded for Riding School at 08.00 hours. Last joined reinforcements paraded at 09.00 hours in No.1.Riding School, under the Adjutant.	
"	24th,19.		Band paraded for Riding School at 08.00 hours. Reinforcements of "B" and "C" Squadrons paraded for Physical Training at 18.00 hours.	
"	25th,19.		Band paraded for Riding School at 08.00 hours. Reinforcements of "A" Squadron paraded for Physical training at 18.00 hours.	
"	26th,19.		Band paraded for Riding School at 08.00 hours. Recruits of "A" Squadron paraded for Physical Training at 18.00 hours.	
"	27th,19.		Band paraded for Riding School at 08.00 hours. Recruits of "B" and "C" Squadrons paraded for Physical training in No.1 Riding School at 14.15 hours. Recruits of "B" and "C" Squadrons paraded for Physical Training at 18.00 hours. 101 guns were fired from the bank of the RHINE near the HOHEN ZOLLERN BRIDGE to celebrate the signing of peace.	
"	28th,19.		Exercise under Squadron Leaders. 22 O.Rs from 30th Labour Coy joined for duty. 1 O.R proceeded on leave to ENGLAND.	
"	29th,19.		Church Service was held in the Regimental Canteen at 10.15 hours. Regtl Band played selections on the Square from 12.00 hours to 13.00 hours.	

Army Form C. 2118.

WAR DIARY
or
INTELLIGENCE SUMMARY.
(Erase heading not required.)

Instructions regarding War Diaries and Intelligence Summaries are contained in F. S. Regs., Part II. and the Staff Manual respectively. Title pages will be prepared in manuscript.

12th (Prince of Wales's Royal) Lancers

Place	Date	Hour	Summary of Events and Information	Remarks and references to Appendices
COLOGNE.	June 30th, 19.		Band paraded for Riding School at 08.00 hours. Recruits paraded for Riding School at 08.00 hours. Headquarters of Mobile Force rejoined the Regiment.	
	30/6/1919.		A. J. Dawdge, Lieut. Colonel. Commanding 12th Royal Lancers.	

Army Form C. 2118.

WAR DIARY
or
INTELLIGENCE SUMMARY.
(Erase heading not required.)

Instructions regarding War Diaries and Intelligence Summaries are contained in F. S. Regs., Part II. and the Staff Manual respectively. Title pages will be prepared in manuscript.

Place	Date	Hour	Summary of Events and Information	Remarks and references to Appendices
			12th (PRINCE OF WALES'S ROYAL) LANCERS	
	1st July 1919.		The band paraded for riding drill at 08.00 hours. Recruits paraded for riding drill at 08.00 hours.	JE
	2nd July 1919.		The band paraded for riding drill at 08.00 hours. 1st class ride paraded with all arms under Lieut. R.STRAKER.M.C at 08.00 hours. Recruits paraded for riding school at 08.00 hours. 3 other ranks proceeded on leave. The Mobile Squadron rejoined from Forward area.	JE
	3rd July 1919.		Band paraded for riding drill at 08.00 hours. 1st class ride paraded with all arms under Lieut R. STRAKER.M.C at 08.00 hours. Recruits paraded for riding drill at 08.00 hours. Recruits of "B" and "C" Squadrons paraded for " " " Physical training at 18.00 hours. Captain J.V.ADAIR. M.C inspected all horses of the Regiment detached at the grazing farm. 3 other ranks proceeded on leave.	OF
	4th July 1919.		Band will parade for riding drill at 08.00 hours. 1st class ride paraded with all arms under Lieut R. STRAKER.M.C at 08.00 hours. Recruits paraded for musketry at 10.00 hours. " " " Footdrill 14.00 " " " Physical training at 18.00 hours. 3 other ranks proceeded on leave.	JE
	5th July 1919.		Exercise under Squadron arrangements. 3 other ranks proceeded on leave. 49 other ranks rejoined from 30th Labour Company.	OF

Army Form C. 2118.

WAR DIARY
or
INTELLIGENCE SUMMARY.
(Erase heading not required.)

12th (PRINCE OF WALES'S ROYAL) LANCERS.

Instructions regarding War Diaries and Intelligence Summaries are contained in F. S. Regs., Part II. and the Staff Manual respectively. Title pages will be prepared in manuscript.

Place	Date	Hour	Summary of Events and Information	Remarks and references to Appendices
	6th July 1919.		The day was observed as a day of National Thanksgiving on the signing of the Peace. The following parades were held.	
			Parade service in the Retl. Canteen at 10.30 hours.	↲
			All Roman Catholics attended the local church.	
			3 other ranks proceeded on leave.	
	7th July 1919.		1st class ride paraded at 08.00 hours with all arms.	
			Recruits paraded for riding school at 08.00 hours.	↲
			" " Foot drill. 14.00 "	
			" " Physical Training at 18.00 hours.	
	8th July 1919.		The day was observed as a holiday to celebrate the signing of Peace.	↲
			A short service was held in the Regimental Canteen at 09.00 hours. Regimental Sports were held in the afternoon commencing at 14.30 hours. A smoking concert was held at 17.00 hours. 3 other ranks proceeded on leave to ENGLAND.	
	9th July 1919.		1st class ride paraded for riding drill at 08.00 with all arms. Recruits paraded for riding drill at 08.00 hours.	↲
			Recruits paraded for Musketry at 10.00 hours.	
			" " " Footdrill 14.00 "	
			" " " Physical training at 18.00 hours.	
			Captain D.C.H.RICHARDSON.M.C. 9 other ranks and 5 horses proceeded to PARIS to take part in the Victory march.	
			3 other ranks proceeded on leave.	

Army Form C. 2118.

WAR DIARY
or
INTELLIGENCE SUMMARY.
(Erase heading not required.)

Instructions regarding War Diaries and Intelligence Summaries are contained in F. S. Regs., Part II. and the Staff Manual respectively. Title pages will be prepared in manuscript.

Place	Date	Hour	Summary of Events and Information	Remarks and references to Appendices
			12th (PRINCE OF WALES'S ROYAL) LANCERS.	
	10th July 1919.		1st class ride paraded for riding drill at 08.00 hours with all arms.	
			Recruits paraded for riding drill at 08.00 hours.	
			" " " Musketry at 10.00 "	
			" " " Foot drill at 14.00 "	
			" " " Physical training at 18.15 hours.	
			3 other ranks proceeded on leave to ENGLAND.	JT
	11th July 1919.		Recruits and tranfers paraded for riding drill at 18.00 hours.	
			Recruits paraded for musketry at 10.00 hours.	
			" " " foot drill at 14.00 "	
			" " " Physical training at 18.00 hours.	
			The Medical Officer inspected all W.C.Os and men of the regiment at 14.30 hours.	
			12 W.C.Os paraded mounted under the Adjutant for instruction in riding drill at 06.00 hours.	
			L/4907. Sgt Master Tailor CRUDEN transferred to 2nd Life Guards and proceeded to ENGLAND.	
			3 other ranks proceeded to ENGLAND on leave.	JT
	12th July 1919.		12 W.C.O instructors paraded under the Adjutant at 06.00 hours.	
			2 W.C.Os and 2 chargers proceeded to PARIS with Commander in Chiefs Staff for VICTORY March.	
			2 other ranks proceeded on leave to the United Kingdom.	JT
	13th July 1919.		Church parade at 10.30 hours. 1 other rank proceeded on leave to ENGLAND.	JT
	14th July 1919.		Recruits and transfers paraded at 08.00 hours for riding drill.	
			Recruits and transfers paraded for musketry at 10.00.	JT

Army Form C. 2118.

WAR DIARY
or
INTELLIGENCE SUMMARY.
(Erase heading not required.)

Instructions regarding War Diaries and Intelligence Summaries are contained in F. S. Regs., Part II. and the Staff Manual respectively. Title pages will be prepared in manuscript.

Place	Date	Hour	Summary of Events and Information	Remarks and references to Appendices
	14th July 1919.		12th (PRINCE OF WALES'S ROYAL) LANCERS	
			(Continued). Recruits and Transfers paraded for foot drill at 14.00 hours.	
			Recruits and Transfers paraded for physical training at 18.00 hours.	
			W.C.Os ride paraded at 06.00 hours under the Adjutant. 10 other ranks of the band went on leave to ENGLAND.	
			Mentioned in despatches. March 1919.	
			The following Officers and other ranks were mentioned in despatches.	
			Lieut Co.onel.C.FANE.C.M.G..D.S.O.	
			Major (T/Lt.Col) A.B.REYNOLDS.D.S.O.	
			Bt.Major.H.V.S.CHARRINGTON.M.C.	
			Lieut.F.F.SPICER.D.S.O.	
			Lieut J.H.LECHE.	
			L/12972. Staff Sgt Farrier BIRD.J.C.	5/-
			L/3264. SS.Cpl. SMITH.G.F.	
			L/12058. Col. SUMMERS.T.	
			L/11378. Pte LAW.W.C.	
	15th July 1919.		Recruits and Transfers paraded for riding drill at 08.00.	
			" " " " " Musketry at 10.00 hours.	
			" " " " " Footdrill at 14.00 hours.	
			" " " " " Physical training at 18.00.	5/-
			Lieut F.T.BAINES and 10 other ranks of the Band proceeded on leave to ENGLAND.	
	16th July 1919.		W.C.Os ride paraded under the Adjutant at 06.00 hours.	
			Recruits and transfers paraded for riding drill at 08.00.	
			" " " " " Musketry at 10.00 hours.	
			" " " " " Foot drill at 14.00 hours.	5/-
			" " " " " Physical training at 18.00 hours.	

Army Form C. 2118.

WAR DIARY
or
INTELLIGENCE SUMMARY.
(Erase heading not required.)

Instructions regarding War Diaries and Intelligence Summaries are contained in F. S. Regs., Part II. and the Staff Manual respectively. Title pages will be prepared in manuscript.

Place	Date	Hour	Summary of Events and Information	Remarks and references to Appendices
12th (PRINCE OF WALES'S RMAL)LANCERS.				
	16th July 1919	(Continued). Lieut H.H.L.HIGGINS and 5 other ranks reported to Horse Show ground for duty. 10 other ranks of the band proceeded on leave to ENGLAND.	JT
	17th July 1919.	W.O.Os ride under the Adjutant paraded at 06.00 hours. Recruits and transfers paraded at 08.00 for riding drill " " " " 10.00 for Musketry " " " " 14.00 for Foot drill. " " " " 18.00 for physical Tr. All horses of the Regiment were re-classified by the Commanding Officer and the Veterinary Officer. The Commanding Officer inspected the W.C.Os ride at 16.00 hours. The Commanding Officer eliminated entries for the horse show at 16.30 hours. 2 other ranks proceeded on leave to ENGLAND.	JT
	18th July 1919.	The G.O.C., Cavalry Division of the Rhine inspected the system of training in the Regiment. The following programme was carried out :- Recruits at Riding drill at 09.30 hours. W.C.Os instructors ride under the Adjutant at 10.00 hours Recruits foot drill at 10.30 hours. Recruits Musketry at 10.45 hours. The G.O.C inspected expressed his satisfaction of the system carried out.	JT
	19th July 1919.	The day was observed as a holiday to celebrate Peace day.	JT

Army Form C. 2118.

WAR DIARY
or
INTELLIGENCE SUMMARY.
(Erase heading not required.)

Instructions regarding War Diaries and Intelligence
Summaries are contained in F. S. Regs., Part II.
and the Staff Manual respectively. Title pages
will be prepared in manuscript.

Place	Date	Hour	Summary of Events and Information	Remarks and references to Appendices
	20th July 1919.		12th (PRINCE OF WALES' ROYAL) LANCERS. Church parade at 10.30 hours. 2 other ranks proceeded to ENGLAND on leave.	
	21st July 1919.		Recruits and transfers continued training. 1 other rank proceeded to ENGLAND on leave.	JT
	22nd July 1919.		Recruits and transfers continued training. 2 other ranks proceeded on leave to ENGLAND.	JT
	23rd July 1919.		Recruits and transfers continued training. 2 other ranks proceeded on leave to ENGLAND.	JT
	24th July 1919.		Recruits and transfers continued training. Captain. KELLET, R.A.V.C and 2 horses attached to the regiment for duty. 1 other rank proceeded on leave to ENGLAND.	JT
	25th July 1919.		Recruits and transfers continued training.	JT
	26th July 1919.		All officers mounted on their own chargers paraded under the adjutant for riding drill at 09.00 hours. 2 other ranks proceeded to ENGLAND on leave.	JT
	27th July 1919.		Church service was held in the canteen at 10.30.	JT
	28th July 1919.		Recruits and transfers continued training. Veterinary officer carried out preliminary classification of horses. 2 other ranks proceeded on leave.	JT

Army Form C. 2118.

WAR DIARY
or
INTELLIGENCE SUMMARY.
(Erase heading not required.)

Instructions regarding War Diaries and Intelligence Summaries are contained in F. S. Regs., Part II. and the Staff Manual respectively. Title pages will be prepared in manuscript.

Place	Date	Hour	Summary of Events and Information	Remarks and references to Appendices
12th (PRINCE OF WALES ' ROYAL)LANCERS				
	29th July 1919.		Recruits and transfers continued training. 1 other rank proceeded to ENGLAND on leave.	
	30th July 1919.		Recruits and transfers continued training. 2 other ranks proceeded to ENGLAND on leave.	
	31st July 1919.		Recruits and transfers continued training. All officers chargers were paraded for inspection by the Commanding officer at 10.00 hours.	

CWWilton Lieut Colonel,
Commanding 12th Royal Lancers.

WAR DIARY or INTELLIGENCE SUMMARY.

Army Form C. 2118.

12th (PRINCE OF WALES' ROYAL) LANCERS.

Place	Date	Hour	Summary of Events and Information	Remarks and references to Appendices

COLOGNE.	August 1st 1919.		The Cavalry Division of the Rhine held a horse show on the COLOGNE race course. The Regiment was placed in the following events:-
			 1. Best trained troop horse open to Warrant Officers, N.C.Os and men.
			    L/12928. F.Q.M.S.G.ASHBY. 2nd prize.
			 2. Warrant Officers and N.C.Os jumping.
			    L/12977. SSM.H.GREEN. 2nd prize.
			 3. Team of 4 best trained troop horses that have been with the regiment since 1914.
			    "C" Squadron. 3rd prize.
			 4. Team of 4 best overseas troop horses.
			    "C" squadron. 1st prize.
			 Sanitary inspection.
			 The following report was received from the A.D.M.S, Cavalry Division of the Rhine on his inspection of the sanitary arrangements of the regiment.
			 "It affords me great pleasure to be able to say that on inspecting the barracks of the 12th Royal Lancers yesterday, everything was found to be in a most satisfactory state. The absence of flies was most noticable and the cleanliness of all cook houses, mess rooms, latrines etc is a credit to all concerned. Everything seems to be done to make the men, including the Indian personnel comfortable. One other rank proceeded to ENGLAND on leave.	

COLOGNE.	August 2nd 1919.		Recruits paraded for riding drill at 08.00 hours. The remainder of the day was observed as a holiday. The Cavalry Division of the Rhine held a race meeting on the COLOGNE race course. The Cavalry cup was won by Captain J.V.ADAIR's "John Cording". Two other ranks proceeded to ENGLAND on leave	
COLOGNE.	August 3rd 1919.		Church service at 10.30 hours. One other rank proceeded to ENGLAND on leave.	
COLOGNE.	August 4th 1919.		Cavalry Division of the Rhine Horse show continued. Two other ranks proceeded to ENGLAND on leave.	

Army Form C. 2118.

WAR DIARY
or
INTELLIGENCE SUMMARY.
12th (PRINCE OF WALES' ROYAL) LANCERS

(Erase heading not required.)

Instructions regarding War Diaries and Intelligence Summaries are contained in F. S. Regs., Part II. and the Staff Manual respectively. Title pages will be prepared in manuscript.

Place	Date	Hour	Summary of Events and Information	Remarks and references to Appendices
COLOGNE.	August 5th 1919.		Exercise under Squadron arrangements. The rest of the day was observed as a holiday. 2nd day of the Cavalry Division of the Rhine Race meeting. Lieut S.R.F.SPICER's "NABOTH" won the subalterns cup. 8 other ranks proceeded to ENGLAND on leave.	57
COLOGNE.	August 6th 1919.		All horses of the regiment were classified and placed in the following classes:- T- Horses to be retained in Regiment. T- Horses to be transferred. E. Horses for sale in GERMANY. S. Horses for sale in ENGLAND. B. Horses for butchery. Escort duty. Two troops of 40 strong under Captain R.S.T.MOORE formed a Guard of Honnour to General GOURAUD, Commanding French Army on a visit him to the British Army of the Rhine.	57
COLOGNE.	August 7th 1919.		A composite squadron of 6 Officers and 80 other ranks paraded under Captain D.C.H.RICHARDSON.M.C to take part in a review order parade with a Lancer Composite Regiment formed of 9th, 12th and 17th Lancers commanded by Lieut Colonel.C.FANE.C.M.G.,D.S.O which practiced the march past with the 6th Corps to be reviewed by the Army Council on August 18th 1919. One other rank proceeded on leave to ENGLAND.	57
COLOGNE.	August 8th 1919.		Recruits and transfers paraded for riding drill at 08.00 hours. Recruits paraded for musketry at 10.00 hours. Recruits and transfers paraded for foot drill at 14.00 hours. Recruits paraded for Physical training at 18.00 hours. 7 other ranks proceeded to ENGLAND to join 5th Lancers as serving soldiers. 1 other rank proceeded on leave to ENGLAND	57
COLOGNE.	August 9th 1919.		Exercise under Squadron arrangements. All pack ponies of the regiment were inspected by the Commanding Officer at 11.00 hours. One other rank proceeded to ENGLAND on leave.	57
COLOGNE.	August 10th 1919.		Church service at 10.00 hours. 3 other ranks proceeded to ENGLAND on leave.	57

WAR DIARY
INTELLIGENCE SUMMARY

(Erase heading not required.)

Army Form C. 2118.

Instructions regarding War Diaries and Intelligence Summaries are contained in F.S. Regs., Part II. and the Staff Manual respectively. Title pages will be prepared in manuscript.

Place	Date	Hour	Summary of Events and Information	Remarks and references to Appendices
			12th (PRINCE OF WALES' ROYAL) LANCERS	
COLOGNE.	August 11th 1919.		The Composite regiment under Lieut Colonel.C.FANE.C.M.G.,D.S.O paraded at 09.30 hours and carried out a rehearsal of the Review order parade. Recruits and transfers paraded for lance drill at 14.00 hours. Recruits paraded for physical training at 18.00 hours. 3 other ranks proceeded to ENGLAND on leave. Major H.V.S.CHARRINGTON.M.C rejoined the regiment for duty.	5↑
COLOGNE.	August 12th 1919.		Recruits and transfers paraded for riding school at 08.00 hours. "C" Squadron horses were inspected in watering order by Major General Sir.W.H.BIRBECK.K.C.B., C.M.G, Director of Remounts.	5↑
COLOGNE.	Aug.13.		Recruits and transfers paraded for lance drill at 14.00 hours. All N.C.Os not in possession of 2nd or 3rd class certificates of Army Education, paraded in the lecture room for a lecture by the Commanding Officer. 3 other ranks proceeded to ENGLAND on leave.	5↑
COLOGNE.	August 14th 1919.		Recruits and transfers paraded for riding drill at 08.00 hours. Recruits and transfers paraded for lance drill at 14.00 hours. Recruits paraded for physical training at 18.00 hours.	5↑
COLOGNE.	August 15th 1919.		Recruits and transfers paraded for riding drill at 08.00 hours. All N.C.Os paraded for instruction under SSM.I.F&G.MARTIN at 10.00 hours. Recruits paraded for physical training at 18.00 hours.	5↑
COLOGNE.	August 16th 1919.		The Composite regiment paraded under Lieut Colonel.C.FANE.C.M.G.,DS.O. at 09.30 hours and carried out a rehearsal of the review order parade with the remainder of the Cavalry Division of the Rhine. Special Message. The following message was received by Major General W.H.GREENLY.C.M.G.,D.S.O in reply to the regiments' wire of congratulations to H.R.H,The PRINCE OF WALES. " I thank you and all ranks, past and present of my regiment the 12th Royal Lancers for good wishes on my birthday, EDWARD, P., Colonel, 12th Lancers."	5↑
COLOGNE.	August 17th 1919.		Church parade at 10.30 hours.	5↑

Army Form C. 2118.

WAR DIARY
or
INTELLIGENCE SUMMARY.

(Erase heading not required.)

Instructions regarding War Diaries and Intelligence Summaries are contained in F. S. Regs., Part II. and the Staff Manual respectively. Title pages will be prepared in manuscript.

12th (PRINCE OF WALES'ROYAL)LANCERS.

Place	Date	Hour	Summary of Events and Information	Remarks and references to Appendices
COLOGNE.	August 18th 1919.		The Composite Lancer Regiment paraded under Lieut.Colonel.C.FANE.C.M.G.,D.S.O, and took part in the review of troops by the Army Council at 11.00 hours on the EXERCISER PLATZ north of COLOGNE. Army horse show took place at MULHEIM.	ot
COLOGNE.	August 19th 1919.		Exercise under Squadron arrangements. Orders were received that the regiment would proceed to IRELAND on or about 1st and 2nd September 1919.	ot
COLOGNE.	August 20th 1919.		Exercise under Squadron arrangements. Recruits paraded for foot drill at 08.00 hours. 126 horses were sent to the Animal Collecting Camp at COLOGNE DEUTZ for sale in GERMANY.	ot
COLOGNE.	August 21st 1919.		Recruits paradedefor riding drill at 06.00 hours. N.C.Os class for under SSM.I.F.G.Martin paraded at 09.45 hours. The remainder of the regiment exercised under Squadron arrangements. Recruits paraded for physical training at 18.00 hrs.	ot
COLOGNE.	August 22nd 1919.		Recruits paraded for rifle drill at 08.00 hours. N.C.Os class under SSM.I.F.G.Martin paraded at 09.45 hours. Exercise under Squadron arrangements.	ot
COLOGNE.	August 23rd 1919.		Recruits paraded for rifle drill at 06.00 hours. N.C.Os class under SSM.I.F.G Martin paraded at 09.45 hours. The 1st August Race meeting took place on the Race Course at COLOGNE.	ot
COLOGNE.	August 24th 1919.		Church parade at 10.30 hours. A Very wet day.	ot
COLOGNE.	August 25th 1919.		Recruits paraded for rifle drill at 08.00 hours. N.C.Os class paraded at 09.45 hours. All equipment held on charge on shown on G.1095 was handed in, in the riding school, packed and labelled and ready for despatch to ANTWERP.	ot

WAR DIARY
or
INTELLIGENCE SUMMARY.

(Erase heading not required.)

Army Form C. 2118.

Instructions regarding War Diaries and Intelligence Summaries are contained in F. S. Regs., Part II. and the Staff Manual respectively. Title pages will be prepared in manuscript.

Place	Date	Hour	Summary of Events and Information	Remarks and references to Appendices
			12th (PRINCE OF WALES' ROYAL) LANCERS.	
COLOGNE.	August 26th 1919.		Recruits paraded for rifle drill at 08.00 hours. N.C.Os class paraded at 09.45 hours and 14.00 hours for instruction in Lance, Sword and Rifle drill. A Board of Officers consisting of Major H.V.S.CHARRINGTON.M.C, Lieut R.S.T.MOORE and Captain T.H.KELLETT,R.A.V.C assembled at the Forge to examine No.L/5150.Pte SAMUELS and L/16780.Pte RAYNER as to their fitness to become shoeing smiths. These two men were passed fit and appointed shoeing smiths. Medals and Awards. The following extract appeared in the LONDON GAZETTE dated 21/8/19. L/12881. SQMS.EVANS.J, 12th Royal Lancers awarded the Military Medal.	ST
COLOGNE.	August 27th 1919.		Recruits paraded for rifle drill at 08.00 hours. N.C.Os class paraded at 09.45 hours and 14.00 hours for instruction.	ST
COLOGNE.	August 28th 1919.		Recruits paraded for Rifle drill at 08.00 hours. N.C.Os paraded at 09.45 hours and 14.00 hours for instruction.	ST
COLOGNE.	August 29th 1919.		Recruits paraded for rifle drill at 08.00 hours. N.C.Os class paraded for instruction at 09.00 hours and 14.00 hours. The Regimental equipment laid down in A.F.G.1098 was despatched to ANTWERP enroute for AINTREE under Lieut S.R.F.SPICER and 7 other ranks.	ST
COLOGNE.	August 30th 1919.		Recruits paraded for rifle drill at 08.00 hours. N.C.Os class paraded for Commanding Officers' inspection at 10.00 hours. The remainder of the day was observed as a holiday. Race meeting on COLOGNE race course.	ST
COLOGNE.	August 31st 1919.		The day was given over prior to packing prior to leaving for IRELAND on Sept.1st 1919.	ST

Cecil Howe
Lieut Colonel,
Commanding, 12th Royal Lancers.

BEF
Cav Div
Lancer Bde

17 Lancers

1919 Apr to 1919 Aug

From 3 Cav Div 7 Bde
Box 1155

OR66

Army Form C. 2118.

WAR DIARY
or
INTELLIGENCE SUMMARY.
(Erase heading not required.)

17th Lancers V.F.
Part II P.6. April 1917

Instructions regarding War Diaries and Intelligence Summaries are contained in F. S. Regs., Part II. and the Staff Manual respectively. Title pages will be prepared in manuscript.

Place	Date	Hour	Summary of Events and Information	Remarks and references to Appendices
COLOGNE	2.		2nd Cd. Bgde. W.O. there ached the Regt. hd. been allocated to Cologne there came to the Lancer Bks. Lg. infm. D.A.J.G. 1/12 to Lancer	
	3.		Lt. M.G. Nicholls landed at 8 p.m. Regt. went out for Route march, esp. F. to G - B. aft. 13.00 set for 16 Light Bu.Fd. to revert to being after the Lines - Regt to Officers 134. O.R. -	
	9.		12 O.Rs. & 16 horses arrived from J.MP - the Reed. of Rfts. C.-i.-C. Depot Front.	
	23.		Regt supports Sgt. no for mid establishment - 67 ORs. were left to lose to and establishment 67 ORs. who Lpt. W.B. Turner M.C. + A.D.C. 6/ + 7 Dr. L.-S. Burry opined to ADC 62 + 9w. Insp.: unanimously named that entirely want + body to keep horse order for men — Endurance Struggle to keep horse order for men	
	26.		Strength Offs - 34 O.Rs - 155 Animals 536	

2 MAY 1919
ORDERLY O
17TH LANCERS

O.W. Griffith
Lt Col.
17 Lancers

Confidential.

V.F.

War Diary of the 17th Lancers.

Cavalry Division, Army of the Rhine

late 7th Cav. Bde

Contents:— Vol. VI. page Y. for period 1st to 31st May 19.

—oOo—

To, Lancer Brigade.

— Forwarded. — Original Copy.

Arthur D
Captain & Adjutant
for O.C. 17th Lancers.

Cologne.
1/6/1919.

WAR DIARY or INTELLIGENCE SUMMARY

17th Lancers
Vol VI
p 7
May 1919.

Army Form C. 2118.

Place	Date	Hour	Summary of Events and Information	Remarks and references to Appendices
COLOGNE	4th 7 12 13 19		Capt C.L. WYNNE-JONES apptd G.S.O.3 Cavalry Division. H.R.H. Duke of Connaught inspected the Regt. Received a contingent of 5 officers & 10 O.R. keys all 13th Hussars. 2 Horses & Mules. 12 Their late were prepared to join at HQ for the Lancer Regt. They were confined to &c. from the rest. Regt. This nedischin was appointed closed on the Regt. being regarded this boots the Roll D.C. BOLES ...	att att
	22		... released to command the Horse Exhib. i.e. 2 troops of the first rest Regt. was held ready to advance in the road of the enemy (trying) to hold field places from the side of the cavalry regt.) to hold rock between the advance guard & (Kosta i rest troops) & the main army ...	att
			There seemed a likelihood that the scheme would emerge but a further extension of time was granted for the discussion of the terms.	att
	27		G.O.C. El Corps (General Holsham) visited tomorrows.	att
	29 30		2nd SIR W ROBERTSON visited barracks, 2nd Cavalry reinforcements arrived during the month. L/Cpl QUINLEY rejoined. Two officers & 24 of the Oxlam Light infantry were attached to Learn horse management & details in R.B. 25 Lt Col OXLADE & Lt/Lieut N ALFORD rejoined, the command of the Regt. T.O. MERRILL 250 or about the Lt & Explorer 075.	att att

Strength 32 officers 449 O.Rs 543 and—
2 Mules 3 H.T. 160 O.R.T.

[signature] A W H Jelf Lt Col

Confidential.

A.2.95.

War Diary of the 19th Lancers
Cavalry Division, Army of the Rhine.

Contents: Vol. VI. 1 page. for period 1st to 30th June 1919.

To Lancer Dn.

Forwarded.

M W Turner
for Captain & Adjt.
for Officer Commanding 19th Lancers.

Cocogne
14/7/1919.

WAR DIARY or INTELLIGENCE SUMMARY

Army Form C. 2118.

17th Lancers. Vol VI. p 8. June 1919.

Place	Date	Hour	Summary of Events and Information	Remarks and references to Appendices
COLOGNE	1.		L/H. etc still awaiting to move	n5
	4.		61 O.Rs 51st 13th O.Rs (attached to Regt) Ren transfer to re-precedent	az
	6.		L.Ht. 26. O.Rs (17th L) futur to Regt for offices transfer	az
	7.		6 O.Rs 51st + 52 "" O.Rs police in Regt for journey to BERLIN	
	8.		Lt J.M. HEDLEY to GHQ Army of Rhine. Special duty	az
	16.		Dept. move from CURDASH. ISMAN NIKKES Y110 O.Rs. all non remts.	
	17.		Only 2 duty & signature of June note Lt. (3 W. OFFENL Curry) + Lt. OL HARRIS + Lt. Ol. DENGHAM) + 75 O.Rs Regt Dept ←	CoLN Jun 59 OTZ
			Penn & 3o(?) detached from Regt. v/e. Laun no/m to VOLRERE. The felling day 16 marched to ENGELSKIRCHEN.	otz
			The Regt now the Dept without any horses duty in billets.	OTZ
	18.		Capt. H.A.H. PLENDEN signed for ENGLAND + not bound of 13 Lct	
	28.		Peace was signed at VERSAILLES by delegates between the Allied + Associated Powers + GERMANY	w757

Strength of Regiment 30/6/19

	Officers	Other Ranks	Animals
	34	267	493
attached	2 officers	128 OR	

Rifle Brigade

A/W/Gordon GRAHAM
Lt. Col. 17 Lancers

CONFIDENTIAL.

WAR DIARY of the 17th LANCERS.

Cavalry Division.   British Army of the Rhine.

CONTENTS:-   Vol. VI.   page   for period 1st to 31st JULY 1919.

****

To:-

Lancer Brigade.

Forwarded.

Cologne.
1/8/1919.

[signature]
Captain and Adjutant,
for Officer Commanding 17th Lancers.

Army Form C. 2118.

WAR DIARY
or
INTELLIGENCE SUMMARY.
(Erase heading not required.)

17ᵗʰ Lancers.

July 1919 pg 9.

Place	Date	Hour	Summary of Events and Information	Remarks and references to Appendices
COLOGNE	1.		11 N.CO's rejoining from ENGLAND:-	A.2
	3.		Details of Rifle B'ns. Dn. have left Kamphansen region their unit.	A.2
	6.		Retained photographing day for Peace-	A.2
	14.		An escort of 14 O.Rs attached to Douglas Haig in Victory march. Hd.Qrt PARIS. 2ⁿᵈ D.R. HARRIES A.D.C & O.C. Roller Drivers - Trans of recruits.	A.2
	14. & 30. & 31.		Reclassification of horses with a view to the return of the Can. Div. It had been now a few officers announced that an reduction of the Army of Occupation Rgt. until again supplied with 10: Horses & mustering Diagram.	A.2
			Lᵗ O.C. DIGHTON to the U.K. Gents resignation of commission.
			Strength O.R.
			H 33 366 537.
			174
			74 native 2700.
			Attached.

C O N F I D E N T I A L.

WAR DIARY OF THE 17TH LANCERS.
CAVALRY DIVISION
BRITISH ARMY OF THE RHINE.

Contents -

Vol. VI, pages ___ , for the period 1st to 31st August, 1919.

oR 10 y.

To, Lancer Brigade

Forwarded.

Cologne.
1/9/1919.

Captain & Adjutant,
for O.C., 17th Lancers.

Army Form C. 2118.

WAR DIARY
or
INTELLIGENCE SUMMARY.
(Erase heading not required.)

17th Lancers
1st VI
August 1919
p. 10

Instructions regarding War Diaries and Intelligence Summaries are contained in F. S. Regs., Part II. and the Staff Manual respectively. Title pages will be prepared in manuscript.

Place	Date	Hour	Summary of Events and Information	Remarks and references to Appendices
COLOGNE	12th		It became known that the Regiment was to leave, & that the Brigade would take the 2nd Cavalry Regt to remain in Germany. The Regt was to test to go. The Lone Rain was scheduled to go Sept 23rd. It was intimated that the Regt was to go to CATTERICK BRIDGE directly to YORK later, & to be officered & equipped as for Heavy –	
	18.		2 Captains & Sgt. & 80 ORs who Capt H.R. PLOWDEN paraded for review in occasion of visit of any Council to COLOGNE	OR
	19 to 26		Preparation for the entrainment of all Govt. stores –	OR
	27.		Equipment train left for ANTWERP. Lt. H. J. H. VERNEY M.C. I/C. 1 N.C.O. + 60 O.R.	OR
	31.		Strength – 32 Officers 326 ORs. 487 horses –	

R.W. West Capt.
A/ Adjt.
17th Lancers.
17

BEF

CAV. DIV.

LANCER BDE.

2 MACHINE GUN SQN

1919 APR. to 1919 AUG.

FROM 1 CAV DIV 2 BDE
Box 1111

Became LANCERS BDE

WAR DIARY
or
INTELLIGENCE SUMMARY.
(Erase heading not required.)

2nd. MACHINE GUN SQUADRON. Army Form C. 2118.

VOLUME No. 39.

APRIL 1919.

Instructions regarding War Diaries and Intelligence Summaries are contained in F. S. Regs., Part II. and the Staff Manual respectively. Title pages will be prepared in manuscript.

Place	Date	Hour	Summary of Events and Information	Remarks and references to Appendices
DEUTZ.	1st.		Usual Routine. C.O. inspected all recently joined horses for selection of suitable L.D. and Packs. Afternoon. All saddles and harness surplus to present establishment, put into oil and dubbin and stored.	
DEUTZ.	2nd.		Usual Routine. Afternoon. All Spare Saddlery and harness cleaned and stored.	
"	3rd.		Usual Routine. Afternoon. Usual Routine.	
"	4th.		Stables 09.15 hours. G.O.C. Cavalry Division (Major General Sir W.E. Peyton) visited the Squadron at 10.00 hours and inspected the men and horses during stables, also Canteen, barracks and rooms etc.	
"	5th.		Usual Routine. 29 N.C.O's and men proceeded to U.K. for demobilization, yesterday.	
"	6th.		Sunday Routine. 9 Riding horses taken on the strength from "H" Battery R.H.A. yesterday. 15 Riding horses class "Z" cast and despatched to Animal Collecting Camp, Cologne.	
"	7th.		Usual Routine. Squadron provides 22 men (in addition to men for our own horses) for Hussar Brigade horses at Animal Collecting Camp, Cologne. Remain there until 15-4-19. 1 O.R. leave to U.K.	
"	8th.		No Exercise. Stables 10.00 to 12.30 hours being short of men.	
"	9th.		Exercise in 3 parties for each Sub-Section and Headquarters before and after breakfast. Stables on completion of same. 15 men returned from A.C.C. for duty in afternoon. Still very short of men. 1 O.R. leave to U.K. and 1 officer leave to U.K.	
"	10th.		Usual Routine. Medical Inspection at 10.30 hours. Lieut. (T/Capt) D.F.G. Duff to 9th Lancers and struck off the strength of M.G.C. Cav. 1 officer leave to U.K.	
"	11th.		Exercise 08.30 hours. All thin horses parade at same hour daily for grazing, separate to Exercise Party. 1 officer and 1 O.R. leave to U.K.	
"				

Sheet 2.

Army Form C. 2118.

WAR DIARY
or
INTELLIGENCE SUMMARY.
(Erase heading not required.)

2nd. MACHINE GUN SQUADRON.

VOLUME NO. 39.

APRIL 1919

Place	Date	Hour	Summary of Events and Information	Remarks and references to Appendices
DEUTZ.	12th.		Exercise at 15.00 hours. Stables on return. (No Midday stables) Funeral of No. 41287 Sergeant Walton, who died at No.44 C.C.S. yesterday morning, took place at Cologne Cemetery at 10.00 hours. Firing Party of 1 sergeant and 12 rank and file from Squadron. All Officers and many O.Ranks also present.	
"	13th.		Sunday Routine. Church parade C of E. 09.30 hours. Stables 11.15 hours. 3 Riding horses from 9th Lancers taken on the strength. 1 O.R. leave to U.K.	
"	14th.		Usual Routine. 1 O. R. leave to U.K.	
"	15th.		Exercise and grazing at 08.30 hours. Dismounted Parade full strength. C.O's inspection. Sundry orders read out. 1 O.R. leave to U.K. 30 L.D. and 6 Riding horses from "H" Battery taken on the strength.	
"	16th.		Routine altered as follows:- Reveille 06.00 hours. Early stables 06.20 hours. Breakfasts 07.00 hours. Parades or Exercise 08.00 hours. Usual Routine. 1 O. R. granted leave to U.K.	
"	17th		Usual Routine. 1 O.R. leave to U.K.	
"	18th		Good Friday. Exercise on blankets 06.30 hours. Stables 08.30 hours.	
"	19th		Usual Sunday Routine.	
"	20th		Easter Sunday. Church Services.	
"	21st.		Race Meeting.	
"	22nd.		Usual Routine. Infantry Officers ride 14.30 hours.	
"	23rd.		Major Wathen leave to U.K. Inspection by A.D.V.S. at 14.30 hours. Small exercise party 06.30 hours. Breakfast 07.30. Large exercise party 08.30 hours. Usual Routine.	
"	24th.		Usual Routine. Soccer Match Squadron v 17th Lancers. Infantry Officers ride 14.30 hours.	

Sheet 3

WAR DIARY
or
INTELLIGENCE SUMMARY.

(Erase heading not required.)

2nd MACHINE GUN SQUADRON. Army Form C. 2118.

VOLUME No. 39.

APRIL 1919

Place	Date	Hour	Summary of Events and Information	Remarks and references to Appendices
DEUTZ.	25th.		G.O.C.'s inspection of Mobile Section. Highly complimented. 3 horses sent to R.A.F. 11th Wing. Usual Routine. 15 O.Rs. sent to help 12th Lancers with horses.	
"	26th.		Usual routine. Very short of men. A few Officers of the Riding School Course attended voluntary ride in school 9.am.	
"	27th		Sunday. Parade Service C. of E. 11.30 hours. Usual Holy Communion and Evening Services. Stables 09.10 hours.	
"	28th.		Exercise as usual. Stables 10.30 to 12.20 hours. Dinners 12.30. London Divisional Races 14.00.	
"	29th.		Exercise as usual. Stables and Races same as yesterday.	
"	30th.		Exercise as usual. Stables 11.00 hours. Usual Routine. Officers ride 14.30 hrs.	

Arthur Shaw. Captain.
Commanding 2nd Machine Gun Squadron.

Army Form C. 2118.

WAR DIARY
or
INTELLIGENCE SUMMARY.

2ND. MACHINE GUN SQUADRON. VOLUME NO 40

(Erase heading not required.)

MAY, 1919

Instructions regarding War Diaries and Intelligence Summaries are contained in F. S. Regs., Part II. and the Staff Manual respectively. Title pages will be prepared in manuscript.

Place	Date	Hour	Summary of Events and Information	Remarks and references to Appendices
COLOGNE	1		Usual Routine. Very wet. Main Guard Mounted all night. day	
	2		Usual Routine. Cavalry Memorial Service 10.30 hours. No one from the Squadron present. Owing to lorry not arriving. Officers Riding Class 14.30 hours	
	3		Usual Routine.	
	4		Sunday. No Church Parade Service. 4 O.Rs gone on leave to U.K.	
	5 May		Usual Routine. 4 O.Rs. leave to U.K. Subsection Football Match H.Q. versus B section.	
	6		Usual Routine. 2 O.Rs. leave to U.K.	
	7		Usual Routine. 1 O.R. to Concentration Camp. O.C.'s Conference 17.00 hours.	
	8		Usual Routine. Riding School for Officers. 1 O.R. demobilised. Medical Inspection. 2 OR'S leave to U.K. 1 Riding horse struck off.	
	9		Usual Routine. 2 O.R's from Base Depot Boulogne. Mobile Subsection standing to 2 hours notice	
	10		Usual Routine.	
	11		Sunday Routine. Pte Levett committed suicide in Barracks.	
	12		Usual Routine. Funeral of above man. Major L.W.D Watnen returned from leave in U.K. and assumes command.	
	13		Usual Routine. Court of Enquiry held at Squadron Headquarters on pte Levetts death.	
	14		Usual Routine. Ride of Army Headquarters Officers in afternoon	
	15		Usual Routine.	

Army Form C. 2118.

WAR DIARY
or
INTELLIGENCE SUMMARY.
(Erase heading not required.)

2nd. Machine Gun Squadron
VOLUME 40
May 1919

Instructions regarding War Diaries and Intelligence Summaries are contained in F. S. Regs., Part II. and the Staff Manual respectively. Title pages will be prepared in manuscript.

Place	Date	Hour	Summary of Events and Information	Remarks and references to Appendices
COLOGNE	16		Usual Routine.	
	17		Usual Routine. G.O.C. Lancer Brigade (Brigadier General Neil Haigh) inspected No 1 Section and Transport at Stables. 29 O. Ranks (Labour Co., Agriculturists) taken on the strength, all men of low medical category cannot ride. useful as grooms. Grooming strength up to now 49 horses per man .	
	18		Sunday Routine.	
	19		Usual Routine. G.O.C. Lancer Brigade inspected No. 2 and 3 Sections at stables, Barrack Rooms and the Messroom during dinner hour.	
	20		Usual Routine. Court of Enquiry on death of Pte Levett reassembled. Canteen Accounts audited by Squadron Board of Officers.	
	21		Usual Routine. G.O.C. Cavalry Division visited the Squadron during mid-day stables and inspected the horses and newly joined Labour Corps men	
	22		Usual Routine. Attached Infantry in Riding School 08.30 hours. Medical Inspection 10.30 Leave considerably curtailed owing to uncertainty regarding acceptance of peace terms.	
	23		Usual Routine. 11 O.Ranks sent up from 6th M.G. Squadron taken on the strength temporary pending permission to retain permanently. Grooming strength now 3 horses per man.	
	24		Usual Routine . 45 men inoculated	
	25		Sunday Routine. C of E. parade service at 09.30 .	
	26		Inspection by C.O. of Mobile Section. Find one Section complete as per W.E. Lt. Roberts M.C In Command (standing to with a view to a move over Frontier, part of composite Brigade found by the Cavalry Division) in Barracks at 09.00 hours. Exercise afterwards .	
	27		Usual Routine. i.e. exercise at 07.00 hours again at 08.30 hours. for remaining horses latter combined	

Army Form C. 2118.

WAR DIARY
or
INTELLIGENCE SUMMARY.
(Erase heading not required.)

2nd. Machine Gun Squadron.
Volume 40
May 1919

Place	Date	Hour	Summary of Events and Information	Remarks and references to Appendices
COLOGNE	27		Combined with grazing and occasional drill. 2 O.R.s from 6th M.G. Squadron.	
	28		Usual Routine. Squadron now providing (1) Mobile Section see entry for the 26th. (2) A duty Subsection not standing to but personally detailed for same to turn out if required to meet trouble in the Area of Cologne.	
	29		Usual Routine. G.O.C. VI Corps visited the Squadron at 12 noon and inspected Rooms, Canteen cook-house etc., Medical Inspection 10.30 hours.	
	30		Usual Routine. Cricket begun Inter Squadron game.	
	31		Usual Routine. Usual weekly inspections of Arms Kit and Equipment 10.30 hours. Cricket Match Squadron versus H.Q. in the afternoon.	
			NOTE. The weather has been very mild and warm throughout the month. No rain.	

L.E. Nichols Lieut
for Major.
Commanding 2nd. Machine Gun Squadron.

WAR DIARY or INTELLIGENCE SUMMARY.

LANCER MACHINE GUN SQUADRON.

VOLUME 41. JUNE 1919

Army Form C. 2118.

(*Erase heading not required.*)

Instructions regarding War Diaries and Intelligence Summaries are contained in F. S. Regs., Part II. and the Staff Manual respectively. Title pages will be prepared in manuscript.

Place	Date	Hour	Summary of Events and Information	Remarks and references to Appendices
DEUTZ.	1st		Usual Routine.	JCM
COLOGNE.	2nd		Usual Routine.	JCM
	3rd		Kings Birtaday. Usual Routine.	JCM
	4th		Usual Routine.	JCM
	5th		Usual Routine.	JCM
	6th		Usual Routine.	JCM
	7th		Usual Routine.	JCM
	8th		Usual Routine.	JCM
	9th		Usual Routine.	JCM
	10th		Usual Routine.	JCM
	11th		Usual Routine.	JCM
	12th		Usual Routine	JCM
	13th		Usual Routine.	JCM
	14th		Usual Routine.	JCM
	15th		Usual Routine.	JCM
	16th		Usual Routine.	JCM
	17th		Usual Routine.	JCM

Sheet 2.

WAR DIARY
Lancer Machine Gun Squadron   Army Form C. 2118.
or
INTELLIGENCE SUMMARY.

(Erase heading not required.)

Instructions regarding War Diaries and Intelligence Summaries are contained in F. S. Regs., Part II, and the Staff Manual respectively. Title pages will be prepared in manuscript.

Place	Date	Hour	Summary of Events and Information	Remarks and references to Appendices
BHUT 2	18th.		Usual Routine.	JCH
COLOGNE.	19th.		Mobile Section moved out to form part of Mobile Machine Gun Squadron with 1st and 9th Squadrons.	JCH
	20th to 28th		Billet Routine.	JCH JCH
	29th		Peace signed 6 P.M.	JCH
	30th		Usual Routine. Mobile Section returned.	JCH

J.C.Humfrey
Major.
Commanding Lancer Machine Gun Squadron.

Army Form C. 2118.

WAR DIARY
or
INTELLIGENCE SUMMARY.
(Erase heading not required.)

LANCER MACHINE GUN SQUADRON.

VOLUME 42.   JULY 1919.

Place	Date	Hour	Summary of Events and Information	Remarks and references to Appendices
DEUTZ. COLOGNE.	1st.		Usual Routine.	
	2nd.		Usual Routine. Classes for training N.C.O's as Instructors in Riding and Gunnery.	JCM
	3rd.		Usual Routine. Classes for training N.C.O's as Instructors in Riding and Gunnery.	JCM
	4th.		Usual Routine. Classes for training N.C.O's as Instructors in Riding and Gunnery.	JCM
	5th.		Usual Routine. Classes for training N.C.O's as Instructors in Riding and Gunnery.	JCM
	6th.		Sunday Routine. Church Parade. 35 O. Ranks joined from 30th. Labour Company.	JCM
	7th.		Usual Routine. Classes for training N.C.O's as Instructors in Riding and Gunnery.	JCM
	8th.		Observed as a holiday for the celebration of the signing of Peace.	JCM
	9th.		Usual Routine.	JCM
	10th.		Usual Routine.	JCM
	11th.		Usual Routine.	JCM
	12th.		Usual Routine. Classes for training N.C.O's as Instructors in Riding and Gunnery.	JCM
	13th.		Sunday Routine.	JCM
	14th.		Usual Routine. Classes for training N.C.O's as Instructors in Riding and Gunnery. Inspection of all horses.	JCM
	15th.		Usual Routine.	JCM
	16th.		Usual Routine.	JCM
	17th.		Usual Routine.	JCM
	18th.		Usual Routine.	JCM
	19th.		Usual Routine.	JCM
	20th.		Sunday Routine. Church Parade.	JCM
	21st.		Usual Routine.	JCM
	22nd.		Usual Routine.	JCM
	23rd.		Usual Routine.	JCM
	24th.		Usual Routine. Classification of Horses.	JCM
	25th.		Usual Routine. Classification of Horses.	JCM
	26th.		Usual Routine. Classification of Horses.	JCM
	27th.		Sunday Routine. Church Parade.	JCM
	28th.		Usual Routine.	JCM
	29th.		Usual Routine. Lecture on War Savings Certificates and War Bonds.	JCM
	30th.		Usual Routine. Classification of Horses.	JCM
	31st.		Usual Routine.	JCM

J C Hunt Major.
Commanding Lancer Machine Gun Squadron.

Army Form C. 2118.

WAR DIARY
or
INTELLIGENCE SUMMARY.
(Erase heading not required.)

LANCER MACHINE GUN SQUADRON
VOLUME 43.   AUGUST 1919.

Instructions regarding War Diaries and Intelligence Summaries are contained in F. S. Regs., Part II. and the Staff Manual respectively. Title pages will be prepared in manuscript.

Place	Date	Hour	Summary of Events and Information	Remarks and references to Appendices
	1st.		Usual Routine.	
	2nd.		Usual Routine.	
	3rd.		Sunday Routine. Church of England Parade Service.	
	4th.		Usual Routine.	
	5th.		Usual Routine.	
	6th.		Observed as a holiday as a special/for the work done in preparation for the entry of a sub- reward. Section for the Cavalry Division Horse Show.	
	7th.		Usual Routine.	
	8th.		Usual Routine. Lecture given by Major. Johnson of G.H.Q. on War Savings Certificates.	
	9th.		Usual Routine.	
	10th.		Sunday Routine. Church of England Parade Service.	
	11th.		Usual Routine.	
	12th.		Usual Routine.	
	13th.		Usual Routine.	
	14th.		Usual Routine. Classes for the training of N.C.O's in Musketry.	
	15th.		Usual Routine. Classes for the training of N.C.O's in Musketry.	
	16th.		Usual Routine. Classes for the training of N.C.O's es in Musketry.	
	17th.		Sunday Routine. Church of England Parade Service.	
	18th.		Usual Routine. Classes for the training of N.C.O's in Musketry.	
	19th.		Usual Routine. Classes for the training of N.C.O's in Musketry.	
	20th.		Usual Routine. 70 'S' horses despatched to the Rhine Army Animal Collecting Camp, Cologne for sale.	
	21st.		Usual Routine.	
	22nd.		Usual Routine.	
	23rd.		Sunday Routine. Church of England Parade Service.	
	24th.		Usual Routine.	
	25th.		Usual Routine.	
	26th.		Usual. Routine.	
	27th.		Usual Routine.	
	28th.		Usual Routine.	
	29th.		Departure of all limbers and wagons with Squadron equipment to U.K. Entrained at NIPPES STATION, COLOGNE.	
	30th.		Usual Routine.	
	31st.		Sunday Routine. Church of England Parade Service.	

J. Chumfrey
Major.
Commanding Lancer Machine Gun Squadron

www.ingramcontent.com/pod-product-compliance
Lightning Source LLC
Chambersburg PA
CBHW080806010526
44113CB00013B/2335